Spassky's 100 Best Games

Spassky's 100 Best Games

Bernard Cafferty

Boris Spasskii

Foreword by Leonard Barden

THE MACMILLAN COMPANY • *NEW YORK, NEW YORK*

ACKNOWLEDGEMENTS

The author wishes to thank R.G. Wade and D.T. Fairbank, Librarian of the Birmingham Chess Club, for access to sources not available in his own library. Thanks are also due to Messrs. A.J. Gillam, R.D. Keene and D.N.L. Levy for their assistance and advice. Particular mention must be made of J.M. Ripley who first suggested that the author should undertake the task of providing the English speaking chess public with an up to date record of the world champion's career.

The Macmillan Company
866 Third Avenue, New York, N.Y. 10022

Library of Congress Catalog Card Number: 72-76277

Second Printing

Printed in the United States of America

CONTENTS

FOREWORD

by Leonard Barden

Boris Spassky has had a curiously uneven chess career for a world title holder. Teenage prodigy, junior world champion, and the youngest ever qualifier for the interzonal at 18 (Fischer later lowered this record to 14), Spassky was already the crown prince of international chess before he was twenty. Then came years of disappointments, quarrels with his trainer and chess officials, divorce, before a second surge carried Boris to the summit in 1969. As this book goes to press, the lack of conviction in Spassky's play seems to have returned in the face of the challenge from Bobby Fischer.

These ups and downs in his career illustrate a personal paradox which Spassky himself appreciates. The handsomest chess champion since Capablanca, with a deserved reputation as a friendly, affable, easy-going swinger, is also more prone to inner self-doubt than any champion since Morphy, more involved with the psychological aspects of chess than any champion with the possible exception of Emanuel Lasker.

Your first impressions of Spassky are of charm, relaxed good looks, and an easy acceptance of strangers: Boris is informal, likes to talk, make new friends and visit new countries. He is five feet ten inches tall, with the athletic build of a high jumper and volleyball halfback now just showing the first hints of middle-aged spread. The face is handsome, distinguished by reflective green eyes and impeccably groomed reddish-brown hair which in recent years he has lengthened with neatly trimmed sideburns. His voice is deep, masculine rather than musical.

Boris smokes, usually two an hour but occasionally over-heavily. Once I asked him what advice he would give to a young player who wanted to become a chess master. Boris raised his hands in mock horror. "No, please, not this question. Capablanca gave very good advice: to study chess from the endgame. It's the kind of advice which everybody gives to everybody else, like 'please don't smoke'" — and Boris smilingly emptied the last of his cigarette packet and lit up. He likes such sardonic humour. Another time he described to me how his family had been short of food during the second world war, how his mother had been ill and how his father had been unable to help. "Little boys should be warned," commented Boris as an afterthought, and grinned. His irony extends to mimicry: Spassky could have had a successful career as an actor, and was once even offered an acting job. Now he confines this talent to imitating other grandmasters — his favourite sketch is an impression of Botvinnik giving a solemn lecture on how to train for tournaments and beat Petrosian.

The Melancholic Charmer

Boris speaks good English, even though his vocabulary and intonation are generally better than his grammar. Ask him a question, and you will discover his, at first, disconcerting habit of looking quite expressionless while he considers a reply, almost as if the question were some theoretical novelty in the Ruy Lopez. Probing deeper, you notice his keen awareness of feelings and emotions as well as the natural politeness and modesty which makes him a hit with women. U.S. journalist Beth Cassidy, reporting the Tel Aviv Olympiad in 1964 for *Chess Life*, wrote: "I had a few words with Boris Spassky who speaks excellent English and is an absolute charmer. When I approached him he was working on a problem which he promptly handed to me, asking my opinion. I looked at him to see if he was serious, and loved him when I realised he was. In our chess club they wouldn't even ask me if it was raining outside let alone the answer to a problem!"

Many leading chess masters have a day to day, materialistic, attitude to their careers typical of professional sportsmen who belong to an international circuit. It is just that their chosen field of activity happens to be mental rather than physical. Spassky is emotionally more complex. On the surface, there is irony and charm; Robert Byrne recently called him a gentleman, which must be about the supreme compliment an Anglo-Saxon can make to a Slav. Yet Spassky often shows in his personality a kind of deep introspective and rather sorrowing quality, even at what might seem inappropriate moments. It suggests that much of his life, like that of an artist, is lived below the surface. The *Tass* commentator remarked that Petrosian appeared relaxed and satisfied when he arrived at the Central Chess Club in Moscow to resign the eighth game and go two down in the 1969 world title match, but that the winner looked careworn and depressed. A Yugoslav journalist asked Boris after he won the title: "Do you ever lose your zest for life?" "Yes, when I get depressed, my coach Bondarevsky becomes the optimist, and vice-versa. We complement each other nicely." The melancholic side to Spassky's nature is also reflected in a modest appraisal of his own successes; it is significant that he has always claimed that the 'game of my life' is a defeat — his loss to Polugaevsky in the USSR Championship in January 1961.

Boris's family background provided few clues that the Spasskys were to produce both a chess and a checkers champion in the same generation (Boris's attractive 27-year-old sister Irina has more than once won the USSR women's draughts or checkers championship). Boris's grandfather on his father's side was an orthodox priest, while his other grandfather, though a rather poor man, was elected a delegate from his local district of Kuvsky Guberna (about 250 miles from Moscow) to one of the elected assemblies at St. Petersburg. He was probably on the Jewish side of Boris's ancestry. Both the grandpaternal families were, in Boris's words, "very enormous." Boris's father, who became a construction engineer in Leningrad, was one of eleven children, while his mother, who taught the first four grades in an elementary school, was the eldest of a family of nine.

The Spassky's met and married at the beginning of the 1930s and, in Boris's usual ironic words, "they decided to produce children." Boris's older brother is 36 and works as an electrician in a factory. English chess writer David Hooper has a theory that a significant proportion of great chess masters are second children and more especially second sons in a family: Spassky,

Alekhine, Botvinnik and Fischer are among the known instances.

Boris was born on 30 January 1937, and was only four years old when there occurred the first crisis of his small life. The Germans invaded the Soviet Union in 1941, and the Spassky's home city of Leningrad soon came under siege. Boris was evacuated to Moscow two months after the outbreak of war, and returned to Leningrad only five years later. The war and the siege brought stresses which strained the Spassky marriage beyond breaking point. Boris's mother was the stronger character, a woman with firm, uncomplicated emotional beliefs. She was a Komsomol leader when a young teacher, likes revolutionary songs, yet is also puritanical and religious. "She has the deepest beliefs that everything is very good in the world," Boris told me, "and that a human being must take a very calm attitude to life." Mrs. Spassky has a stubborn streak, and it is stubbornness which Boris singles out as his own outstanding characteristic as a chessplayer. It is certainly a factor Spassky admires: reporting the Petrosian v. Korchnoy match for *Chess Life and Review* in 1971, he described Korchnoy as "a fighter with stubbornness that anyone could envy. He is tenacious in defence and can become quite 'angry' — in the sports sense of that word."

Boris's parents were divorced in 1944. The three children stayed with their mother, and Boris has since then only seen his father once or twice a year, though they both live in Moscow. Spassky senior has been twice divorced; the absence of a strong masculine figure in his early formative years was probably a factor which caused Boris, much later, to look for a chess trainer whom he could also admire as a father and family man. The comparison is obvious between Spassky, whose greatest chess victories coincided with his happy period working with his coach grandmaster Bondarevsky, and Fischer, whose father also disappeared from the family scene in early childhood and whose genius has come to full flower in the last two years with another strong character, USCF Director and former US Army Colonel Ed Edmondson, acting as his manager. In the writer's opinion, this similarity of family background is one of the reasons for the underlying and unexpected sympathy and friendship which existed between Spassky and Fischer before their great struggle in 1972.

Learning the moves

Boris learned to play chess at the age of five. It was a happy accident rather than family design, for Boris's father preferred dominoes to chess, while his mother was too absorbed in her work and struggle to bring up a family to have time for games. When Boris was evacuated from Leningrad, he was billeted in a private house with other children. "I remember that my favourite piece was a rook, because I liked very much that it moves in a straight line. Hop! But then I completely forgot about chess until our family returned to Leningrad after the war." Boris was probably fortunate to learn the moves so young, for recent research by the world champion's psychologist-trainer Nikolai Krogius in the Latvian magazine *Sah* has shown a distinct correlation between grandmasters who have learnt the moves of chess before the age of eight and those whose chess careers have remained at peak performance for extensive periods of years.

When the family returned to Leningrad after the war, Boris occasionally saw a chess club and "felt a great passion and a great respect for it. Then I began to visit a special summer chess pavilion in Central Park, Leningrad. The most interesting thing, which I remember very well, was that I was very afraid to ask anyone to play with me and my first two months were spent only as a spectator. Then I began to learn my first moves. The club was only open during the summer, and it was tragedy for me when it closed down in September. It was like a death, with no chess. I remember that I used to go to the pavilion at eleven in the morning and only came back at eleven at night. I was nine. We had very little food, for the period immediately after the war in 1946 was a very hungry time."

Next year, Boris joined the Leningrad Palace of Pioneers, and began to play chess more systematically. He started to improve, but didn't really believe he was a strong player: "when you are obtaining good results you begin to understand that you do not play chess so well." At the Palace of Pioneers, Boris met his first chess trainer, Vladimir Zak, a candidate master and the senior coach at the Palace. Boris remembers him as "a very interesting, very sympathetic man. Sometimes he gave me chess lessons. He showed me opening variations and perhaps he noticed that I had a chess talent. He understood that probably in the future I should be rather strong. He was my trainer and teacher for five years; a rather good time." It was Zak who first thoroughly analysed a move in the Nimzoindian (1 P—Q4 N—KB3 2 P—QB4 P—K3 3 N—QB3 B—N5 4 B—N5) which Boris later adopted and with which he scored his first notable victory against a grandmaster in his game with Smyslov at Bucharest 1953.

The Young Master — Passionate Calculator

The nine-year-old Boris had a curious mixture of passion within and dryness without in his approach to chess. He loved the game rather than the results, although after a defeat he was angry and often cried. In 1947, when he was ten, he had an encounter with a curious portent of the future. Victor Korchnoy, a gifted teenager, was the Soviet junior champion and gave simuls against the younger pioneers. Boris was his fan: "at that time he was for me like a chess God." At one of Korchnoy's exhibitions against fifteen opponents the young candidate master decided to take on a blindfold game, and by chance it was Spassky who was the opponent. Korchnoy won quite easily, and Boris wept as usual. 21 years later, in the final match of the challengers series, he got his revenge.

The tough practice in the Palace of Pioneers, coupled with Zak's intelligent coaching, soon developed Boris's talents, but it was still a hard period for him. "In 1946 I was a very weak player, in the third category. But I achieved successes because in 1947 I was promoted to the second category, the next year to the first, and in 1949 I became a candidate master; rather good! I played, though, like an old man; very positional and solid. You can understand this better if I tell you that when I was six or seven years old I was the chief in my family. My mother had a very difficult position; she was alone in Moscow with three children and she could not work after she was forty, as she had strained herself lifting a heavy weight. My father couldn't do anything for his family, and friends helped my mother to get by. No good for chess!"

Krogius, writing in the *British Chess Magazine* in May 1971, related how Spassky appeared to his opponents at the time: "People started talking about him as a prodigy. However, he was an unusual kind of *wunderkind,* as he was remarkably calculating and unchildlike at the board. His early games were too dry. I remember our game in the 1947 USSR Junior Championship. Boris was White, got a better ending, and then . . . offered me a draw. I asked him why and he gave me the business-like reply, 'I had already planned a draw in this game when I was considering the general situation in the tournament.' As you can see it was the reply of an experienced person, hardly that of a ten-year-old boy!" concludes Krogius.

Within himself, Boris was still emotional about chess. As he told me: "I got quite passionate when I was very young, up to the age of nine or ten. Between 1946 and 1950 I regularly played up to five hours a day. After that the emotion diminished and chess became a day to day habit. Probably love between people develops in the same way. As a young boy, I never thought that I should become a strong chessplayer or a professional. Later, when I grew up, I understood that it was necessary for me to take chess more seriously; but I continued to be very lazy about it — this is a contradiction, but it's in my nature to be like a Russian bear."

"What do you mean, a Russian bear?"

"Someone who is very calm and lazy, and who even finds it an effort to spend the time to stand up!"

Bucharest to Amsterdam — the Crown Prince

Despite the young Spassky's cautious appraisal of his results, his reputation grew steadily after 1950. He was second in the 1952 Leningrad championship, behind Taimanov but ahead of both Levenfish and Korchnoy; Botvinnik, who was at the centre of Soviet chess administration as well as world champion, praised him highly. In 1953, before even taking part in a USSR championship semi-final, he was selected as one of the Soviet players in the strong Bucharest international. The chess world started to sit up and pay attention when Spassky drubbed Smyslov in the very first round with Zak's move 4 B—N5. The tournament finished with Spassky sharing fourth with Boleslavsky and Szabo, who both played in the Candidates' tournament later in 1953.

Boris was 16, the age at which Bobby Fischer dropped out of high school to concentrate on chess. Boris, too, preferred chess and outdoor sports to the academic life, as he explained when I asked him his best school subjects. "I very much liked history, and I still do. But my best subject was mathematics, and I began my university course in that. I gave it up after two months and changed to journalism, as I couldn't work systematically at maths. I was a very lazy schoolboy, but sport took a lot of my time. I reached second category as a high jumper; I could clear five feet eleven and a half inches, that is one and a half inches more than my own height. I swam, and was a volleyball halfback. At junior school I sang patriotic songs and was quite a good orator."

"Why did you change your university course?"

"In mathematics it was necessary to work every day; but I often had to interrupt my studies to go to tournaments. So I switched courses and changed to a softer option in journalism. I got my degree, but the exams were easy. Actually, I am not a journalist by spirit; I don't even enjoy writing about chess. At one time I had a chess column in a Leningrad newspaper, but I gave it up. My time at university was not very useful — probably I even lost five years. Fischer is completely right when he says that it is a bad idea for a chess master to study hard at school or college."

After Bucharest, F.I.D.E. awarded Spassky the international master title. His first USSR championship strengthened his image as the crown prince of world chess. Equal with Botvinnik, Petrosian, and Ilvitsky and only half a point behind the joint winners Geller and Smyslov, Boris had become the youngest player at the time to qualify for the world title interzonal. Next, he became the first Russian to take part in the junior world championship and the only Russian to win it until Anatoly Karpov did so in 1969. Aside from an embarrassing moment in the preliminaries when his long side castled position was wrecked by the unknown West German Klages, he was never in difficulty and won the final with 8 out of 9.

A few days after the world junior, Spassky was playing in the interzonal. Again like Bobby Fischer in his first interzonal three years later, Spassky only narrowly scraped in the Candidates' tournament, tying seventh with Pilnik and Filip. But now he was an international grandmaster, and already accepted as one of the world's top ten. Next year, in 1956, he was third in the Candidates' tournament in Amsterdam, still only nineteen years of age. Astonishingly, he had none of the dreams of actually winning the highest title that you would expect from a young player in such a situation.

"I don't believe I ever considered the possibility (of becoming world champion). I used to play from tournament to tournament and from game to game. My outlook only changed much later, in 1964, when I was a main referee of the match Russian Republic v. Budapest. I decided to make a joke and I told Bondarevsky 'I shall be world champion.' Then I saw that my joke was coming rather good, and that I had a strong position. That was the first time I thought seriously about the title."

"You must have thought a little before then — after all, in 1956 you were one of the eight challengers."

"No, I didn't have any illusions about my result, although it was very interesting for me to play in such a tournament with grandmasters like Keres and Smyslov. It was a revelation to me how seriously and nervously the other candidates took their tournament work. I remember especially Bronstein one evening wanted to reassure himself about his prospects. He took three dice and threw them three times. Each time three fives came up, and Bronstein decided this was a lucky omen. Next round he had to play against Smyslov and he lost, completely killed. I tried to understand this situation; I was very young and I saw that the other candidates were very nervous and excited. I felt quite calm, and I understood that I was a very weak player in this company but had to fight-attack."

Despite his modest hopes in Amsterdam, Boris finished third equal, with only Smyslov and Keres in front of him. He lost only to Geller and Szabo. As Wade writes in *Soviet Chess*, "It seemed only a matter of time before the youngest grandmaster would follow with the sureness of Capablanca on to the world championship throne."

The Tragedy of Riga, 1958

Boris's less favourable results in the next couple of years seemed at first just natural reaction from his brilliant achievements in 1955 and 1956. He tied with Averbakh and Taimanov in the 1956 USSR championship, but was ill in the play-off and had to default one game. The 1957 championship was the first brilliant success for Mikhail Tal, who was soon to usurp Boris's position as the hero of the young generation. Tal won the title, with Spassky a useful equal fourth. Yet the start of the 1958 championship in Riga, which was another zonal tournament for the world title, seemed to indicate that Boris was again surging forward. A powerful win from Bronstein in the tenth round gave him the fine score of 7-2 (he had an early bye). Then came ominous signs of nerves and interzonal jitters, losses to Gurgenidze and Kotov. What went wrong?

"First of all, I possessed poor fighting spirit. If I lost a game, I could not sleep; whereas now, if I am beaten, I feel a great energy to fight again and I believe that the defeat is even helping me. In 1958 I became more ambitious, in fact over-ambitious. When you play in a tournament you should think about your result, but I made the mistake of expecting more than I could reasonably achieve."

It was in the last round at Riga that Boris played a game which became an omen of his lack of success in the next few years, and for a time threatened to blight his self-confidence in the same way that Cardoso-Bronstein, Portoroz 1958 and Quinones-Stein, Amsterdam 1964 did to two other world title contenders. Spassky met Tal, who needed to win to stay champion while Spassky also required the full point to make sure of an interzonal place. Spassky refused an early draw and obtained a much superior position. The bitterly fought game was adjourned after 40 moves, and both players stayed up all night to analyse.

Boris described to me what happened next day: "The game was adjourned, and I had a good position; but I was very tired from analysing and went to resume next morning unshaven. Before I played important games I usually tried to bathe, to put on a very good shirt and suit, and in general to look *comme il faut.* But on this occasion I had analysed incessantly and came to the board looking very dishevelled and fatigued. Then I was like a stubborn mule. I remember that Tal offered me a draw, but I refused. Then I felt my strength ebb away, and I lost the thread of the game. My position deteriorated. I proposed a draw, but Tal refused. When I resigned, there was a thunder of applause but I was in a daze and hardly understood what was happening. I was certain the world went down; I felt there was something terribly wrong. After this game I went on the street and cried like a child. I remembered that in 1951 when I lost to Smyslov in his clock simultaneous was the last time I cried, and I promised myself then never to cry again, but after losing to Tal I couldn't keep my word."

The Tal episode was still decisively influencing Boris's self-control three years later in the next zonal tournament in the spring of 1961. He had to win against Stein in the last round to qualify for the interzonal, but he attacked nervously and unsoundly to adjourn with a lost position. He analysed, found no chances to draw, went to Stein's room and offered to resign. Stein could not understand. "What is the proposal?" he asked. Boris resigned, and then asked Stein how he intended to continue after the adjournment. Stein then showed him "something terrible." Boris drew his own moral: "I understood that I resigned too early; it is necessary to fight to the last drop of blood in chess."

A Double Divorce

Spassky's recession period, climaxed by the failures in the vital games against Tal and Stein, coincided and was largely caused by personal problems on two fronts. In 1952 he had changed his trainer from Zak to Alexander Tolush, a fiery and brilliant player. The partnership worked well at first. Tolush went with Spassky to his first international at Bucharest, where Tolush himself also scored the success of his life by capturing top place.

"Tolush was very involved with chess," Boris told me. "He was a brilliant player who loved to sacrifice pieces, and he helped me very much. When I first met him in the early 1950's

I had a great desire to work with him, and I changed my style because my trainer was an attacking player. I began my first chess steps as a positional player, but when I was fourteen I felt there was something wrong with this approach. I felt a revolution — I didn't like my old way. I came to understand that chess has something extra besides sound strategy — attacks, sacrifices, creative ideas.

"It was then that I met Tolush, and it seemed natural that we should work together. He continued as my trainer from 1952 to 1960. It became a hard time for me, because I didn't find a good personal contact with Tolush. He was rather a brutal man and he liked very much to give advice to me." Boris mimicked Tolush's tone of voice: "I don't like that position! I've always tried to teach you; you are a very stupid boy; you make mistakes here, there, this time, that time; you must think, watch your step . . .   It was terrible! Eight years is a very long time, you know. I had nobody to turn to at that time except my mother. I didn't have contact with my brother and sister and was alone. That man . . . I still had respect for him, of course."

In the same period, Boris's first marriage was unhappy. "I had a very hard three years from 1959 to 1961. My nervous energy was completely destroyed for three years, and I could do nothing right. For example, I had some very good form in our national championship in Moscow in January 1961. I remember two very nice games: against Polugaevsky, which I lost, and against Smyslov, which was drawn. Despite the results, these were probably my best games. But at the end of them, I could do nothing right. I felt at the time that I had a talent, but I was very nervous. In that tournament I proposed a draw twelve times. Twelve times! It's terrible; now I never do it."

Boris and his wife were divorced in 1961; they had become, as Boris puts it, "like bishops of opposite colours." His wife has remarried (funnily enough her second husband is also named Boris Vasilievich) and she now lives in the south of the USSR with Boris's 11 year old daughter Tanya.

The divorce coincided with a final break with Tolush. In 1961 Spassky took what he thinks was the most positive step in his chess career; he started to analyse and work with Igor Bondarevsky, the grandmaster who is still his coach and trainer.

"Bondarevsky did a lot not only for my chess knowledge and understanding of positions, but also for my character. I admired him less as a grandmaster than I did Tolush. Bondarevsky used to be a combination player, but then he decided to become like Capablanca and now his chess is rather dull. But when I first got to know him well, I was drawn to him, felt a great respect and saw that this was a very interesting man."

"Every trainer gave me a lot in their different ways, and I respect all of them. But I quarrelled with Zak and Tolush, who probably didn't like my switch to Bondarevsky. Also I made the mistake of leaving Tolush at the time of my divorce, when I was in a very nervous state. I should have had a special meeting with him to explain what I was doing, but instead I refused to speak to him. At the time, I had five civil courts before my divorce — very bad situation!"

During his recession period, Spassky was also out of favour with the Soviet Chess Federation. If a USSR master misbehaves, he is suspended from play abroad for a year, and Boris was kept at home three times. One instance was after the 1960 world students championship in Leningrad, when Spassky, the Russian top board, lost the key game of the event with the white pieces to William Lombardy, the United States No. 1, in only 29 moves. The Americans won the tournament and the student team title, and Spassky was among those blamed for the USSR failure. It was said that he had not prepared properly and had failed to takē the training sessions seriously.

In 1961, he was dropped from the USSR student team which regained the championship at Helsinki. A year later, he was due to play as one of the Russian representatives in the traditional New Year tournament at Hastings, but was pulled out just before the start and substituted by Kotov.

Boris's description of his results in 1958-61 makes them sound a straight catalogue of defeat. In fact the overall impression is no worse than inconsistent, and reads remarkably well considering his difficulties at the time. A year after the Riga failure, he tied for second with Tal in the 1959 Soviet championship at Tiflis, a point behind Petrosian; in the same year he tied with Bronstein and Smyslov in the Moscow Central Chess Club's first international tournament. The feature of 1959 was Tal's brilliant success in winning the Candidates', twelve months after winning the Portoroz interzonal. At the time it looked as if the dramatic last round game at Riga 1958 had marked a decisive turn in the fortunes of the two young stars, but a year later Boris got consolation in the same city when he won an international tournament with 11½ out of 13, a full 2½ points ahead of the Tal who had just returned in triumph from the Candidates'.

Boris's win from Tal at Riga was an omen of recovery, and another significant encounter took place at Mar del Plata 1960. Boris and Bobby Fischer had a hectic race from start to finish, as they outclassed the other competitors and tied with 13½ out of 15. Spassky won their individual game with a King's Gambit to take a lead in his personal duel with his later challenger which by the start of 1972 he had extended to 4-1.

The Road to the Title: "It is awful."

Starting from late 1961, the curve of Spassky's career sets out on a fresh upswing. At Baku, he won the national title for the first time, holding off Polugaevsky's challenge in the closing rounds to capture the championship by half a point. Bondarevsky was now his main coach, but also between the two 1961 championships he trained for some months with the Leningrad master Klaman "to sharpen my style." Boris told me during the 1962 Varna Olympiad when commenting on his game there with Lothar Schmid: "Klaman, a highly original and daring player, taught me a lot about complicated sacrificial attacks on the king, and this sharp style which I choose in the Schmid game is perhaps a reflection of his teaching." Evidently Boris, despite the quarrel, was still nostalgic about his days with Tolush.

David Levy asked Boris in 1970 (the complete interview is in *Siegen Chess Olympiad*, by Keene and Levy) what he thought about the method of qualifying for the world championship. It's a subject about which Boris, like Bobby Fischer, is a trifle bitter: "I think it is necessary to change it because the challenger has to spend a lot of nervous energy and this is very hard. I know this because I was qualifying for six years and it is awful. The challenger comes to the match for the title completely ruined because he has spent his ideas and he is completely empty inside."

Boris's long trail began with a modest second place in the Kharkov semi-final of the 1963 USSR championship. The championship final qualified six players for a special zonal tournament (together with Korchnoy, who was ill during the championship). Boris shared first place, and in the play-off for the title was second to Stein. The double round zonal, with three players from seven qualifying for the 1964 interzonal, was a desperate affair, with only two points covering all the players at the finish. Boris suffered from his memories of 1958 and 1961: "I started very badly. I began to think it was the finish for me, but Bondarevsky helped me. It was a very hard time for both of us."

A closing spurt brought Boris through to qualify and even win the tournament, aided by Korchnoy's weak resistance in his final game. The interzonal at Amsterdam was another nerve-wrecker, as Boris handicapped himself by a slow start of 4 out of 7, which he drily described as "another type of sickness" from his old habit of cracking at the finish. "Probably this is psychological, because I have a very slow type of emotions. They take a long time to rouse, but then they become steadily stronger." The closing rounds were very tense, with the five Russian grandmasters fighting desperately among themselves because of the rule that only three of them could qualify. I was in Amsterdam at the time, and remember how Bronstein, during his game with Quinones of Peru, was fidgeting around the hall, talking to anyone who would listen about his crash against Cardoso at Portoroz 1958 . . . Smyslov adjourned against another tail-ender, Vranesic of Canada, more upset and agitated than I have ever seen him as he swapped variations in a difficult knight endgame with his trainer Polugaevsky. . . .

Boris is blessed with a poker face in such situations, so much so that Bobby Fischer once commented that "Spassky sits at the board with the same dead expression whether he's mating or being mated." I asked Boris if he was really as calm as he looked. "Actually I feel very nervous inside during a game, as if there was an explosion in progress. But when I make a mistake I try to keep myself under control, to remain quiet and calm and to find the best way out of a difficult situation. When I play chess probably I seem rather unruffled, but this is not really so. It is like a clown's face which is put on specially for the occasion; when I appear particularly calm I am really feeling specially nervous."

The clown's face was needed when Larsen stretched Boris to defeat in the second session: "I decided that it was the finish for me because I didn't know that Stein had failed to win against Quinones." Even in a 1971 interview, Boris described Amsterdam as the most difficult tournament of his life.

Until 1965 Spassky had never played a match. In the Candidates' encounters, he found it hard at first to adjust to the rhythm of a man-to-man encounter, and was surprised to find when he played Keres that he was already tired after seven or eight games. The Keres match proved to be a sharp fight, starting and ending with a tactical climax. Spassky typically described the first game, which he lost, as the most satisfying for him: "I made a very good sacrifice, but made a mistake and was crushed. Instead of R—R3, P—Q5 would have been strong." Keres' lead with this game was brief, for Spassky, playing Zak's 4 B—N5 in the Nimzoindian, equalised the score in the third game and then won two in a row with his opponent's favourite Ruy Lopez. Keres fought back to 4-5 with one game left, then went down in a maze of complications in the final game.

Spassky's impressive play against Keres made him the general favourite to beat Geller in the semi-final, and he was full value for the winning score of 5½-2½. Meanwhile Tal had beaten Portisch and Larsen in the other half of the draw to ensure a final match eagerly awaited by the chess public. Tal, handicapped by kidney disease, was no longer quite the player who had swept to the world title in 1960, but it looked a very open and interesting contest. Boris had prepared thoroughly. In view of his tendency to start badly, he stopped following Botvinnik's advice to rest for a week before an event and trained intensively beforehand by playing blindfold exhibitions against candidate masters. He would have liked to have played open games against Tal, but decided that it was necessary to use waiting tactics: "draw, draw, and draw again, reserving my final kick for the end of the match when I was gaining in strength and Tal was becoming weaker."

Spassky surprised his opponent and the chess world by playing the Marshall against the Ruy Lopez in three of his games with Tal. Tal failed to progress with the white pieces against it, and this was a decisive factor in the match. Said Boris: "I believe that the Marshall is good enough for a draw, which was of course all I aimed for with Black. After this match Bondarevsky and I thought we should erect a statue to Frank Marshall; a very sympathetic player!" Boris's tactics succeeded brilliantly and, following a run of five successive draws in the middle of the match, Tal's nerves broke in the latter stages of the ninth game enabling Spassky to win the final three games.

Claws of the Tiger

When I talked to Boris at Hastings three months before the 1966 title match, it was possible to sense a tide of rising eagerness in his thoughts. He quoted a comment by Tal that Petrosian was a very careful player; not passive, but a little bit cowardly. "I am a little younger, seven years, and my advantage is in the fifth hour of play. I have to think how to organise the games in such a way that the climax will come at the end of the session." It was generally expected in 1966 that Spassky's ability to combat Petrosian's favourite Caro-Kann 1 P—K4 P—QB3 would be one of the technical keys to the match, and I offered Boris a file of all known Caro-Kann variations to take back to Moscow. He thanked me, and said he felt that the defence to 1 P—K4 was Petrosian's major weakness in the openings. "I think it will be unwise for Petrosian to play the Caro-Kann in the match. 1 . . . P—QB3 is an unpositional move; he believes in it, though, and that's my chance. I feel very much at ease in such openings as the Caro-Kann and the French Defence. They don't seem to solve Black's centre problems; maybe I'm wrong, of course. Probably Petrosian's best chance is to meet 1 P—K4 with 1 . . . P—K4, for in the Ruy Lopez Black has good chances to equalise. But I doubt if Petrosian will play 1 . . . P—K4 because it will be a kind of psychological defeat for him.

Boris's hopes and forecasts started to go wrong from the first game, where Petrosian played the Caro-Kann, improved on a variation in the Barden file, and scored an easy draw. The first six games were all drawn, and Spassky in a recent article in *Chess Life and Review* pinpoints the fifth as the turning point of the match: "When I failed to win the 'won' fifth game, to a certain degree I lost confidence in myself and my opponent was right there to pick up his own confidence. It was by no means coincidental that after the twelfth game he was leading the match with a two-point margin." Boris's play in the seventh game, which he lost with the white pieces, shows something of the same loss of patience after a run of draws as happened to Tal in the ninth game of the 1965 match.

Petrosian's brilliant win in the tenth game showed not only that the champion was in his best form since he beat Botvinnik in 1963, but that Spassky was feeling the reaction from the long series of elimination events before the title. Boris recovered bravely in the second half of the match. He won at last against the Caro-Kann (at the fifth attempt) game 13 in a marathon 91 moves, but Petrosian wriggled, ducked, and weaved to stop or delay his efforts to level the scores. When Spassky at last struck convincingly against Petrosian's French Defence in game 19 to make it 9½-9½, it was also his final effort. In game 20, Petrosian trampled on the challenger's Nimzoindian to virtually ensure the title's stay in Armenia for another three years.

Taming of the Tiger

Before the 1966 match, I asked Boris how he would feel if he lost. "For me personally it will not matter too much if I lose; if I am defeated in this match, I shall still have hopes to meet Petrosian again." For the next two years, Boris's tournament results gave the impression that he was husbanding his resources, ready for a fresh assault on the title in 1969. His personal life was also changing, this time for the better. When I interviewed him at Hastings 1965-66, he told me that it was difficult to organise his time to prepare properly for the Petrosian match. "When I live alone a lot of time is spent on everyday practical problems; I have to wash my shirts and look after myself."

"You need a woman," I commented. "You're right," Boris replied, and laughed as I added "Only to wash your shirts?"

"I don't like this kind of life when it is so disorganised. A bachelor's life is very bad. But now that I am so involved with the world championship I don't like to spend a lot of time with girls — just enough to say how-do-you-do and goodbye." A year after the 1966 match he was married again, and his wife Larissa often came to the tournament hall in 1969 to watch the return with Petrosian. By 1970 he was telling David Levy that "I am never afraid about anything in my life. Only my young boy, he is three years old. Maybe he will be a bandit or something like that."

It was a successful period for him in tournaments, too, even though he was often not full out. His fine victory at Santa Monica 1966, ahead of both Petrosian and Fischer, was achieved in a style typical of several of his best results: a fair percentage of draws, but wins in the key games and of sufficient numbers to show who was the tournament boss. After another good win in early 1967 at Beverwijk, he was sufficiently inactive for the rest of the year before the 1968 Candidates' matches for Korchnoy to write that "Spassky's results have shown a noticeable downward trend in recent years." Boris had treated the Alekhine Memorial and Sochi in 1967 partly as training events. As he told me earlier: "Sometimes I find it difficult to play well against a close friend. In Sochi when I had a bridge foursome with Malich, Damjanovich and Jansa, I couldn't play against them seriously in the tournament, and proposed draws."

The 1968 Candidates' matches quickly showed that Boris had maintained his strength since the 1965-66 series. He defeated Geller by the same score of 5½-2½ as in their previous match, though the success was less convincing and depended on Geller's stubbornness in persisting with the black side of the Closed Sicilian which he handled poorly. Spassky's next match with Larsen was eagerly awaited, for the Danish grandmaster was telling the world of his intention to become world champion, and many believed him. Boris won the first three games, outplaying Larsen in both simple positions and tactical complications, and the match was virtually over. It was around this time that many commentators began to remark on Spassky's 'universal style' as his major strength. Fischer might calculate better, Tal might have more flair for sacrifices, and Korchnoy might be a better defender, but Spassky was the greatest all-rounder.

The Spassky v. Korchnoy match, the final eliminator of 1968, was an impressive example of Boris's resilience after a defeat compared with the 'latter round jitters' which affected him in the early 1960's. He reached a 3½-1½ score smoothly enough, then wrecked a winning position by a series of errors in the sixth game. Korchnoy, scenting a chance to come back, abandoned his usual Grunfeld for a King's Indian in the seventh game, but was beautifully smashed by the eager Boris, who finished with an elegant queen sacrifice. A notable indication of the sharp play in the Spassky-Korchnoy match was that queen's side castling occurred more often than in all the other six challengers' matches combined. "Spassky at the present time is superior to all his contemporaries . . . I do not doubt for a minute that we are going to have a new World Champion," said Korchnoy after the match — the same pundit who had commented just three months previously that "Spassky is in poor form."

Spassky's preparations for the 1969 match against Petrosian were more thorough than in 1966, when he was tired by the long series of elimination contests. He spent three months in early 1969 studying the openings and Petrosian's games. The team of helpers now included Nikolai Krogius, a psychology lecturer as well as a grandmaster. Boris also worked hard for physical fitness: a cross-country run each morning and Yoga exercises were part of his programme.

Spassky was the general favourite to win in 1969 and after a nervous defeat in the first game (what happened to the blindfold displays against candidate masters?) he drilled holes in the weak squares around Petrosian's castled king in the fourth and showed the most elegant play of the match in the fifth. When Petrosian lost game 8 by an opening blunder and the ninth was adjourned with Spassky the exchange up for a pawn, the results seemed flowing smoothly in favour of the challenger.

The next phase of the match, from the second session of the ninth game until game 17, was Spassky's last crisis before winning the title and poses some interesting questions. Spassky delayed a winning break-through in the ninth game and allowed Petrosian to build a blockade defence; and lost the tenth and eleventh to enable Petrosian to square the match. Now came a curious run of draws, with Spassky making only token efforts to win with the white pieces in games 13 and 15 against Petrosian's Petroff Defence. Krogius later claimed in his *British Chess Magazine* article that Spassky "did right from a psychological point of view. During that period Spassky was in boxing parlance 'groggy' because of the outcome of the tenth and eleventh games. He needed time to come round, recover his composure and then begin the real fight at the end of the match. It is curious that Petrosian failed to realise this, apparently thinking that Spassky had finally lost control of himself. I feel that Petrosian's only chance was to increase pressure in the 13th to 17th games. Instead he temporised, thinking as the proverb puts it 'that the apple would fall on itself'. That was why Petrosian did not withstand this fresh challenge and the match was decided."

It is suggestive to compare this account from a man who was at Spassky's side during the match with Boris's quick recovery from his setback in the Korchnoy match and Fischer's rapid bounce from a defeat during his 1971 encounter with Petrosian. The notable feature of games 9-17 was that Boris's weak period was relatively long — more than a third of the match. Spassky's current high esteem for Petrosian's play seems to date from this time. He told Ray Keene during the Siegen interview: "I think that perhaps the most interesting individuality is Petrosian's. . . . Because his play is deep, and he has very original ideas — strategical, but of course a little bit pragmatical. During the game he plays like a very nice cat. But this is not real because after that he becomes like a tiger."

In the final third of the match, the tiger was tamed. Spassky won game 17 when Petrosian lost his footing in complications, and increased his lead in game 19 with a slashing king's side attack. Petrosian revived briefly by winning game 20, but after rejecting a tactical chance to complicate, lost game 21 to go two down once more. It was the end. After two fairly uneventful draws, the match finished 12½-10½ in the challenger's favour. Dr. Euwe presented Boris Spassky with the gold medal of World Champion and the victor's laurel wreath.

Shadow over Olympus

Boris's first interviews after winning the championship sounded optimistic. He spoke of playing 100 tournament games a year, and of continuing to treat chess normally. He told Bertok of Yugoslavia that "I shall be afraid neither of draws with weaker players, nor of defeats . . . my preparations for chess events will be better and more thorough in future." Yet in fact he has played less since becoming champion than in earlier periods. He has aimed to win tournaments, but without trying to dominate the field — a feature of his play highlighted by the Leiden quadrangular of 1970 where he finished first with two wins and ten draws.

The years of a championship which promised to be a glamourous age for Soviet chess, judged by the adventurous approach which brought Boris to the title, have been overshadowed by the massive challenge from Bobby Fischer. Petrosian in his time found the role of world champion a hard one and his tournament results made it easy for critics to suggest that he was not really the World's No. 1. Boris himself, before becoming champion, did not envisage dominating his contemporaries. Realistically he accepted his own laziness as a restricting factor, and his answer when I asked him what he would expect from himself as world champion could prove an astute assessment of his future: "I hope I shall be stronger in three of four years' time than now (that was in 1966); but after that I shall decline and another strong player will take my place. Chess is an abnormal way of life, and to remain at the top you need to be very self-disciplined. Botvinnik is a very dedicated man, and has this discipline, but it is a quality you need to be born with. I am quite the opposite; very impractical and completely disorganised."

Boris's dramatic win over Fischer at Siegen 1970 has been the high point of Spassky's career as world champion before the match against the young American in 1972. The quality of the game, its importance in the struggle to win the Olympiad, and the tense emotional circumstances, all combined temporarily to hush the growing body of Fischer supporters. After Siegen Spassky again seemed briefly not only the world champion, but convincingly the world's best player. Between then and this book going to press, eighteen months have passed in which Boris seems, for whatever reasons, to be going through a period of self-doubt reminiscent of his crisis years around 1960. He did not play for nine months after Siegen, and his results during 1971 were in a subdued key which was emphasised by their contrast with Fischer's brilliance. He was equal second behind Hort in a small event at Gothenburg, struggled to tie with the Dutch international master Hans Ree at Vancouver after surviving a lost position against Suttles, and ended the year with sixth place in the Alekhine Memorial. Russian commentators grumbled at his dull performance and seeming lack of enthusiasm in the Alekhine. "I'm still king, you know," he told a reporter at the Alekhine, but added "I have very much work to do. I have many problems at the moment." Grandmaster Jan Donner of Holland commented after Fischer's match wins, but before the Alekhine Memorial: "I still think that Spassky will win (the match) because he has a deeper knowledge of chess and a bettter understanding of quiet positions. But Spassky has a great respect for Bobby's ability and I fear that subconsciously he may desire him to become the next champion."

Boris is an avid reader; a Yugoslav journalist described his flat as "books, books everywhere — but far from confined to chess as their subject." One of his favourite writers is Dostoevsky, and he also likes both Solzhenitsyn and Bulat Okudzhava, a poet and short story writer who renders ironic topical songs to his own guitar accompaniment. It often seems that Boris himself possesses Dostoevskyan personality features. He likes to say that "every man is full of contradictions" and in Boris there is a tug of war between the outward charm and irony and an almost harsh underlying self-criticism. Perhaps this is the reason why so far the creative flow and subtle positional understanding which has won him the world title has shown patchily. Yet another feature of his chess career is an ability, certainly in recent years, to produce his best on the biggest occasions. The Candidates' matches, the final games of the second Petrosian series, and the personal struggles with Fischer at Santa Monica 1966 and Siegen, all these indicate that the 1972 match may stimulate Spassky to peak form. Boris himself said last year that he welcomed the prospect of Bobby as his challenger: "Fischer would be a new opponent. A match against him would arouse great creative elan. It would be an interesting test." The 1972 match will be fought at an emotional level as well as on the battlefield of the Exchange variation of the Grunfeld, and it promises to be a struggle fascinating both from the technical viewpoint and the human.

(The writer wishes to thank the U.S. Chess Federation for permission to quote from 'Portrait of a world champion' published in *Chess Life*, 1970; the *British Chess Magazine* for extracts from 'A close-up on Spassky' by N. Krogius, published in their May 1971 issue; and R.D. Keene and D.N.L. Levy for extracts from their interview with Spassky in *Siegen Chess Olympiad;* and last, but not least, to Boris Spassky for spending several hours with my tape recorder when he visited England for the Hastings tournament of 1965-66.)

1949-57 CONTINUOUS IMPROVEMENT

Spassky himself admits that in his early period he had a cautious approach to the game. This was partly the result of coaching with its inevitable emphasis on sound play. Yet it is a surprise that the early games (Nos. 1-8) given here do not include a single King's Pawn opening while in his defence to the Queen Pawn he chose the solid Slav Defence (game 4).

In 1951 however Spassky changed trainers and the able pedagogue Zak was replaced by the attacking genius Tolush, who, if he had not been let down by bad health, would have made a far greater mark on the chess world than his isolated successes such as first prize at Bucharest 1953. This change bore fruit and as early as 1953 a tactical mastery began to show up ever more frequently in Spassky's games. Perhaps the best game in this period is his counter-attacking master-piece against Geller (game 11), as despite this defeat the Ukrainian was to go on and win the title in what was I believe the strongest ever Soviet Championship. The game against Stahlberg (No. 17) is also of considerable interest as in it Spassky adopted the Modern Benoni in the form that Tal was to adopt with great success in the late fifties.

1 Leningrad Junior Championship 1949
Black: Avtonomov
Queen's Gambit Accepted

1	P—Q4	P—Q4
2	P—QB4	PxP
3	N—KB3	N—KB3
4	P—K3	P—B4
5	BxP	P—K3
6	0—0	P—QR3
7	Q—K2	

The impeccably played opening suggests that both young players had been well coached!

7	....	P—QN4
8	B—N3	N—B3

An error, which commits Black too soon. 8 ... B—N2 is correct, retaining the option of QN—Q2.

9 N—B3

Failing to exploit his opportunity. The energetic move 9 P—QR4 forces the reply 9 ... P—B5 and after 10 B—B2 B—N2 11 PxP PxP 12 RxR followed by 13 N—B3 White has some advantage in view of his attack on the QNP and generally superior development.

9 ....   PxP?

Opening the position at a time when he cannot meet White's pressure on the Q file with QN—Q2. As 9 ... P—N5 10 N—QR4 produces a similar opening of lines (9 ... PxP 10 R—Q1) Black's only good move is to close the position by 9 ... P—B5.

10 R—Q1   B—N2

Black should try 10 ... B—K2, preparing to castle, or 10 ... P—Q6. Now White opens the K file and after the inevitable P—Q5 the whole centre bursts apart while the Black monarch is still dozing at home.

11 PxP   N—QN5

A desperate attempt to prevent P—Q5, which would in fact be the answer to 11 ... B—K2. However, although Black now has four units controlling his Q4 (the pinned KP must be disregarded in this count) the central breakthrough is still feasible, and indeed very strong.

12 P—Q5!   QNxQP

13 B—N5!

Now Black suffers from no less than three pins!

13 ....   B—K2

14 QBxN   PxB

Other moves just lose material at once.

15 NxN   BxN

If 15 ... PxN, to retain his bishop for defensive purposes,

then again 16 N—Q4 and as 16 ... B—B1 allows 17 N—B6 Q—Q3 18 BxP with a threat to the QR Black is no better off than in the actual game.

16 BxB   PxB

17 N—Q4

An ideal square for the knight. White could win the QP by 17 Q—Q2 or Q—Q3, but he already has enough advantage to play more ambitiously.

17 ....   K—B1

Not 17 ... 0—0? 18 N—B5 threatening the bishop as well as mate. If 17 ... Q—Q2 then 18 R—K1 with great pressure e.g. 18 ... R—R2 19 R—QB1 K—B1 20 Q—R5 followed by 21 N—B5 and wins easily since Black's scattered forces cannot cope with all the White-square pressure.

18 N—B5   P—KR4

To prevent 19 Q—R5, but now White has a neat sacrifice. Black could try 18 ... B—B4 but then comes 19 P—QN4 BxP (19 ... B—N3 20 RxP as in the game.) 20 Q—N4, while if 18 ... R—R2 then 19 Q—K3! and White penetrates with 20 Q—R6+.

19 RxP!	QxR
20 QxB+	K—N1
21 QxP(6)	Resigns

White threatens both 22 Q—N7 mate and 22 N—K7+ winning the queen. A most convincing final attack!

2 Quarter-final XX USSR Championship, Riga 1951
White: Estrin
Ponziani Opening

1 P—K4	P—K4
2 N—KB3	N—QB3
3 P—B3	

Estrin is the Soviet specialist on the open game and therefore normally prefers 3 B—B4 to 3 B—N5. Here his calculation seems to be that the fourteen year old schoolboy sitting opposite him would hardly be familiar with a genuine 19th century opening.

3	P—B4

Estrin is proved correct, since either 3 ... P—Q4 or 3 ... N—B3 are the only moves approved of by theory. However the text also seems playable.

4 P—Q4	

Best. After 4 PxP Q—B3 Black has a satisfactory game.

4	BPxP
5 NxP	Q—B3
6 N—B4	

The crucial line is 6 N—N4 Q—N3 7 P—Q5 (7 N—K3 preventing 7 ... P—Q4 is also good by analogy with the line 1 P—K4 P—K4 2 N—KB3 P—KB4 3 NxP Q—B3 4 P—Q4 P—Q3 5 N—B4 PxP when Nimzovich recommended 6 N—K3) 7 ... N—Q1 8 B—K2 B—B4 9 B—K3 with some advantage to White.

6	P—Q4
7 N—K3	B—K3
8 B—N5	B—Q3
9 0—0	

Too early. 9 P—QB4 gives White more options e.g. 9 ... N—K2 10 PxP (10 P—B5 B—B5 11 P—KN3 also comes into consideration) 10 ... 0—0 11 0—0 KNxP 12 NxN BxN 13 N—B3 with a fair game.

9	N—R3!

Fresh thinking. With his centre under less pressure than in the last note he can avoid the stereotyped N—K2 in favour of a more aggressive development.

10 P—B3?	

This leaves him exposed to a strong attack. 10 P—QB4 was better.

10	Q—R5!
11 P—KN3	

11 P—KR3 Q—N6 is certainly no more exciting a prospect.

(See diagram next column.)

11	BxP!
12 PxB	QxP+
13 N—N2	

After this he can never play PxP because of ... N—N5 when

KR2 cannot be defended along the second rank because of the blocking action of the knight at KN2. However 13 K—R1 is no better because then comes 13 ... 0—0 14 N—Q2 (14 PxP N—N5! 15 Q—K2 loses to 15 ... R—B7, and if White tries ti improve with 15 NxN? BxN 16 Q—K1 he loses his queen to 16 ... B—B6+!) 14 ... R—B5 15 N—N2 QR—KB1 with a decisive attack. e.g. 16 B—K2 P—K6!

13 ....   B—R6
14 Q—K2
Or 14 R—B2 0—0 and Black threatens 15 ... N—KN5.

14 ....   0—0
15 Q—KB2
Not 15 QBxN PxP! 16 Q—KB2 (16 RxP RxR 17 B—Q2 QR—KB1 18 B—K1 Q—N3 19 N—Q2 R—K6! wins) 16 ... QxN+

17 QxQ PxQ wins.
15 ....   Q—N3
16 B—K2
Or 16 N—Q2 P—K6!
16 ....   R—B3
17 P—KB4
Playing for exchanges is still no good as after 17 BxN QxB there is no defence to 18 ... R—N3..

17 ....   N—B4
Now the threat is 18 ... N—R5.
18 K—R2
Or 18 R—Q1 N—R5 19 B—B1 N—B6+ 20 K—R1 Q—R3.
18 ....   Q—R3
19 R—R1
Loses at once but there was no defence e.g. 19 R—N1 R—N3 20 N—K1 B—B8+ mates or 19 K—N1 R—N3.

19 ....   BxN+
     Resigns
Because of 20 KxB R—N3+.

This tournament was the first time that Spassky met Tal — but not over the board. As the Soviet master Chapiinsky puts it "Misha Tal was one of the regular audience for this tournament. In those days he was noticeably weaker than Spassky. Often after the round was over the two young players would analyse the games together. It was nice to see the tact with which Spassky explained things to Misha."

3 USSR Junior Team Championship, 1952
Black: Juchtman
Nimzoindian

| 1 P—Q4 | N—KB3 | 3 N—QB3 | B—N5 |
| 2 P—QB4 | P—K3 | 4 P—K3 | 0—0 |

5 P—QR3   BxN+
6 PxB   P—B4
7 B—Q3   P—Q4

Long experience has shown that Black does better to leave White with the doubled pawn and try 7 ... N—B3 or 7 ... P—QN3 meeting 8 P—K4 with 8 ... N—K1 in order to avoid the pin: 9 B—N5.

8 BPxP   KPxP
9 N—K2!

The knight is best placed here guarding the weakness at QB3 and preparing to control K4 with P—B3.

9 ....   P—QN3
10 P—QR4

The first sign of inexperience from the young master. All White's chances are on the K side and so he should simply castle. The plan of developing his bishop at QR3 is irrelevant to the demands of the position.

10 ....   B—R3
11 B—R3   Q—B1

A good move, emphasising his control of the White squares and ready to meet the immediate 12 N—N3? with 12 ... PxP 13 BPxP?? Q—B6+ winning material.

12 0—0   R—K1
13 N—N3   BxB
14 QxB   P—B5

A risky move. Black was probably worried about the possibility of 15 PxP PxP 16 P—QB4, but simply 14 ... QN—Q2 followed by 15 ... Q—N2 or even 14 ... Q—R3 would leave him with equality. Now, however, that Black has removed the tension from the centre White can easily prepare the thematic advance P—K4.

15 Q—B2   P—N3?

Black pays dearly later on for this weakening of his black squares. The threat of 16 N—B5 was better met by 15 ... N—R3 16 N—B5 R—K3 and then Q—Q2 followed by QR—K1, so as to attack White's K3 and K4 and thus restrain the advance of the KP.

16 QR—K1   P—KR4

A further weakening of his K-side, though with the laudable objective of reducing White's central control by driving his knight to the edge of the board.

17 P—B3   Q—B3

An inconsistency, but probably dectated by the fact that after 17 ... P—R5 18 N—R1 the knight will quickly emerge again from his stable via KB2.

18 Q—B2!

Now White forces P—K4 when the pressure of his queen down the soon-to-be-opened KB file becomes decisive.

18 ....   QN—Q2

18 ... QxP is too great a luxury given Black's backward development. White replies 19 B—B1 and then 20 P—K4 and the absence of the queen from the Q side renders Black's defensive task even more onerous.

19 B—B1   R—K3
20 P—K4!

Now White has concentrated all his forces where they matter: on the K side and in the centre. Black is lost.

20	P—R5
21 N—R1	PxP
22 PxP	RxP
23 RxR	QxR

Or 23 ... NxR? 24 QxBP+ K—R1 25 Q—K7 Q—Q3 (otherwise 26 R—B7) 26 QxP+ K moves 27 QxN.

24 B—N5

The bishop was needed on the K side!

| 24 .... | P—R6 |

Black has been outplayed and tries for traps.

25 PxP

Black has no justification for playing on now since 25 ... Q—B4 is met by 26 Q—R4 and 27 RxN!

25	R—KB1
26 N—N3	Q—Q6
27 BxN	NxB
28 QxN	

Black soon resigned as he has no defence to 29 K—R1 followed by 30 N—R5 or 30 N—B5 depending upon the position chosen by his queen.

4 Leningrad Championship 1952
White: Furman
Queen's Gambit Declined

1 P—Q4	P—Q4
2 P—QB4	P—QB3
3 N—KB3	N—B3
4 N—B3	P—K3

Inviting White to play the complicated line: 5 B—N5 PxP 6 P—K4 P—QN4 7 P—K5 P—KR3 8 B—R4 P—KN4. Furman who is known for his strong preference for steady positional play chooses a quieter line.

5 PxP	BPxP
6 B—B4	N—B3
7 P—K3	B—K2
8 B—Q3	B—Q2
9 P—KR3	R—QB1
10 0—0	N—QN5
11 B—N1	

White must retain this bishop if he is to strive for an advantage.

| 11 .... | 0—0 |

| 12 N—K5 | N—B3 |
| 13 Q—Q3 | |

Black's knight manoeuvre has given White a strong attacking position, but in view of the symmetrical pawn formation and the absence of an open K file for White the following forced weakening move does not entail particularly serious consequences.

13	P—KN3
14 B—R6	R—K1
15 P—B4	

A double-edged move weakening his KN3 and K4 squares. It is far from certain that White will enforce P—B5, so 15 P—R3 intending to gain space on the Q side by P—QN4, is a sounder plan.

| 15 .... | N—KR4! |

16 P—KN4

Otherwise N—N6—B4 exploits the exposed QB.

16	N—N2
17 Q—K2	

White realises that he has weakened his position somewhat and plays to consolidate. The impetuous 17 P—B5 is met by 17 ... NxN 18 PxN B—KN4! 19 BxB QxB and if 20 P—B6 simply 20 ... N—B4!. but not 20 ... QxKP 21 K—N2! winning a piece for two pawns

17	NxN
18 BPxN	P—B3
19 PxP	BxP

Now the attack has been liquidated and White must be content with steady play in an attempt to preserve equality.

20 B—B2	B—KN4
21 BxB	QxB
22 K—R2	B—B3
23 B—N3	

Otherwise 23 ... P—K4.

23	R—B1
24 R—B3?	

24 QR—K1! intending to guard his main weakness by N—Q1 and then to exchange both pairs of rooks would keep the game level.

24	RxR
25 QxR	R—B1
26 Q—N3	P—KR4!

Thus Black takes the initiative, exploiting his command of the KB file and the weakness of White's K3.

27 R—KN1?

Too passive. He had a better chance of drawing in the variation 27 PxP QxQ+ 28 KxQ N—B4+ 29 K—R2 PxP 30 R—K1 so as to protect his K3 and KB2 by N—Q1. Then if 30 ... N—R5 31 R—K2.

27	P—R5!

28 Q—K1	R—B6
29 N—Q1	Q—K2
30 N—B2	

Otherwise 30 ... Q—Q3+ winning the KRP.

30	P—K4
31 B—Q1	

White has gone over completely to defence.

31	R—N6!

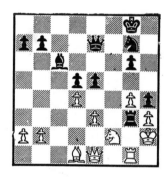

This move demonstrates that White's defensive play is inadequate to hold the game. White's best now was to go into the ending a pawn down by 32 RxR PxR+ 33 KxP PxP 34 N—Q3 though it is doubtful if he can successfully blockade the passed pawns for long, since P—Q5 will soon make Black's bishop very mobile.

32 N—Q3	PxP
33 PxP?	

Missing his last chance of prolonging resistance by 33 RxR which would transpose into the last note.

33	R—K6!
34 Q—Q2	

The knight has to be guarded and 34 Q—B1? B—N4 loses a piece.

34 ....   Q—K5
35 R—K1

"Pinning" the rook but the knight is attacked by the queen as well. However, 35 N—B2 loses

White's queen after 35 ... Q—B5+

35 ....   RxN
36 Q—KB2   QxQP
Resigns

5 Bucharest 1953
Black: Smyslov
Nimzoindian

1 P—Q4   N—KB3
2 P—QB4   P—K3 .
3 N—QB3   B—N5
4 B—N5

The Leningrad system, successfully introduced into grandmaster play by Keres against O'Kelly in the 1952 Budapest Maroczy Memorial Tournament. Spassky has often employed it.

4 ....   P—KR3
5 B—R4   P—B4
6 P—Q5

Not 6 P—K3? Q—R4! and Black has much the better of it.

6 ....   PxP

O'Kelly played 6 ... BxN+ 7 PxB P—K4 but after 8 P—K3 P—Q3 9 Q—B2 QN—Q2 10 B—Q3 Q—K2 11 P—B3! P—KN4 12 B—N3 N—R4 13 N—K2 White stood better. Against the very dangerous pawn-sacrifice 6 ... P—QN4!? Spassky might well have continued: 7 PxKP BPxP 8 PxP 0—0 9 P—K3 P—Q4 10 N—B3 QN—Q2 11 B—Q3 as he did against Liebert at Sochi 1967.

7 PxP   P—Q3
8 P—K3   QN—Q2
9 B—QN5

The Chigorin influence at work. In the forties and fifties Soviet methodologists laid great stress on Chigorin's view that the supposed advantage of bishops over knights was ofter overestimated, and in Spassky's games there are a number of cased where he had two knights against two bishops and won (see game 24). The point of the text is to take the sting out of a possible 9 ... Q—R4 which could follow in answer to 9 B—Q3. Now, however, 9 ... Q—R4 is met by 10 BxN+ BxB 11 N—K2 with some advantage. In later games Spassky came to the conclusion that Q—R4 was no great threat and reverted to 9 B—Q3 (see game 15).

9 ....   0—0

Black probably does better to accept the weakening of his K side by 9 ... P—KN4; after 10 B—N3 Q—R4 11 BxN+ BxB 12 N—K2 B—N4 Black has equality (Spassky-Porath, Amsterdam Interzonal, 1964). This line, however, has a bad reputation for Porath soon went wrong: 13 P—QR3 BxN+ 14 NxB B—B5? when 15 Q—B3! K—K2 16 BxP+ KxB 17 QxN+ K—B2 18 QxBP+ gave

White an easy win.

10 N—K2	N—K4
11 0—0	N—N3
12 B—N3	N—R4

A possible improvement here is 12 ... B—B4 and if 13 P—B3 then 13 ... P—R3 to exchange white-squared bishops.

13 B—Q3

Before Black gets his Q side majority moving by means of P—R3 and P—QN4. However, the text admits that his 9th move was probably not best.

13	NxB
14 NxN	N—K4
15 B—K2	BxN
16 PxB	Q—R5

At first sight Black has got over the opening difficulties by exchanging White's superior bishop, but now he has to face the threats arising from White's mobile centre pawns.

17 P—KB4!	N—N5
18 BxN	BxB
19 Q—R4!	

Threatening the curious long lateral pin 20 P—B5. Thus 19 ... P—R3? 20 P—B5 P—QN4 (or 20 ... Q—N4) 21 Q—KB4! and White wins material.

19 ....   B—B1

Clearly this is a game out of the ordinary. White moved his KB four times in the opening and now Black finds nothing better than playing right back home so as to maintain his queen in its attacking position.

20 P—K4	Q—N5
21 Q—B2	P—KR4

Ambitious play that ultimately tells against Black, as he weakens his K side without really achieving his object of driving the knight to an inferior square. But 21 ... P—B3, to restrain the

advance of the KP, is met by 22 P—K5! vacating K4 for the knight, so 21 ... B—Q2 seems best.

22 R—B2	P—QN4
23 P—K5	P—R5
24 N—B1	

Not 24 N—K4 B—B4.

24	B—B4
25 Q—Q2	PxP

In the higher sense the losing move as it opens the KB file for White and also gives him use of his KB4 square. The strictly defensive 25 ... QR—Q1 26 R—K1 KR—K1 is the correct strategy.

26 PxP   B—N3

He had to meet the threat of 27 N—K3, but now the bishop is not available for the blockade of the formidable centre pawns.

27 R—K1	P—R6
28 P—Q6	B—K5
29 N—K3!	Q—K3

Or 29 ... Q—N3 30 R—B4! BxP 31 R—KN4 with a strong attack. 29 ... Q—N4 looks better, but after 30 P—N3 Black still has to face the awkward threat of 31 R—B4 as 30 ... QxKP loses material to 31 N—B5!

30 R—B4!   BxP

Not 30 ... QxKP 31 N—N4.

31 N—B5!

Now White has a winning

attack for if 31 ... P—N3 then 32
R—K3! KR—K1 33 N—K7+
K—N2 34 R—B6 followed by 35
R—N3, while, as an alternative,
White has 32 R—KR4 PxN (other-
wise 33 Q—R6) 33 R—R6! P—B3
34 PxP etc.

   31 ....   KR—K1
   32 R—K3   QR—Q1?

Black mobilises his rooks too
late. However he could still put

up some resistance with 32 ...
P—N3, whereas the text loses at
once.

   33 NxP!   RxP

Or 33 ... KxN 34 R—N3+
K—B1 35 RxP+ KxR (35 ... QxR
36 Q—R6+) 36 Q—B4+ and mates.

   34 NxQ   Resigns

34 ...RxQ allows a beginner's
mate in two with the two rooks
at the edge of the board.

6 Bucharest 1953
Black: Golombek
Nimzoindian

1	P—Q4	N—KB3
2	P—QB4	P—K3
3	N—QB3	B—N5
4	B—N5	P—B4
5	P—Q5	P—KR3
6	B—R4	P—K4
7	P—K3	P—Q3
8	B—Q3	P—QN4

A mixture of systems. The
gambit is normally tried at move
six when the more fluid nature of
the centre gives it a better chance
of success. The text involves
Black in the weakening move
P—KN4, therefore 8 ... BxN+
seems best.

   9 PxP

White could also play 9 N—K2
P—N4 10 B—N3 P—K5 11 B—B2
PxP 12 0—0 as Black's KP would
be a convenient object of attack.

   9 ....   P—N4
   10 B—N3   B—N2

10 ... NxP is better e.g. 11
B—K4 (11 Q—B3 N—N3) 11 ...

BxN+! (11 ... NxN 12 PxN BxP+
13 K—K2 is good for White even
after Black's best reply 13 ...
P—Q4 14 QxP! QxQ 15 BxQ
BxR 16 N—B3!) 12 PxB NxBP 13
Q—Q3 NxB 14 QxN Q—R4+ 15
K—Q1 QxNP 16 QxR Q—Q6+
with a formidable counter attack
that should be worth at least a
draw. White in fact would do
best to meet 10 ... NxP with the
quiet 11 N—K2.

Once Black has missed this
chance his position rapidly
deteriorates.

   11 N—K2   NxP
   12 0—0   N—Q2?

He must play 12 ... N—KB3 to
rule out White's powerful reply.

   13 B—K4

Now it becomes clear that
Black has lost the opening
struggle. He has not yet removed
his king into safety, his QP
becomes exposed to attack along

the open file and his pieces are not very safely placed.

In contrast White has no weak points in his position.

13 ....   BxN

Trying to get rid of one liability. 13 ... NxN 14 NxN BxN 15 BxB BxP (otherwise he loses a pawn with no compensataion) 16 R—N1 R—QN1 17 RxB RxB 18 QxP is no better since after 18 ... R—N3 (18 ... Q—K2 19 Q—QB6 R—N3 20 Q—R8+ and 21 QxP) 19 Q—Q5 he still cannot castle because of the killing pin 20 R—Q1.

14 BxN!

Not 14 PxB N(2)—B3.

14 ....   BxB
15 QxB   BxP
16 QR—Q1

Now White threatens not so much 17 QxQP as 17 Q—N3 harrying the lame duck of a bishop.

16 ....   B—R6

Or 16 ... P—K5 17 BxP with a quick win.

17 QxQP   Q—K2
18 Q—QB6   R—Q1

I wonder if Harry Golombek began to realise at this stage that his position bore some resemblance to the famous game between Morphy and the aristocratic consultation team?

19 N—B3   0—0

The Duke and the Count never managed to castle!

20 N—Q5

The crude 20 QxRP was equally strong, but the text is much more aesthetic — a real chess player's move!

20 ....   Q—K3

Or 20 ... Q—K1 21 QxN (21 QxRP P—B3 22 N—B7 is also an easy win) 21 ... RxQ 22 N—B6+ K—R1 23 NxQ RxR 24 BxP+ P—B3 25 BxP+ with a straightforward win in the ending.

21 QxQ   PxQ
22 N—K7+   K—B2
23 N—B6   K—K1
24 R—Q3

Stronger than taking the exchange as the text again has aesthetic arguments in its favour since it exploits the leitmotiv of the whole game — pressure on the Q file combined with harrying the misplaced bishop.

24 ....   B—N7

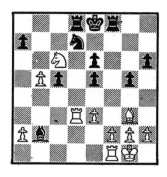

25 KR—Q1

This is the move given in the Rumanian tournament book and Black then resigned. However, as Black in fact could prolong the game a little by 25 ... P—B5 26 NxR PxR 27 NxP R—B3 I feel this may well be a misprint. The strongest move is of course 25 R—N3! which would indeed force immediate resignation (but not 25 R—N1 P—K5!).

7 Bucharest 1953
White: L. Szabo
King's Indian Defence

1 P—Q4	N—KB3
2 P—QB4	P—Q3
3 N—KB3	P—KN3
4 N—B3	B—N2
5 P—K4	0—0
6 B—K2	P—K4

The most common position in the King's Indian Defence over the last two decades. We now have the great parting of the ways. White can close the centre with Petrosian's favourite move 7 P—Q5 intending 8 B—N5, or play for a more flexible type of game by castling. The third lalternative 7 PxP is not good as White stands to get the worst of it due to the weakness of his Q4 square. Both players would be well aware of this for they would be familiar with the game Grunfeld-Geller, Szczawno- Zdroj 1951 which went 7 PxP PxP, 8 QxQ RxQ 9 B—N5 '(9 NxP NxP!) 9 ... QN—Q2 10 QR—Q1 R—B1! 11 N—Q5 P—B3 and White's temporary initiative petered out.

    7 0—0   N—B3

A comparatively new move at the time putting more pressure on White's centre than the traditional 7 ... QN—Q2 and so forcing White's hand.

    8 P—Q5   N—K2
    9 N—K1

Clearly Szabo intends following the plan which was successful in the Taimanov-Bronstein game played in the XX USSR Championship 1952, of which more anon. Taimanov, who has had more experience of this position than anyone else, has oscillated over the years between the text, 9 P—QN4 and 9 N—Q2. In his 1971 Candidates Match with Fischer he obtained a good game from his latest idea 9 B—Q2, a neutral developing move, that retains the option of answering Black's eventual P—KB4 with N—KN5.

    9 ...   N—Q2
    10 B—K3

This allows Black to gain a tempo with P—KB5 later. 10 N—Q3, in order to force P—QB5 without committing his bishop, seems White's best.

    10 ....   P—KB4
    11 P—B3   P—B5
    12 B—B2   P—KN4
    13 P—QN4

Szabo finally deviates from the Taimanov-Bronstein game which had continued: 13 N—Q3 R—B3 14 P—B5 R—R3? 15 PxP PxP 16 N—N5 B—B1 17 B—K1 and Black's attack develops much too slowly since he has wasted time in placing his rook on a poor square. The correct Black defence is 14 ... N—N3 15 R—B1 R—B2 16 R—B2 B—B1 using his passive bishop to defend his weak Q3 and then attacking later by R—N2 and P—N5.

    13 ....   R—B3
    14 N—Q3?

Inconsistent. The knight could well be left at home for the defence of the K side. 14 P—B5 at once was the logical move.

14 ....   R—N3!

Spassky does not make the same mistake as Bronstein and soon drums up a formidable attack on the KN file.

15 P—B5   N—KB3
16 Q—N3

Another careless move which weakens his control over KN4 and does nothing to advance his Q side attack. 16 R—B1 looks best, intending the standard follow-up PxP and then N—N5—B7.

16 ....   K—R1

Not so much to avoid a possible check on the White diagonal QR2/KN8 as to make room for a major piece at KN1.

17 KR—B1   P—N5!
18 KBPxP

A serious concession, weakening his KP, but after his previous· inaccuracies White had only a choice of evils. Thus P—N6 was a serious threat and after 18 PxQP PxQP 19 N—N5 P—N6! 20 PxP PxP 21 B—K3 (21 BxP RxB! or 21 B—K1? Q—N3+) 21 ... B—R3 22 N—K1 (22 BxB? RxB intending. 23 ... Q—B1 and then R—R8+! mating) 22 ... K—N1 23 NxRP B—Q2 Black has a winning attack due to his threat of N—N1 followed by Q—R5 when the advanced KNP *"wirkt wie eine Figur,"* as Dr. Tarrasch so nicely put it.

18 ....   BxP
19 B—B1

The KP was threatened as well as 19 ... P—B6

19 ....   B—B6

The tempo gained by attacking the KP allows a decisive strengthening of the pressure against the KNP

20 Q—B4

A menial role for the queen, but 20 R—K1 BxNP 21 BxB P—B6 is ·no improvement.

20 ....   BxNP
21 BxB   P—B6
22 N—K1

Or B—N3, which would almost certainly transpose into the game.

22 ....   PxB
.23 NxP

In such situations the enemy pawn in front of the king can sometimes be left as a self-block to the attacking pressure along the file. Here, however, this is not the case since Black threatens to extend the conflagration to other points in the vicinity of the king by 23 ... N—N5 in combination with B—R3.

23 ....   B—R3

The problem child of the closed King's Indian Defence formations at last gets a chance to play an active role.

24 R—B2   Q—KN1
25 B—N3

After 25 B—K1 Black simply trebles on the file by 25 ... Q—N2 when the knight will not be able to move in view of the check threat at KN1. The counter 25 B—R4, hoping to exchange minor pieces and discourage N—N5 because of the hanging knight at Black's K2, fails to 25 ... N—N5! 26 BxN N—K6 or 26 K—R1 N—K6 27 NxN BxN N—K2 Q—B2 29 N—N1 (otherwise 29 ... Q—B6+) 29 ... QR—KN1 30 B—N3 RxB 31 PxR RxP with a winning attack after 32 R—KB1 Q—N2 or 32 Q—K2 Q—N3.

(See diagram next column.)

25 ....   RxB!
26 PxP

Or 26 PxR QxNP and the threat of 27 ... N—N5 decides e.g. 27 N—K2 B—K6+ and mate next move.

26	PxP
27 Q—B7	R—N2
28 QxQP	N—N5

Defending the KP and threatening 29 ... N—K6.

| 29 K—R1 | R—Q1 |
| Resigns | |

---

8 Semi-final XXII USSR Champ., Leningrad 1954
Black: Byushev
Grunfeld Defence

1 P—Q4	N—KB3
2 P—QB4	P—KN3
3 N—QB3	P—Q4
4 B—N5	

A move played infrequently until it was adopted by Taimanov in the 1969 USSR Championship and in the subsequent USSR-Rest of World match, after which it became all the rage.

| 4 .... | N—K5 |
| 5 B—B4 | |

Taimanov's idea is 5 B—R4 to maintain pressure on the KP.

5	NxN
6 PxN	B—N2
7 P—K3	0—0
8 N—B3	

Up to now the play has been quite correct and with 8 ... P—QB4, the key move in this defence, Black could secure comfortable equality. Instead he plays a much more passive move that fails to challenge White's centre.

8	P—QB3?
9 B—Q3	PxP
10 BxP	N—Q2

It was still better to challenge in the centre with 10 ....P—QB4.

| 11 0—0 | N—N3 |
| 12 B—QN3 | N—Q4 |

By 'forking' the QBP and QB Black forces the exchange of a White bishop but this is very poor compensation indeed for the central advantage which he has conceded.

| 13 N—K5 | NxB |

Not 13 ... NxBP 14 NxKBP! RxN (14 ... NxQ 15 NxQ+ K—R1 16 N—B7+ winning the exchange) 15 BxR+ KxB 16 Q—N3+ N—Q4 17 P—K4 winning material.

| 14 PxN | Q—Q3 |
| 15 R—K1 | P—K3 |

After this Black remains very cramped. His 14th move is only logical when followed by 15 ...

B—K3, though after 16 R—N1
White has awkward pressure
along the two files occupied by
his rooks.

16 Q—B3   R—K1

Inaugurating a completely incorrect plan intended to drive
away White's knight with P—B3.
Black's passive play has left him
with the type of lifeless position
in which it is better to avoid all
pawn moves as weakening. The
purely Steinitzian manoeuvre 16
... R—Q1 followed by B—Q2—K1
seems his best chance, putting the
onus on White to break through.

17 P—KR4   P—B3?

Consistent but bad. Despite the
threefold protection of his K3 it
soon becomes a clearly weak
point.

18 N—Q3   P—N3
19 P—R5   PxP

Positionally bad, but Black
would also have · a vulnerable
KN3 if he allowed PxP, after
which White would continue
with Q—N3 and B—B2.

20 P—B5!

(See diagram next column.)

Of course this possibility ex-
plains the · choice of Q3 as the
retreat square for his knight at
move 18.

20 ....   K—R1
21 N—B4   B—N2

Nor 21 ... P—K4? 22 QxRP
and 23 N—N6 mate. Black could
quite easily resign at this stage.
As usual we now see how crisply

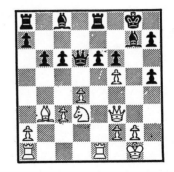

Spassky finishes off an opponent
who "is dead, but won't lie
down."

22 PxP   R—K2
23 NxP   R—KB1
24 N—N3!   P—QB4

Black's only really active move
of the whole game!

25 P—Q5!   P—B5
26 N—B5   Q—B4
27 BxP   RxP

A psychologist rather than an
annotator is required to explain
Black's last few moves of this
game.

28 RxR   QxB
29 Q—N3   Resigns

My own observations seem to
show that those players who like
to play on longer than is really
necessary seem unable to bring
themselves to persist in the habit
when the opponent is about to
administer the coup de grace! (29
... R—KN1 30 R—K8! QxQP 31
QxB mate or 29 ... R—B2 30
R—K8+ B—B1 31 RxB+!).

9 Semi-final XXII USSR Champ., Leningrad 1954
Black: Zurakhov
Sicilian Defence

1 P—K4	P—QB4
2 N—KB3	P—Q3
3 P—Q4	PxP
4 NxP	N—KB3
5 N—QB3	P—QR3
6 B—KN5	P—K3
7 Q—B3	

Once thought very strong this move has nowadays been rejected in favour of 7 P—B4. The theory is that piece pressure alone is not sufficient to open up the game and White must mobilise his pawns, in particular aiming for P—K5.

7 ....   P—R3

Considered strongest. Black must have a chance of breaking the pin later by P—KN4, and meanwhile does not fear doubled pawns because of their strong influence in the centre.

8 B—R4   B—K2

More exact is 8 ... QN—Q2 when after 9 0—0—0 N—K4! 10 Q—K2 (10 Q—R3 N—N3!) 10 ... P—KN4! 11 B—N3 B—Q2 12 P—KR4 R—KN1 13 PxP PxP 14 N—B3 Q—B2 Black had an equal game (Spassky-Petrosian XXII USSR Championship 1955).

9 0—0—0   Q—B2

There was already a threat of 10 P—K5.

10 B—K2   N—B3

This lets White get in a promising pawn sacrifice. 10 ... B—Q2 first was more accurate.

11 NxN   PxN

11 ... QxN was feasible. White would continue 12 P—KN4 trying to open lines on the King side.

12 P—K5!

This leaves Black with a poor pawn structure and a weak square at his QB4. The move is often feasible in the Sicilian. Compare for example with the game Fischer-Nichevsky Zagreb 1970 which went 1 P—K4 P—K3 2 P—Q4 P—QB4 3 N—KB3 PxP 4 NxP P—QR3 5 N—QB3 Q—B2 6 P—KN3 N—KB3 7 B—N2 N—B3 8 0—0 P—Q3 9 R—K1 B—Q2 10 NxN PxN 11 P—N3 B—K2 and now 12 P—K5! PxP 13 B—N2 0—0 14 Q—K2 N—Q4 15 NxN KPxN 16 BxKP and White has the better of it.

12 ....   PxP

13 KR—K1   0—0

14 B—Q3

A useful move as his bishop may come into play at K4 and his rook is now attacking the weak pawn at K5.

14 ....   R—N1

15 B—N3   B—Q3

16 Q—K2

The alternative plan was 15 N—K4 and if 16 ... NxN 17 BxN B—N2? (17 ... P—KB4!) 18 RxB! QxR 19 BxKP QxB? 20 B—R7+ However, the text keeps up the tension as Black's ·minor pieces are forced into awkward positions to defend his extra pawn.

16 ....   N—Q2

17 B—QB4!

Now 17 ... B—N2 loses material after 18 Q—Q2! N—N3 19 BxP(K6) PxB 20 QxB. Note that 17 BxRP would ease Black's game by removing his weak QB and ceding him another open file on the Q side along which his rooks could operate against the White king.

17 ....   N—N3
18 RxB   QxR
19 BxP(K5)   Q—B4

Black had relied on this as a saving clause, but Spassky is not interested so much in material as in an attack based on his strong bishops.

20 Q—N4!   P—B3

After 20 ... P—N3 21 BxR QxB 22 Q—R3 White has powerful threats on the black squares, (22 ... K—R2 23 R—K4 and 24 R—KR4, 22 ... N—Q2? 23 B—Q6 and 24 QxRP).

21 BxP+   BxB
22 QxB+   K—R1
23 BxR   RxB
24 N—K4   Q—QN4

Black's only counter chance is on the QN file.

25 R—Q1   N—Q4

Or 25 ... N—B5 26 P—QN3 and Black has nothing.

26 P—QN3   N—N5

Apparently strong, this move loses at once since it weakens his KB3 square. 25 ... Q—K7 was his best chance.

27 Q—Q6   NxRP+
28 K—N2   N—N5

White's 28th ruled out 28 ... Q—QR4.

29 NxP!   Q—N3

29 ... PxN 30 QxP+ and 31 R—Q7 decides at once, while 30 Q—Q8+ mating was a threat.

30 N—Q7

Black lost on time.

10 XXII USSR Championship, Moscow 1955
White: Shcherbakov
Sicilian Defence

1 P—K4   P—QB4
2 N—KB3   P—Q3
3 P—Q4   PxP
4 NxP   N—KB3
5 N—QB3   P—QR3
6 B—K2

A quiet move, but no less strong for that.

6 ....   P—K4
7 N—N3   B—K2
8 0—0   0—0
9 B—K3   QN—Q2
10 P—QR4   P—QN3

Black must not allow the

blockading move P—R5.

11 P—B3

All part of White's quiet system, strengthening his centre and playing to control Q5.

11 ....   B—N2
12 Q—Q2   Q—B2
13 KR—Q1   QR—B1

As White can threaten Q—K1—B1 it seems better for the other rook to be played to this square.

14 B—B1

14 Q—K1 or Geller's 14 N—B1 intenidng N—R2—N4—Q5 were also very strong.

14 ....   P—Q4

Premature. 14 ... KR—Q1 is correct.

15 NxP

Not 15 PxP B—N5! with counter play.

15 ....   NxN
16 PxN   QxP
17 QxQ   RxQ
18 QR—N1!

Yet another quiet move underlining White's advantage. Black's Q side pawns are objects of attack and the possession of the seventh rank is not sufficient compensation.

18 ....   R—Q1
19 P—Q6!   B—KB1
20 N—Q2

Quite playable, but 20 P—R5! was a more energetic way of bringing his knight into the attack. Then after 20 ... P—QN4 (20 ... PxP 21 NxP B—B1? 22 B—Q3!) 21 B—Q3 QR—B1 22 B—KB5 R—N1 23 QR—B1 White stands clearly better having taken over the QB file.

20 ....   N—B3
21 N—B4   P—QN4
22 PxP   PxP
23 NxP?

Going for the wrong pawn. 23 N—R3! QR—B1 24 NxP N—Q4 (24 ... B—R3? 25 N—R7!) 25 B—B2 BxP 26 NxB RxN 27 P—QN4 leaves White a strong passed pawn and the two bishops.

23 ....   N—Q4
24 B—Q4   RxQP!

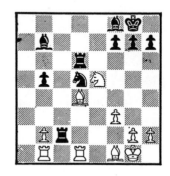

Now Spassky begins to get into the game exploiting his rook on the seventh for an attack on the king. Thus 25 BxP is parried by 25 ... N—B5! 26 B—B2 (26 B—KB1 RxB! 27 RxR B—B4) 26 RxP! with some advantage. 25 B—Q3 first, to drive the aggressive rook away, is best, though after 25 ... R—B1 26 BxNP N—B5 Black has good counter-play with his threats of RxB, R—B7 and QR—Q1.

25 B—B2

Hoping to close out the effect of the rook on the seventh; Spassky could now try 25 ... N—B5, but foreseeing the chance of a pawn fork on his QB7 advances his vulnerable pawn.

25 ....   P—N5
26 N—B4   R—K3
27 B—Q3   P—N6!

Now the rook obstinately

refuses to give way!

28 N—R5

Or 28 N—Q2 N—N5! 29 NxP NxB 30 RxN R(3)—K7! gives Black strong pressure so White attacks the pawn in a different way with a simultaneous threat to the bishop.

28 ....   RxB!

A striking reply that builds the tension up even further.

29 NxB?

Failing to spot that Black can now play his rook back to the protected square so beginning a decisive attack against White's king. White had to accept the sacrifice, and after 29 KxR B—B4+ 30 K—N3 (30 K—B1 N—K6+) 30 ... B—Q3+ 31 K—B2 (31 P—B4 B—R1 32 R—KB1 N—N5 with a strong attack) 31 ... B—B4+ the game would be drawn by perpetual check.

29 ....   R—B7!
30 N—R5   N—K6!
31 NxP

Too late!

31 ....   RxKNP+
32 K—R1   R—KR3
      Resigns

An ingenious tactical recovery!

11 XXII USSR Championship, Moscow, 1955
White: Geller
Nimzoindian

1 P—Q4   N—KB3
2 P—QB4   P—K3
3 N—QB3   B—N5
4 P—QR3

Geller favoured this sharp line at the start of his career, despite some notable reverses with it against positional players (Geller versus Smyslov and versus Euwe, Zurich Candidates, 1953 and Geller-Smyslov, Amsterdam Candidates, 1956).

4 ....   BxN+
5 PxB   P—B4
6 P—K3   N—B3

A more accurate move here is 6 ... P—QN3 so as to meet 7 B—Q3 with 7 ... B—N2 when 8 ... BxP is a more serious threat.

7 B—Q3   P—Q3
8 N—K2   P—QN3

9 0—0   Q—Q2

An original plan giving himself the option of castling long and also preparing 10 ... B—R3, which, if played at once, is met by 10 Q—R4.

10 P—K4   B—R3
11 B—N5   0—0—0
12 N—N3?

Quite the wrong plan, as a result of which he opens lines against his own king. Instead of trying to exploit the pin he should aim for the enemy king with 12 N—B1, as he in fact played in a later round against Lissitsyn. After 12 ... N—QR4 13 N—N3! Q—R5 14 NxN QxN? (better to exchange queens) 15 Q—K2 White gradually developed a powerful attack on the Q side.

12 ....   P—R3!

Before White can play N—R5.

13 BxN   PxB

14 N—R5

Consistent in his error. Perhaps he only expected the defensive move 14 ... Q—K2, whereas Spassky finds a much better idea.

14 ....   PxP

15 PxP   NxP

16 NxP   Q—K2

17 Q—R4

Typically aggressive play from Geller, but the absence of the queen from the centre is soon felt. The defensive 17 N—N4 followed, if necessary, by N—K3 would enable White to consolidate.

17 ....   B—N2!

18 N—R5

Now 18 N—N4 only helps Black to open his bishop's diagonal by 18 ... P—B4 and if 19 PxP PxP 20 N—K3 (20 KR—K1? Q—N2! 21 N—K3 N—B6+ or 21 ... P—B5) 20 ... KR—N1 and Black already threatens 21 ... QxN! amongst other things.

The sacrifice 18 N—Q5?! to close the diagonal is met by 18 ... Q—R5 19 QxP N—B6+ 20 PxN KR—N1+ 21 K—R1 Q—R6 22 NxP+ K—B2 23 N—Q5+ PxN and it is Black's attack which gets in first. Finally 18 QxP QxN 19 QxP is an unsound sacrifice as Black again gets in first by 19 ... N—B6+ 20 K—R1 Q—Q5 beating off the attack.

18 ....   KR—N1

(See diagram next column.)

Black still has no need to worry about the QRP, such is the impetus of his attack. Thus 19 QxP? loses the queen to 19 ... RxP+! 20 KxR (20 K—R1 RxP+!

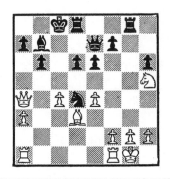

21 KxR Q—R5+ 22 K—N2 QxN and 23 ... R—N1+) 20 ... BxP+.

19 Q—Q1

A confession of defeat. 19 N—N3 is met by 19 ... P—KR4 continuing the attack.

19 ....   P—B4

20 R—K1

Not 20 P—B3? Q—N4 21 N—N3 P—B5 winning the knight.

20 ....   Q—R5!

Every move a hammer blow! 20 ... Q—N4 is less exact since after 21 P—N3 P—B5 22 K—R1 P—B6 23 N—B4 Black has no follow-up.

21 P—B4

Trying to buy Black off with an offer of the exchange (21 QxR+ 22 QxQ N—B6+). If 21 P—N3 then 21 ... P—K4 safeguarding his knight and renewing the threat of PxP. Now K—R1 allows 22 ... PxP 23 PxQ PxB+ 24 P—B3 BxP+ 25 QxB NxQ.

21 ....   P—K4!

Here too this move is the quickest win. Thus 22 R—KB1 loses to 22 ... BPxP 23 B—K2 N—B6+.

22 R—QB1   KPxP

23 B—B1   QxR

Otherwise the threat to his knight has to be watched.

24 QxQ	N—B6+
25 K—B2	NxQ
26 RxN	P—B6!

Accurate play. 26 ... BxP 27 NxP is not so decisive. The text opens the KB file, enabling Black to deploy his rooks actively.

27 NPxP	PxP
28 PxP	QR—B1+

29 K—K3	BxP!
30 B—R3+	B—B4
31 BxB+	RxB

Resigns

The exchange of rooks is forced. It says much for the young Geller's resilience that after this disastrous loss he went on to win the title.

12 XXII USSR Championship, Moscow 1955
White: Simagin
English Opening

1 P—QB4	N—KB3
2 N—KB3	P—K3
3 P—QN3	

The late grandmaster Simagin was noted for his original play. Nimzovich was quite fond of this move, but 3 P—KN3 to try for a Catalan is much more popular nowadays.

3	P—Q4
4 B—N2	P—B4
5 P—K3	N—B3
6 P—QR3	

With the double purpose of preparing P—Q4 (6 P—Q4 BPxP and 7 ... B—N5+ with a good game) and tempting Black into 6 ... P—Q5 when 7 PxP PxP 8 P—QN4 or 7 P—QN4 at once would give White a useful reversed Benoni.

6	B—K2
7 PxP	PxP
8 P—Q4	PxP
9 NxP	0—0
10 B—K2	B—Q3

Playing for a K side attack. Black could immediately demonstrate the drawback to White's opening play by 10 ...: NxN 11 BxN N—K5 12 N—Q2 B—B3 with complete equality.

11 N—Q2	NxN
12 BxN	B—KB4
13 0—0	R—B1

This way too Black stands quite well and his threatened occupation. of QB7 with the QB forces an awkward-looking defensive move.

14 R—R2	B—N1
15 Q—R1	Q—Q3
16 P—N3	

This weakening would be forced anyway after 16 N—B3 N—N5 and on 17 P—N3 (17 P—R3? N—R7!) 17 ... Q—KR3 Black has the attack.

16	KR—K1
17 N—B3	

17 BxN was a better chance of reducing the pressure.

17	B—R6
18 R—K1	

Intending to discourage 18 ... N—K5. He would do better to try

18 R—Q1 N—K5 19 N—Q2 and
if 19 ... N—B3 then 20 B—KB3
consolidating on the white
squares.

18	N—K5!

19 BxNP?

Based on an error in analysis.
19 N—Q2 was still correct.

19	Q—KN3

20 B—K5

As Simagin explained later,
only now did he see that in
answer to his intended 20 B—Q4
Black has 20 ... BxP 21 BPxB (21
RPxB? NxNP 22 K—R2 NxB 23
KxB Q—B4+ 24 K—N2 Q—N5+
or 23 N—R4 Q—N5 24 B—B6
RxP! 25 R(2)xN — 25 PxR?
Q—N6+ 26 K—R1 B—N7+ 27
NxB Q—R6 mate — 25 ... RxR
26 RxR QxR 27 Q—KN1+
Q—N5) 21 ... NxP 22 B—B1 (22
K—B2 N—K5 mate) 22 ... NxB+
23 K—R1 R—B7! It was this last
quiet line-intercepting move that
Simagin had failed to foresee
when considering his 19th move!

20	BxB
21 NxB	Q—B4
22 P—B4	

This seems to lose. Instead he
should try 22 N—Q3 N—B6 23
N—B4! when after 23 ... NxR 24
B—Q3 Q—K4 25 QxN White has
definite compensation for the
exchange.

22	P—B3
23 N—B3	N—B6
24 N—R4	

Simagin gave this a "?" and
wrote that after 24 N—Q4!
Q—K5 25 B—B3 Q—Q6 26
K—B2! NxR 27 BxP+ K—N2 28
QxN White has material compensation for the exchange and only
a slightly worse position. This is
incorrect however, as Black now
plays 28 ... RxP! shattering·
White's game (29 RxR? Q—B8
mate, or 29 N—B5+ BxN 30 RxR
R—B7+ 31 K—B3 QxB+ or 29
B—B4 RxB).

24	Q—K3!
25 B—R5	

He cannot let the KP go.

25	NxR
26 BxR	

Both players had seen this far
but Simagin's analysis stopped
here, whereas Spassky had gone
further.

26	R—B8!

This would also have been the
answer to 25 QxN.

27 QxR	

Or 27 RxR QxP+ 28 K—R1
NxR and then 29 ... Q—K8 mate.

27	NxQ
28 B—N5	P—QR3

Resigns

13 Students' Olympiad, Lyons 1955
Black: Kajan (Finland)
Sicilian Defence

1 P—K4	P—QB4
2 N—KB3	N—QB3
3 P—Q4	PxP
4 NxP	N—B3
5 N—QB3	P—K4

First played by Lasker as a surprise move in his 1910 match
with Schlechter. The text has
always been considered inferior
but in recent years it has been employed as the introductory move
of the so-called Pelikan system (6
KN—K5 P—Q3 7 B—N5 P—QR3
8 BxN PxB 9 N—R3 P—Q4?!).

6 N—N3

Also considered inferior, but as
a subsequent note shows Spassky
had a special idea in mind.

| 6 .... | B—N5 |
| 7 B—QB4! | |

Schlechter played 7 B—Q3
which allowed Black to free himself completely by 7 ... P—Q4.

| 7 .... | NxP |

Accepting the offer. Gligoric
and Sokolov recommend 7 ...
P—Q3 8 0—0 B—K3 when Black
has a perfectly satisfactory position. Spassky must have known
of a game between two fellow
Leningrad players in which Black
refused the offer by 7 ... 0—0 and
after 8 0—0 BxN 9 PxB NxQP 10
B—R3 P—Q3 (10 ... R—K1 11
BxP+ KxB 12 Q—Q5+ forcing the
king to come forward) 11 Q—Q3
B—B4 12 QR—K1 Q—R5 White
got the better of it with 13
P—KB4! (Kopaev-Korchnoy, 1952).

| 8 0—0 | |

8 Q—Q5 N—Q3! beats off the
attack, while 8 BxP+ KxB 9

Q—Q5+ K—K1 10 QxN(K4)
BxN+ 11 PxB P—Q4 12 Q—K2
does not offer much for White.

| 8 .... | NxN |

8 ... N—Q3 9 B—Q5 leaves
Black with some development
difficulties, while 8 ... BxN 9
Q—Q5! is awkward to meet (not
9 PxB NxQBP 10 Q—B3 P—Q4!).

| 9 PxN | B—K2 |

This safety-first play is feasible
if followed up correctly. Black
could also play 9 ... BxP 10
Q—B3 P—Q4! the usual antidote
to open-game gambits. Then after
11 BxP 0—0 12 BxP+ RxB 13
QxB the game is about even. In
this White cannot play more
ambitiously 12 R—Q1 as Black
closes the Q file with the effective
counter-stroke 12 ... N—Q5!

10 P—KB4!

Now White gets his rook into
play quickly before Black can
mobilise his Q side.

| 10 .... | 0—0 |

"Castling into it". 10 ... P—Q3
is a much better defensive move.
Then if 11 Q—R5 not 11 ... 0—0,
with transposition to positions
akin to the game, but instead 11
... P—KN3 12 Q—R6 (12 Q—B3
B—K3!) 12 ... B—B1 ·and 13 ...
B—N2 with a stronger defensive
position for the king when
castling follows.

11 P—B5

Playing to ensure a safe square
at KR3 for his rook.

| 11 .... | P—QN4? |

The move of an inexperienced
player. His bishop can do little at

QN2 and the paralysis that settles on his position after White's next move could be avoided by the freeing 11 ... P—Q4 12 BxP N—Q5! and if 13 BxP+ RxB 14 PxN BxP keeping level material in a position where Black has finally completed his development. White would do better to continue 13 B—K4 and after 13 ... NxN 14 BPxN he would retain some advantage due to his powerfully placed KB.

12 B—Q5

Naturally to this square, even if 12 BxP did not lose his bishop to 12 ... Q—N3+.

12 ....   B—N2

13 Q—R5

(See diagram next column.)

Now the simple transfer of rook to KR3 cannot be countered.

13 ....   N—R4
14 BxB   NxB
15 R—B3   P—N3

If 15 ... R—K1 or 15 ... B—B3 then 16 R—R3 P—KR3 17 BxP wins, or 15 ... Q—N3+ 16 B—K3 Q—KB3 17 R—R3 P—KR3 18 R—N3 K—R2 19 R—KB1 and 20 R—N6! (18 ... K—R1! 19 R—KB1

and 20 B—N5).

16 Q—R6   Q—N3+
17 B—K3   Q—KB3
18 PxP   Q—N2

Or 18 ... QxP 19 R—N3.

19 PxBP+   K—R1

Forced to prevent the loss of the queen.

20 Q—R5   KR—B1

Or 20 ... P—Q3 21 B—R6 winning the exchange. The text loses much more swiftly.

21 B—R6   Resigns

White mates after 21 ... Q—N3 21 QxP+ B—B3 22 RxB P—Q3 23 RxQ+ PxQ 24 B—N7 — a rather unusual final mating pattern.

14 World Junior Championship, 1955
White: Schweber
Nimzoindian

1 P—Q4	N—KB3	6 N—B3	0—0
2 P—QB4	P—K3	7 0—0	P—Q4
3 N—QB3	B—N5	8 P—QR3	BxN
4 P—K3	P—QB4	9 PxB	QPxP
5 B—Q3	N—B3		

The immediate 9 ... Q—B2 is a

dynamic alternative giving White a wider choice than the text.

10 BxP	Q—B2
11 B—Q3	P—K4
12 Q—B2	B—N5

In the 1950s, the move order thus far was standard play. Only after this and many other games was it realised that 12 ... R—K1 was a more accurate move than the text, since the threat of 13 ... P—K5 forces the exchange 14 NxP (which the text with its threat of 13 ... BxN also provokes). After 12 ... R—K1 ·13 P—K4 P—B5! 14 BxP PxP 15 PxP N—QR4! 16 B—Q3 QxQ 17 BxQ NxP Black has equality, and after 12 ... R—K1 13 NxP NxN 14 PxN QxP Black can play B—Q2—B3 without allowing White to gain a tempo by P—B3.

13 NxP	NxN
14 PxN	QxP
15 R—K1?	

The unguarded rook on this square is a tactical weakness. 15 P—B3 is correct and after 15 ... B—Q2 16 P—K4 or even 16 P—QR4 (Petrosian-Spassky, 20th game of the 1966 World Championship match) White stands slightly better.

Not however, 15 P—B3 B—Q2 16 R—K1? (Geller-Spassky, Amsterdam Candidates 1956) because now 16 ... B—R5! gave the young Spassky a fine game since 17 QxB loses to 17 ... QxBP forking both rooks and the KB.

15	QR—Q1
16 P—B3	B—Q2
17 P—QR4	

The comparatively unknown Argentinian junior sees the threat (17 ... B—R5!) which the Ukranian grandmaster overlooked a year later! In those days the status of the World Junior was much lower than nowadays, and Geller's lapse can be partly explained by the fact that of Spassky's games in this event, only the one-sided effort against van Oosterom (see Winning Practice) which won second brilliancy prize was published in the Soviet press.

17	B—B3
18 P—K4	N—Q4!

19 B—N2

Black threatened 19 ... N—N5 as well as 19 ... NxP or 19 ... QxBP. If 19 B—Q2 then 19 ... N—B5 follows with even greater effect as the White queen would no longer guard KN2.

19	N—B5
20 B—KB1	

Not 20 P—B4? Q—N4 21 B—KB1? (21 QR—Q1? BxRP!; 21 R—K3? N—R6+; or 21 KR—Q1 R—Q3 are both greatly in Black's favour) 21 ... R—Q7! 22 Q—B3 (22 QxR N—R6+) 22 ... RxP+ and mates.

20	KR—K1
21 P—N3	

A slight weakening of the King side but after 20 P—B4 Q—N4 21 QR—Q1 (otherwise 21 ... R—Q7!)

21 ... P—KR4 the knight can be maintained on its post at KB5 for some time. Admittedly White could then play 22 B—B1 to exchange his QB for it, but the resulting black square weakness would be equally serious in the middle game and ending.

21	N—N3
22 P—QB4	Q—K2
23 Q—B3	P—B3
24 B—Q3?	

After the weakening produced by his 21st move this bishop must stay where it is to guard KN2 and KB3. White had to play 24 P—R5 or 24 B—N2 though after 24 ... R—Q2 and doubling rooks, Black retains some advantage — in this rather rigid position White's two bishops do not enjoy any great scope.

| 24 .... | N—K4! |
| 25 B—B2? | |

He had to try 25 B—K2 guarding his most vulnerable spot at KB3. Black would continue 25 ... B—Q2 followed by N—B3 (or even B—K3 envisaging Q—KB2) when his pieces are all very active.

| 25 .... | R—Q7! |

In the 'British Chess Magazine', the British representative K. W. Lloyd described Schweber as a player with a coffee house style. Surprising therefore, that he missed this strong tactical stroke which decides the game in a few moves.

26 R—KB1

The immediate threat was 26 ... RxB 27 QxR NxBP+ winning two pawns, so White must guard the tender spot at KB3.

| 26 .... | KR—Q1 |

27 R—R3

If 27 B—B1 at once to force the intruder to a decision, then 27 ... R(7)—Q6 28 BxR RxB 29 Q—B2 NxP+ with decisive effect as the KP will be lost and the bishop lurking so long at QB3 will come into its own. Hence White must guard his KB3 yet once more. Spassky's next move demonstrates that he is now turning his attention to the weak QBP.

27	K—R1!
28 B—B1	R(7)—Q5
29 P—B4	

In despair, White throws himself upon the sword. 29 B—N3 R—Q6 loses equally quickly.

| 29 .... | NxP |
| 30 P—K5 | PxP |

The knight is too good a piece to contemplate giving up for White's offside rook.

| 31 PxP | QxP |
| 32 B—Q1 | |

To meet 32 ... Q—Q4 by 33 B—B3.

| 32 .... | RxB |
| 33 QxN | |

One of the points of Black's 27th move was that this knight is captured without check being given.

| 33 .... | RxR+ |
| 34 QxR | |

Or 34 KxR R—Q8+ 35 K—B2 Q—K8 mate.

| 34 .... | Q—K5 |
| 35 B—B4 | |

To close the KB file. If 35 R—K3 then 35 ... Q—R8+ 36 K—B2 R—KB1+ etc.

| 35 .... | R—Q8! |
| | Resigns |

36 K—B2 is the only move to avoid immediate mate.

15 Gothenburg Interzonal 1955
Black: Filip
Nimzoindian

1 P—Q4	N—KB3
2 P—QB4	P—K3
3 N—QB3	B—N5
4 B—N5	P—KR3
5 B—R4	P—B4
6 P—Q5	PxP
7 PxP	P—Q3

Modern opinion is that Black can do without this move here and should castle followed by 8 ... R—K1.

8 P—K₃	QN—Q2
9 B—Q3	

In his famous game against Smyslov (see No. 5) Spassky was successful with 9 B—QN5 but now tries another idea offering his QP.

9	0—0?

Better is 9 ... Q—R4! 10 N—K2 NxP 11 0—0 NxN 12 PxN BxP 13 NxB QxN 14 B—K2! 0—0 15 QxP P—QR3 16 KR—Q1 KR—K1 17 QR—B1 Q—N7 18 B—QB4 Q—K4 with equal chances, Portisch-Donner, Madrid 1960.

10 N—K2	N—K4

The traditional way of relieving the pin, but Black is left with an unpromising position. It was still not too late to revert to a Benoni set-up with 10 ... P—QR3 11 0—0 R—K1.

11 0—0	BxN
12 NxB	N—N3
13 B—N3	Q—K2
14 P—K4	

Now White has much the superior position, since Black is restricted to a purely defensive fight against the threat of a cen-

tral breakthrough involving P—KB4 and P—K5.

14	B—Q2
15 R—K1	

The accurate move; the immediate 15 P—B4 would permit 15 ... P—QN4 or even 15 ... B—N5 16 Q—B2 N—R4! exchanging White's fine bishop.

15	N—K4
16 B—K2	

White has no need to hurry with P—B4 as Black's attempt to restrain this advance represents a serious weakening of his K-side.

16	P—KN4

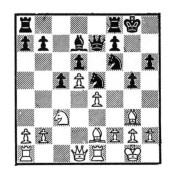

17 R—KB1	

To support the eventual opening of the KB file.

17	K—R2
18 Q—Q2	N—N1
19 P—B4!	PxP
20 RxP	P—R3
21 P—QR4!	

The Q side majority must be held down.

21	P—B3

22 QR—KB1   R—B2
23 B—R5   R—N2
24 P—R5

White gradually increases his command of the whole board. The text ensures that White's knight will reach the strong square QB4.

24 ....   R—KB1
25 N—Q1   R—N4
26 B—K2   N—N3

Black just moves to and fro as he can find no constructive plan.

27 R(4)—B2   N—K4
28 N—K3   R—N2
29 BxN!

The winning move, exchanging Black's only good piece and thus breaking through on the KB file.

29 ....   QPxB

Not 29 ... QxB 30 N—B4 Q—K2 31 Q—B4 winning the QP.

30 P—Q6!

To activate his bishop.

39 ....   Q—Q1
31 B—B4

Simply winning the KBP˙(31 ... K—N3 32 BxN R(2)xB 33 N—.Q5).

31 ....   B—B3
32 N—B5

(See diagram next column.)

Deciding to turn his attention to the KBP.

32 ....   R—N4

33 P—R4   R—N3
34 BxN+   R(1)xB
35 N—K7

Decisive.

35 ....   BxP
36 NxR(6)   RxN
37 P—R5

A fine move constructing a mating net.

37 ....   R—N2
38 RxP!

Spassky rarely misses a tactical point.

38 ....   RxP+
30 QxR   BxQ
40 R—B8!   Resigns

The threatened 41 R(1)—B7 mate can only be parried by the surrender of Black's queen when White's QP will cost the bishop his life.

16 Gothenburg Interzonal 1955
Black: Pilnik
Sicilian Defence

1 P—K4   P—QB4
2 N—KB3   P—Q3

3 P—Q4   PxP
4 NxP   N—KB3

5 N—QB3 P—QR3
6 B—KN5 P—K3
7 P—B4 B—K2

In an earlier round a game Keres-Panno had gone 7 ... Q—N3 8 Q—Q2! (the famous pawn sacrifice!) and after 8 ... N—B3 9 O—O—O QxN 10 QxQ NxQ 11 RxQ Black had a very poor position. The more logical 8 ... QxP was also roughly treated in a later game (Keres-Fuderer) though a decade and a half of analysis since then has not really refuted the cheeky pawn grab. This game was played after Keres-Panno but before Keres-Fuderer and the text was then considered an 'improvement' on the basis of Argentinian analysis.

8 Q—B3 P—KR3
9 B—R4 P—KN4

A very interesting pawn sacrifice to obtain a firm grip on Black's K4 square. However, it gives White a very powerful attacking position as long as he does not shrink from a piece sacrifice.

10 PxP KN—Q2

10 ... PxP 11 BxNP QN—Q2 Olafsson-Pilnik, match 1956 is also playable.

11 NxP!

Credit for having the courage to play this move must go to Geller The point is that the same opening variation had been adopted in two other USSR-Argentinian encounters in this round, Keres-Najdorf and Geller-Panno, and Geller was the first to play the sacrifice.

11 .... PxN
12 Q—R5+ K—B1

The dramatic background to the moves on the board was thus described by Geller in the Soviet tournament book: "At this point Keres and Spassky were still examining the consequences of sacrificing the knight at e6, while their opponents Najdorf and Pilnik were talking in a most animated fashion and looking at my game with Panno. Then Najdorf came over to me and said 'Your game is lost. We have all this analysed'.

If Black were able to establish his knight on K4 then he would repel the attack.

13 B—N5!

"Now, however, this is not possible and Najdorf and Pilnik went back to their boards worried. The text had not been properly assessed by the Argentinians in their preliminary analysis." As Spassky comments in his notes 13 B—K2 or 13 B—Q3 would allow 13 ... N—K4 14 O—O+ K—N2 15 B—N3 QN—B3 safeguarding the knight at K4, while after the text this is not possible.

13 .... K—N2

The parting of the ways. Panno tried 13 ... N—K4 14 B—N3! BxP and lost quickly after 15 O—O+ K—K2 16 BxN Q—N3+ 17 K—R1 PxB 18 Q—B7+ K—Q3 19 QR—Q1+. Forewarned, Pilnik and Najdorf tried the text but only succeeded in lengthening the game without changing its result. The correct defence is 13 ... R—R2 as played by Fischer against Gligoric, Portoroz 1958, and Black seems to have enough resources to draw, though the analysis is very complicated.

14 O—O N—K4

Or 14 ... Q—N1 15 P—N6! BxB 16 QxB! with a winning

attack e.g. 16 ... KxP 17 B—Q3 N—K4 18 R—B6+ K—N2 19 QR—KB1 or 16 ... Q—Q1 17 R—B7+ K—R1 19 RxR+ QxR 20 finally 16 ... PxB 17 R—B7+ QxR (17 ... KxP 18 QR—KB1) 18 PxQ KxP 19 R—KB1+ K—K1 20 NxP!

15 B—N3   N—N3

Now 15 ... Q—N1 loses to 16 BxN+ PxB 17 B—K8 R—R2 18 R—B7+ K—R1 19 RxR+ QxR 20 B—N6 Q—N2 21 R—KB1.

16 PxP+   RxP
17 R—B7+   KxR
18 QxR   PxB

Other defences also lose e.g. 18 ... Q—R1 19 R—KB1+ B—B3 20 B—K8+! KxB 21 QxN+ K—K2 22 RxB! or in this 20 ... QxB 21 Q—R7+.

19 R—KB1+   K—K1

Black's last move gave him this flight square, but he still cannot save the game.

20 QxN+   K—Q2

21 R—B7   N—B3

Black's best chance was 21 ... K—B3 but after 22 Q—R7 P—N5 23 N—Q5! PxN 24 RxB P—Q5 (24 ... Q—R4 R—B7+) 25 Q—B7 R—R3 26 R—K8 or 22 ... B—N4 23 P—K5 PxP 24 B—B2 threatening 25 Q—K4+ he is still lost.

22 N—Q5   RxP

Or 22 ... PxN 23 QxP+ K—K1 24 Q—N6 K—Q2 (24 ... Q—N3+ 25 B—B2 Q moves 26 PxP) 25 PxP RxP 26 Q—B5+ K—K1 27 R—B8+ BxR 28 Q—N6+ K—K2 29 B—R4+ K—Q2 30 PxN+ PxP 31 Q—Q3+.

23 P—R3

Only here did the Soviet duo vary! Keres played 24 P—R4 and after 23 .... Q—R1 24 NxB NxN 25 Q—N5 Najdorf resigned. Spassky's move keeps KR4 available for his bishop.

23 ....   Q—R1
24 NxB   NxN
25 Q—N5   R—R8+

Pilnik decides he will lose a longer game than his two colleagues!

26 R—R2   Q—Q1
27 QxP+   K—B2
28 Q—QB5+!

A plethora of pins.

28 ....   K—N1

Or 28 ... K—Q2 29 QxP+ K—K1 30 R—B8+.

29 BxP+   K—R1
30 BxN   R—R4
31 Q—N4   Resigns

The finish could be 31 ... Q—B2+ 32 B—Q6 Q—Q1 33 R—B8.

17 Gothenburg Interzonal 1955
White: Stahlberg
Modern Benoni

1 P—Q4	N—KB3
2 P—QB4	P—B4

A very uncommon move at the time, yet in the next few years Tal's adoption of it was to make the Modern Benoni very popular.

3 P—Q5	P—K3
4 N—QB3	PxP
5 PxP	P—Q3
6 P—K4	P—KN3
7 N—B3	B—N2

Nimzovich's original idea was to play 7 ... B—N5 here, in order to exchange this bishop for the White KN that can support the breakthrough P—K5 either from its original square, or from QB4.

8 B—K2	0—0
9 0—0	B—N5

Now this move comes too late.

10 B—KN5?

A standard developing move of the sort a club player readily makes. From a grandmaster one expects a deeper penetration into the essence of the position and 10 N—Q2! was called for. After 10 ... BxN 11 QxB R—K1 12 P—B3 QN—Q2 13 N—B4! White has a strong position.

10	QN—Q2

Spassky in his turn omits to play 10 ... BxN and Stahlberg again fails to play the 'programmed' 11 N—Q2.

11 Q—Q2	P—QR3
12 P—QR4	BxN!

13 BxB

Or 13 PxB Q—B2 intending to take control of the black squares by N—R4 and B—K4.

13	P—B5!

Preparing to advance his Q side majority and to play N—B4—Q6 or N6.

14 B—K2	Q—B2
15 K—R1	

White in his turn prepares for his only counter-chance of advancing the KBP and then realising P—K5.

15	N—B4

First 15 ... KR—K1 is better so as to tie White down to the defence of his KP and to provide extra control over Black's K4.

16 Q—K3

White should take his chance to simplify by 16 BxN BxB 17 BxP BxN 18 QxB NxP 19 Q—Q4 when after 19 ... KR—K1 Black still has a superior minor piece, but White may well be able to draw the position.

16	KR—K1

17 P—B3

Now 17 BxN BxB 18 BxP is too late, since after 18 ... BxN 19 QxB RxP Black seizes control of the K file thanks to his constant threat to the QRP from both his knight and his centralised rook.

17	N—N6
18 QR—Q1	QR—N1
19 Q—B2	

Too slow and passive. White's only chance now was to create a threat on the KB file by 19 BxN BxB 20 P—B4 P—QN4 21 P—K5! QPxP 22 N—K4 B—N2 23 P—B5 when, at the cost of a pawn, White has a strong attack. This attacking plan was used subsequently by White in a number of

Benoni games, of which ·the most notable was Penrose's famous win over Tal in the 1960 Leipzig Olympiad.

19	P—N4
20 PxP	PxP
21 P—K5	

White realises that he will gradually be driven back by 21 ... P—N5, forcing the knight to a poor square, so he finally decides on an attacking gesture.

21	RxP
22 P—B4	N—K5!

This takes much of the sting out of the attack.

23 NxN	RxN
24 B—B3	

To avoid the loss of the QNP when Black's pawn majority would be close to queening.

24	R—Q5
25 P—B5	RxR
26 BxR	N—B4
27 P—B6	N—K5
28 Q—K3	NxB
29 PxB	

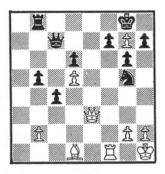

Black, a pawn up, plays consistently for exchanges, while White bases his hopes on an attack. However, 29 QxN was a better chance since Black's knight

remains a fine piece in the rout that now follows. After 29 QxN B—R1 Black can play to tie his opponent down by R—K1 and Q—Q1, but the drawing propensities of opposite-coloured bishops might well show themselves in an ending with major pieces exchanged.

29	P—R3!
30 P—R4	N—R2
31 QxP	

At first sight White has achieved a lot, but deeper judgement reveals a large number of weaknesses in his camp which Spassky now exploits.

31	Q—K2!

Weakness number one is the king. Thus now 32 P—R5 loses to 32 ... Q—R5+ 33 K—N1 Q—Q5+ 34 K—R1 QxKNP.

32 B—B2	R—K1
33 Q—B4	

Otherwise Q—K6 would force an exchange of queens.

33	KxP
34 P—R5	N—N4

Weakness number two is the black squares.

35 PxP	PxP
36 R—R1	

White cannot reinforce his attack on Black's main weakness at KN3 and in time trouble aims to activate his game by attacking Q6.

36	Q—K6!

Now after the forced exchange of queens, 37 QxQ (otherwise 37 ... R—KR1 mating or winning the queen) 37 ... RxQ 38 R—R6 or R5 (38 B—Q1 R—Q6!) R—K7! Black's passed pawns carry the day. Instead of this prosiac end Stahlberg blundered by 37 R—R7+?? and resigned at once before Spassky could reply.

18 Gothenburg Interzonal 1955
White: Ilivitsky
English Opening

1 N—KB3	N—KB3
2 P—KN3	P—B4
3 B—N2	N—B3
4 P—Q4	P—K3

This leaves Black permanently struggling with a cramped game. 4 ... PxP 5 NxP P—K4 is a good system as after 6 NxN QPxN! Black has a sound position, while the superior 6 N—N5 allows Black to play a promising pawn sacrifice: 6 ... P—Q4 7 BxP Q—R4+ 8 KN—B3 B—R6! preventing castling.

5 0—0	B—K2
6 P—B4	PxP

Otherwise P—Q5 is very awkward to meet.

7 NxP	0—0
8 N—QB3	P—QR3
9 P—N3	Q—B2
10 B—N2	P—Q3
11 R—B1	NxN

The only way to complete his development for 11 ... B—Q2 is met by 12 N—Q5 PxN 13 PxP and Black is left with weak pawns.

12 QxN	B—Q2
13 KR—Q1	KR—Q1
14 P—KR3	QR—B1

Black has a very passive game.

15 P—QR4	Q—N1
16 B—R3	B—B3
17 P—K4	N—Q2
18 P—QN4	

White correctly chooses to play for a further squeeze as 18 BxP leaves him with little after 18 ... BxB 19 QxB QxQ 20 RxQ N—B4! 21 RxR+ RxR 22 P—QN4 NxP 23 NxN BxN 24

P—K5 R—Q2

18	N—K4

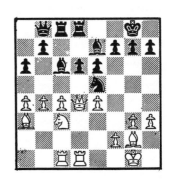

An ingenious attempt to "muddy the water," as the Russian proverb puts it.

19 P—B4	NxP!?

The point. Black gives up some material but releases the bind White has on the position.

20 QxN	BxRP
21 Q—Q3	

Once again the correct decision. 21 QxR RxQ 22 NxB RxR 23 RxR (23 BxR Q—B2 24 N—N2 Q—B7 25 R—B1 B—B3 and the knight has no square) 23 ... P—QN4 24 N—B3 Q—N3+ 25 K—R2 Q—K6 would give Black good counter-chances, as his queen is very active and White's minor pieces cannot easily co-operate.

21	BxR
22 NxB	RxR
23 BxR	Q—B2
24 B—Q2	P—Q4

Playing for further complications, but his centre pawns were an effective defensive barrier and 24 ... P—QN3, in order to create a passed pawn by P—QR4, was objectively a better defensive chance.

25 PxP	BxP
26 BxB	Q—N3+
27 N—K3	QxB
28 K—R2	P—QN4

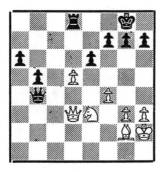

29 Q—B2

In time trouble, White goes seriously wrong and finally justifies Spassky's ingenious resistance. Probably the united passed pawns frightened White into playing a passive move to unpin his QP. Since White must coordinate his three pieces against Black's two he should hardly leave his knight unguarded.

As Bondarevsky points out, 25 P—B5 gives White strong attacking chances on the K side

e.g. 29 ... Q—Q3 30 P—B6! PxP 31 N—N4 P—B4 32 N—B6+ K—N2 33 N—R5+ K—R1 34 Q—Q2 Q—K4 35 Q—R6 R—KN1 36 P—Q6!, or 29 ... PxQP 30 NxP Q—Q3 31 P—B6! PxP (or 31 ... P—N3 32 Q—K3!) 32 Q—B5 K—N2 33 B—K4 R—KR1 34 Q—N4+ and White has perpetual check after 34 .... K—B1 35 Q—B8+, while 34 N—B4 is a good winning attempt.

| 29 .... | PxP |
| 30 BxP | |

A further error. 30 NxP was a better chance.

| 30 .... | R—K1 |

Spassky too goes wrong in the time scramble. 30 ... Q—Q5 was a better way of exploiting White's last move.

| 31 N—N4 | R—Q1 |
| 32 Q—R2 | |

White seems to have obtained some counter-play, as he can play his knight to K5 if Black defends by 32 ... R—KB1. In fact Black can let the pawn go to exploit the weakened position of the enemy king.

| 32 .... | Q—Q5 |
| 33 BxP+ | |

Loses at once, but after the superior 33 B—N2 Black would calmly advance his QNP.

| 33 .... | K—B1 |
| 34 Q—N3 | |

Or 34 N—K5 Q—B6 threatening 35 ... R—Q7+

| 34 .... | Q—Q7+ |
| 35 K—N1 | Q—K8+ |

Resigns

19 Amsterdam Candidates 1956
White: Pilnik
Ruy Lopez

1 P—K4	P—K4
2 N—KB3	N—QB3
3 B—N5	P—QR3
4 B—R4	N—B3
5 0—0	NxP
6 P—Q4	P—QN4
7 B—N3	P—Q4
8 PxP	B—K3
9 P—B3	N—B4

This variation, which has never been refuted, is a fine example of the riches of the game. Black, on successive turns, moves two well-posted pieces instead of completing his development and White is not able to extract any advantage from this infraction of the 'rules'!

10 B—B2	B—N5
11 P—KR3	

White usually plays 11 R—K1 or QN—Q2 continuing development, but it is a useful precaution to be able to break the pin by P—KN4 if required.

11	B—R4

Not 11 ... BxN 12 QxB NxP 13 R—K1 P—B3 14 B—B4 with great pressure for White.

12 B—B4	

A rather 'neutral' move guarding a point that was in no danger. 12 R—K1 or QN—Q2 are more accurate.

12	B—K2

Keres suggests that Black can get a fine game here by 12 ... P—Q5! and if 13 PxP BxN followed by 14 ... NxQP, while 13 P—KN4 P—Q6! (one of Black's trumps in this variation) leaves White with a weak pawn structure on the K side for which he has no compensation, (14 PxB PxB 15 QxP Q—Q2 and 16 ... 0—0—0). Spassky plays the move later when White has a greater choice of counters.

13 QN—Q2	P—Q5

Now the advance is rather risky.

14 N—K4	

Hoping for 14 ... NxN? 15 BxN when the pin is decisive. However, 14 N—N3 looks better and if 14 ... P—Q6 then 15 B—N1.

14	P—Q6!
15 NxN	PxB
16 QxQ+	NxQ

Eschewing the over-exposure of his QRP.

17 B—K3	

The wrong plan. White should simply aim to win the pawn that has strayed so far from home. Thus 17 N—N3! P—QB4 18 QR—B1 and then 19 N—R1 if necessary, when the burden of proof would be on Black to demonstrate that his two bishops are worth the lost pawn. White is far too keen to maintain his knight on its, admittedly fine-looking, square at QB5 thinking that he can pick off the advanced pawn at his leisure. The text has the drawback of weakening his KP.

17	N—B3
18 P—KN4	B—N3
19 KR—K1	P—N5

Thus Black takes the initiative on the Q side forcing the following reply.

20 P—B4	

Otherwise Black exchanges pawns and plays R—QN1—N8.

20 ....   P—KR4
21 K—N2   P—R4

Now the posting of the White knight at QB5 loses its *raison d'etre*.

22 P—N3   0—0—0
23 QR—B1   PxP
24 PxP   P—B4!

Black plays to open the game for his two bishops. White takes the chance to dissolve the liability of his KP, but soon has to meet the nasty threat of B—QN7.

25 PxPe.p.

Not 25 RxP? PxP winning a piece while 25 NPxP BxP gives Black the new threat of advancing his KNP.

25 ....   BxP
26 R—K2

Intending to give up the exchange for a pawn if Black plays 26 ... B—N7, after which the ending would not be easy to win. White once again refuses to retreat his knight from QB5, but even though 26 N—R4 would leave the piece terribly offside it was better than the text. Doubtless Pilnik feared 26 N—R4 B—K5 or even 26 ... N—K4 27 NxN BxN and if 28 P—B4 B—K5+ or 28 B—N5 R—R7+ 29 K—N1 QR—R1! but now White loses without being able to put up much of a fight.

26 ....   R—Q8!

(See diagram next column.)

Winning the exchange in even more favourable circumstances as 27 N—R4 now loses at once to 27 ... KR—R8.

27 QRxP

The pawn so long ignored has extracted its revenge!

27 ....   BxR
28 RxB   N—Q5

The further exchange of minor pieces gives Black more scope to deploy his rooks.

29 BxN   BxB
30 N—K6   B—B6
31 N—B4   R—K1

By retaining the knight and not the bishop at move 29 White has prevented a check on his KN1 after KR—R8, so Black merely occupies both central files with his rooks and waits for White to run out of useful moves.

32 N—Q5   B—Q5
33 NxB   RxN
34 N—K3

Not 34 P—N5 R—N5+ nor 34 P—B3 K—N2 threatening to win the piece by 35 ... P—B3.

34 ....   KR—Q1

Now the rook penetrates to the seventh and it is all over.

35 R—B1

Or 35 N—B5 R—Q7 and Black's pawns are nearer to queening.

35 ....   R—Q7
36 R—QR1   R—B1
37 N—Q1   K—Q2

White has been rendered completely passive, so it time to mobilise the king.

38 K—N3	P—R5!
39 PxP	R—QR1

This would have been the answer to any other reasonable White move and the rook would penetrate as in the game.

40 N—K3	KRxP
41 R—R1	KRxP
42 R—R7	P—N6
43 RxP+	

The time scramble over, White resigned.

20 XXIII USSR Championship, Leningrad 1956
Black: Tal
King's Indian Defence

1 P—Q4	N—KB3
2 P—QB4	P—KN3
3 N—QB3	B—N2
4 P—K4	P—Q3
5 P—B3	P—K4

Modern praxis favours the more flexible 5 ... 0—0 since Black may well do better to put pressure on the centre with a subsequent N—QB3 or P—QN3 and P—QB4. The drawback to P—K4 in the King's Indian is the risk that Black's fianchettoed bishop may be blocked by its own pawns at Q3 and K4 once White closes the centre by P—Q5.

6 P—Q5?

This is a bit rigid — 6 KN—K2! 0—0 7 B—N5! P—B3 8 Q—Q2 gives White a slight advantage. Korchnoi-Olafsson, Wijk aan Zee 1971.

6	N—R4
7 B—K3	P—KB4

In this, the first encounter between Spassky and Tal, the Latvian is not quite true to himself. One would rather expect from him 7 ... N—R3 8 Q—Q2 Q—R5+ 9 P—KN3 NxP!? 10 Q—KB2! NxB 11 QxQ NxB 12

K—B2 NxP with a very complicated position. This was the way a game Spassky-Bronstein, Candidates 1956, went.

8 Q—Q2	N—R3

Black does better to concern himself over his bad bishop. Thus 8 ... P—B5 9 B—B2 B—B3 threatens to exchange it by 10 ... B—R5, and 10 P—N3 to prevent this, will give the bishop a good diagonal at KN4.

9 0—0—0	N—B3
10 PxP	PxP
11 B—Q3	0—0
12 KN—K2	Q—K2

In some variations the queen will support P—K5 so as to bring new life to the black square bishop, even at the cost of a pawn, e.g. P—K5 PxP P—B5! when control of Black's K4 is very useful. However, 12 ... P—B4 followed by N—B2, P—QR3 and P—QN4 reserving the possibility of Q—R4 seems a better plan. As played White gets in more quickly with his attack on the king.

13 QR—K1

To deter P—K5 by the vis-a-vis

of rook and queen on the file. The pawn sacrifice outlined in the last note does not yet work as White has firm control over his own KB4, so perhaps Black should now try the defensive 13 ... Q—B2.

13 ....   P—B4?
14 N—N3!   N—K1

Clearly not 14 ... P—B5? 15 BxKBP.

15 N—R5   QN—B2

It was hardly worth preserving the bishop by 15 ... B—R1. Black strives desperately to create a counter threat on the Q side.

16 P—KN4   K—R1
17 KR—N1   Q—B2
18 NxB   NxN
19 P—B4

White plays to open lines on the K side and Black decides he must give up a pawn to reduce the threats.

19 ....   P—K5
20 B—QB2   P—N4
21 BPxP   R—QN1
22 PxP   BxP
23 KBxP   BxB
24 NxB   QxQP

Exchanging queens is his best chance since both 24 ... NxNP 25 R—N5 and 24 ... N—B4 25 Q—B3+ leave his king in grave danger.

25 QxQ   NxQ
26 NxQP   QR—Q1
27 BxP   NxP

(See diagram next column.)

This is the position for which Tal was aiming several moves ago. He threatens 28 ... N—Q6+ or 28 ... N(5)—K3 with some play for his pieces.

28 B—Q4!

The beginning of a series of accurate moves that force an easily won ending.

28 ....   N—N3

A confession of defeat but 28 ... RxN? 29 BxN+ K—N1 30 BxR+ KxB 31 KR—B1 or 28 ... N—Q6+ 29 K—Q2 NxR (29 ... RxN 30 BxN+ K—N1 31 B—K5+ R—KN3 32 KxN) 30 BxN+ K—N1 31 B—B6+! and mate next move have to be rejected.

29 R—K7   NxR

He could of course end it at once by 29 ... R—KN1 30 N—B7 mate!

30 BxN+   K—N1
31 BxR+   KxB
32 R—B1+   K—N1
33 R—Q1

Now White's pawn superiority comes into its own.

33 ....   R—KB1
34 P—QR4   R—B7
35 N—B4   RxRP
36 R—Q7   N—B4
37 RxQRP   N—Q5
38 R—QB7   Resigns

Now 38 ... R—QB7+ does not win the knight so White pushes home the QNP in very short order.

21 XXIII USSR Championship, Leningrad 1956
Black: Taimanov
Sicilian Defence

1 P—K4	P—QB4
2 N—KB3	N—QB3
3 P—Q4	PxP
4 NxP	N—KB3
5 N—QB3	P—Q3
6 B—KN5	P—K3
7 Q—Q2	P—QR3

Black has the threat of KN—N5 to attend to at some stage.

8 0—0—0	B—Q2
9 P—B4	B—K2

Three rounds later Taimanov preferred 9 ... P—QN4 against Hasin but after 10 NxN BxN 11 B—Q3 B—K2 12 P—K5 PxP 13 PxP N—Q2 14 BxB QxB White secured an advantage with the strong sacrifice 15 B—K4.

10 N—B3!

This threatens P—K5 and so prevents Black from castling in view of the hanging bishop at Q2. 10 B—K2 is much more tame.

10 ....   R—B1

An innovation. The point is that after 11 P—K5 PxP 12 PxP N—Q4 13 NxN PxN 14 BxB (his bishop is *en prise* with check) 14 ... QxB White cannot play 15 QxP because of 15 ... N—N5 attacking QB7.

11 K—N1

Played after long thought. It is a strong move which renews the threat of P—K5. As compared to the variation of the last note White's KB will not be *en prise* with check, nor his QBP. Thus if now 11 ... P—N4 then 12 P—K5 PxP 13 PxP N—Q4 14 NxN PxN 15 QxP BxB 16 NxB QxN? 17 QxB+ while if in this line 15 ...

N—N5 then 16 Q—Q2 NxBP (16 ... RxP 17 QxN!) 17 B—Q3 with much superior development, and after 17 ... BxB (17 ... N—Q5? 18 BxB NxN 19 BxQ NxQ 20 RxN RxB 21 B—K4 threatening 22 KR—Q1 or later on B—N7) 18 NxB N—Q5 White can play 19 BxP or 19 KR—B1 with winning threats. Another point to 11 K—N1 is that after 11 ... P—N4 12 P—K5 PxP 13 PxP P—N5 14 PxN PxP (14 ... PxN 15 PxB wins, as White's queen is *en prise*, but not with check) 15 BxP BxB 16 N—K4 White wins a pawn with the threat of 17 N—Q6+.

11 ....   Q—B2

Thus Black decides that he has to take the sting out of P—K5.

12 P—K5	PxP
13 PxP	N—Q4

Not 13 ... NxP? 14 NxN and 15 BxN followed by 16 QxB+

14 NxN	PxN
15 BxB	

15 QxP is met by 15 ... N—N5 with a threefold attack on QB7.

15 ....   NxB

Thus Black guards his weak centre pawn but he is left with a poor game since White has command of the black squares (Q—N5 and N—Q4 etc.).

16 B—Q3	0—0
17 Q—N5	B—N4

To remove his bad bishop even at the cost of a doubled pawn. After 17 ... B—K3 18 N—Q4 White would have a fine position.

18 BxB   PxB

19 N—Q4

This looks very strong but 19 P—B3 is even better in order to fix the Black QNP. White would also leave Q4 available as a square for his rook with such ideas as R—Q4—KR4 or KN4 with an attack. His KP would then also be twice defended and so Black would have no counter play.

19 ....   N—N3

Black hurries to attack the KP hoping that he will be able to exchange material and be left with fewer weak pawns. However, 19 ... P—N5 was a better chance, after which he might be able to set up counter-play with R—R1 threatening an eventual Q—R4 when White's QRP is hard to defend.

20 P—B3

Correcting his inaccuracy. Strangely enough Boleslavsky in his authoritative "Caro-Kann bis Sizilianisch" (1968) gives 20 R—Q2 as the move played. It would be quite a strong alternative and the only explanation of the grandmaster's "blunder" must be that he worked from private notes made on this game in which he considered that 20 R—Q2 would be a good move. But the golden rule for all writers is "check prime sources"!

20 ....   P—N5

Pursuing the policy of trying to liquidate his weaknesses, but now White is given a powerful Q side majority. He could try 20 ... QxKP 21 QxP NxQ 22 NxP KR—Q1 with an inferior but possibly defensible position.

21 PxP   NxP

22 R—QB1   N—B5

If 22 ... Q—N1 then 23 P—KR4

with strong attacking threats based on N—B5 followed by P—R5.

23 P—QN3   P—KR3

Or 23 ... Q—K4 24 QxQ and 25 N—B5 with advantage due to his threats of N—K7+ and N—Q6.

24 Q—N4!

The right square. From here White defends his knight (which could be pinned after a subsequent N—R6+ K—N2 Q—K4 and then possibly N—N4) attacks the rook on QB8, and forces the Black queen to retreat to a poor square.

24 ....   N—Q7+

25 K—N2   Q—N1

Not 25 ... Q—Q1 when 26 RxR QxR 25 N—B5 wins the queen, while if 25 ... Q—K4? then 26 RxR and Black has no tactical tricks for 26 ... P—R4 (26 ... P—B4? 27 RxP+ and 28 QxP+) fails to 27 RxR+ KxR 28 Q—B8+ and 29 Q—B3.

26 Q—N3!

Another fine queen move just when one would expect 26 N—B5 with an attack. That move, however, is an error for it permits Black to remedy the defects in his position with 26 ... Q—K4+ Now White's blockading knight robs

Black of counterplay, while
White threatens to penetrate to
the seventh with his rook.

26	QxQ

If 26 ... N—K5 then 27 QxQ
RxQ 28 R—B7. so Black decides
on an attempt at maintaining
control of his QB2.

27 PxQ	KR—Q1

Or 27 ... N—K5 28 N—B5!

28 P—N5

The Q side majority begins to
march forward.

28	N—K5
29 KR—K1	P—N3

If 29 ... NxP 30 RxR and 31
R—K7 or 29 ... RxR 30 RxR
NxP 31 R—B7 and in either case
White's pawns on the Q side will
soon storm forward to queen.

30 P—R4	K—B1
31 P—N6	R—R1

Trying to stop the menacing
threat of P—R5, but conceding
the seventh rank in this fashion
loses quickly. He should carry on
with the logical plan set in
motion by his previous move, but
after 31 ... K—K2 32 P—R5
K—Q2 White retains good

winning chances with 33 N—N5
threatening 34 N—B7.

32 R—B7

Now the king is imprisoned.

32	R—Q3

33 R—KB1!

Not 33 RxNP N—B4
threatening N—Q6+.

33	P—B4
34 RxP	N—B4
35 R—QR7	

This is the move Black missed
when analysing his 31st.

35	R—K1

Or 35 ... RxR 36 PxR R—R3
37 N—N5 (37 P—KN4 also wins)
37 ... K—K2 when 38 R—Q1
wins as 38 ... K—K3? allows the
fork 39 N—B7+.

36 P—R5	R—K5
37 R—Q1	K—K1
38 P—N7	R—Q1
39 N—B6	

Now Black could resign with
an easy conscience, but in such
circumstances most players like to
continue until the time control.

39	R—K7+
40 K—R3	R—K6
41 NxR	Resigns

22 XXIV USSR Championship, Moscow 1957
Black: Gurgenidze
Nimzoindian

1 P—Q4	N—KB3
2 P—QB4	P—K3
3 N—QB3	B—N5
4 P—K3	0—0
5 N—K2	

Rubenstein's original idea
which leads to a very difficult

manoeuvring game.

5	P—Q4
6 P—QR3	B—K2
7 PxP	PxP

Black could try to reduce the
pressure by offering the exchange
of knights with 7 ... NxP.

8 P—KN3 QN—Q2

A more promising defensive set-up is 8 ... P—B3 9 B—N2 P—QR4 10 0—0 N—R3 restraining the White pawns. The knight at QR3 may then be usefully transferred to K3.

9 B—N2 N—N3

Not a very impressive move as White has not yet weakened his QB4 square with P—QN4.

10 0—0 P—QR4
11 P—QR4 R—K1
12 P—B3 P—B4

A bold attempt to acquire some initiative, but in the long run the weakening of his QP is very serious. The quiet 12 ... P—B3 waiting for White to declare his intentions looks best; if White plays 13 P—K4 then 13 ... PxP 14 PxP B—QN5! with pressure on the centre.

13 P—KN4!

The most accurate reply. White can no longer achieve P—K4 but the text, threatening N—N3 followed by P—N5 gaining space on the K side, is hard to counter.

13 .... P—R3
14 P—N3 B—Q2
15 PxP! BxP
16 Q—Q3

White's pieces and pawns control nearly all the central squares and his only weak point at K3 cannot easily be attacked once White plays N—Q4 and B—Q2.

16 .... R—QB1
17 B—Q2 B—B3

Obviously Black has no clear plan.

18 N—Q4 QN—Q2
19 QR—Q1 B—R2
20 QN—K2

Overprotection of the important Q4. Quite in accordance with Nimzovich's theories the

White knights subsequently find very useful employment.

20 .... N—K4
21 Q—N1 N—N3
22 N—B5!

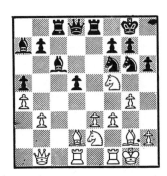

Now the threats accumulate against KN7 and KR6.

22 .... Q—B2

Quite the wrong plan. He must try to get rid of the intrusive knight by 23 ... N—K2 followed, if necessary, by B—Q2.

23 Q—N2 K—R2

The threat was 24 NxP+.

24 K—R1 B—N1
25 N(2)—N3 N—K4

This loses at once since it lets White mobilise his hitherto dormant pawns. 25 ... · N—K2 was still correct.

26 P—B4 N—Q6

Not 26 ... N(4)xP 27 NxNP! KxN 28 N—R5+ K—N3 29 NxN NxN 30 R—KN1 with winning threats of discoveries by his bishop e.g. 30 ... N—N5 31 B—KB3 or 30 ... Q—K2 31 B—K4+ K—R4 32 B—KB3+ K—R5 33 B—K1+ K—R6 34 Q—KN2 mate or 30 ... K—R2 31 B—K4+ PxB (31 ... NxB 32 Q—N7 mate) 32 QxN R—N1 33 B—B3 and mates by 34 R—N7+.

27 Q—Q4	N—N5
28 P—N5	PxP

Or 28 ... N—R4 29 NxN with threats of mate on N7.

29 PxP	N—R4

Now 30 NxN?? allows 30 ...

QxP mate, but Black in fact resigned without waiting for White's reply which would have been 30 Q—R4 P—KN3 31 NxN PxN(R4) 32 QxP+ K—N1 33 N—R6+ etc.

23 XXIV USSR Championship, Moscow 1957
White: Furman
Sicilian Defence

1 N—KB3	P—QB4
2 P—B4	P—KN3
3 P—K4	B—N2
4 P—Q4	PxP
5 NxP	N—QB3

Transposing into a Sicilian Defence Maroczy Bind in which Black has manifold tactical counter-chances.

6 B—K3

6 N—B2 was long held best, but in recent years the text has been considerably more popular. It certainly seems more logical to go for development rather than to retreat the centralised knight.

6	N—R3

In recent years, this has hardly ever been played, preference being given to the crucial variation 6 ... N—B3 7 N—QB3 N—KN5! 8 QxN NxN 9 Q—Q1 and now 9 ... P—K4 or N—K3.

7 N—QB3

7 B—K2 is more accurate, when 7 ... 0—0 8 Q—Q2! N—KN5 9 BxN BxB 10 0—0 is in White's favour.

7	0—0
8 B—K2	P—B4
9 PxP	BxN

An unusual move, offering to give up his strong fianchettoed bishop in the interests of gaining several tempi. 9 ... NxP 10 NxN PxN 11 P—B4 leaves White with the advantage.

10 BxB

Inferior to 10 BxN RxP 11 0—0 when White's knight outpost at Q5 guarantees him a slight plus.

10	NxP
11 B—B5	P—Q3
12 B—R3	KN—Q5
13 0—0	B—B4
14 R—B1	

An obvious move, but 14 B—Q3 was better so that after the exchange of white-squared bishops, Black is weak at his K3 and Q4. Then if 14 ... P—K4 15 B—K4! is strong.

14	Q—Q2
15 N—Q5	R—B2
16 P—QN3	

White clearly expects to get the advantage once he plays his bishop to the long black diagonal, but Black's pieces are all very well placed and he too can look confidently to the future.

16	QR—KB1
17 B—N2	P—K4

18 P—QN4

18 P—B4 to undermine the centre is met by 18 ... B—K3 and Black's play on the KB file gives him the advantage.

The text is too ambitious, however, and the solid defensive move 18 N—K3 was to be preferred. Then 18 ... B—K3 is met by 19 B—N4 while 18 ... Q—K2 19 NxB RxN (19 ... NxN 20 P—B5! threatening 21 B—B4) 20 Q—Q2 Q—R5 21 Q—K3 also leaves White with the better long term prospects.

18 ....   B—K3

Now 19 P—N5 loses its point after 19 ... BxN 20 PxB NxB+ 21 QxN N—K2 and Black has pressure on the QP. Still, this was White's best chance. A subsequent game between Stolyar and Kotkov went 19 N—K3 NxB+ 20 QxN NxP 21 QR—Q1 N—B3 and White did not have much compensation for the pawn he had sacrificed.

19 B—Q3?   B—N5

(See diagram next column.)

20 P—B3

After 20 Q—Q2 Black can continue his onslaught either with 20 ... N—B6+ 21 PxN BxP 22 Q—N5 NxP and if 23 NxN R—B5 etc., or even stronger 20 ... B—B6! and now 21 P—N5 Q—N5 22 N—K3 Q—N4 23 Q—B3 BxP! 24 NxB N—B6+ 25 K—R1 Q—R4 26 P—KR4 Q—N5 or 21 N—K3 (21 Q—R6 or 21 Q—N5 lose the exchange after 21 ... B—K7!) 21 ...

BxP! 22 Q—Q1 R—B5 with a winning attack.

20 ....   BxP!
21 PxB   NxP+
22 K—R1

Or 22 RxN RxR 23 R—B2 Q—R6 24 R—Q2 P—K5 and wins.

22 ....   Q—R6
23 R—KB2

Losing straight away. He had to try 23 Q—K2 when Black does not play 23 ... P—K5 24 BxP NxRP because of the counter 25 N—B6+ RxN 26 B—Q5+ and it is White who stands better, but either 23 ... NxP 24 QxN RxR+ 25 RxR RxR+ 26 BxR QxB+ 27 Q—N1 QxP with four pawns for a piece, or even stronger 23 ... KN—Q5 24 BxN NxB 25 RxR RxR! 26 Q—Q2 P—K5! with a powerful attack:- 27 BxP? R—B8+ mating or 27 N—B4? Q—B6+ or 27 Q—K3 N—B6 28 R—B2 PxB.

23 ....   N—K8!
Resigns

24 Students' Olympiad, Reykjavik 1957
Black: Soderborg
Ruy Lopez

1 P—K4	P—K4
2 N—KB3	N—QB3
3 B—N5	P—QR3
4 B—R4	N—B3
5 Q—K2	

A perfectly playable move ruling out the open variation 5 ... NxP and giving White a lot of scope for manoeuvring as well as some tactical chances based on Q—B4.

5	P—QN4

Not 5 ... B—B4 6 BxN QPxP 7 NxP winning a pawn safely as 7 ... Q—Q5 is met by 8 N—Q3.

6 B—N3	B—B4

A provocative move. 6 ... B—K2 is sounder.

7 P—B3	

White could also try 7 P—QR4 hoping for 7 ... P—N5 8 BxP+! and 9 Q—B4+ but after 7 ...

7	0—0
8 0—0	P—Q3
9 P—Q3	

Restrained play, but the more ambitious 9 R—Q1 gives Black a perfectly sound position after 9 ... Q—K2 10 P—Q4 B—N3 11 B—N5 P—R3.

9	B—K3
10 B—N5	Q—K2

Black's first real inaccuracy. 10 ... R—K1 or first 10 ... P—R3 11 B—KR4 R—K1 would leave it R—QN1 8 PxP PxP White cannot play to win a pawn by 9 N—B3 0—0! 10 NxNP? because of the strong line 10 ... P—Q4 11 PxP P—K5!. The text also rules out a possible N—Q5 which tends to equalise for Black in

some of the B—B4 variations of the Lopez.

equal, whereas now his unguarded queen represents a tactical weakness.

11 B—Q5!	

This exploits that weakness as 11 ... BxB? opens the K file and after 12 PxB N—N1 13 P—Q4 White wins a pawn.

11 .... ⋅	Q—Q2

A second inaccuracy allowing his K side to be broken up. He had to try 11 ... B—Q2 but after 12 N—R4 White already has some K side pressure as 12 ... P—R3 loses the exchange to 13 N—N6! Q—Q1 14 BxKN.

12 BxKN	PxB
13 P—Q4!	PxP

He has to bite the sour apple as 13 ... B—N3 14 BxN QxB 15 P—Q5 just loses a piece.

14 BxN	P—Q6!

Avoiding the loss of a piece as in the last note.

15 QxP	QxB

Now we have the old Chigorin theme — two knights can be stronger than two bishops in closed or semi-closed positions.

16 QN—Q2	K—R1

16 ... P—Q4 to open lines would merely encourage the knights to occupy good squares after 17 N—Q4. So, Black prepares to defend his K side by occupying the KN file.

17 N—Q4	Q—Q2
18 P—QR4	QR—N1

Conceding the file without a fight. 18 ... P—N5 was correct

but not 18 ... PxP 19 Q—B2 P—R6 20 P—QN4!

19 PxP   PxP
20 Q—B3   BxN

Not 20 ... K—N2 21 Q—N3+ K—R1 22 Q—R4 K—N2 23 P—KB4 and then 24 R—B3 with a winning attack, while 20 ... Q—Q1 loses the exchange.

21 PxB   Q—K2
22 KR—B1!

Now the backward QBP is a decisive weakness taken in conjunction with the ruined K side.

22 ....   P—QB4

Or 22 ... R—N2 23 P—K5, or 22 ... KR—B1 23 R—R7 followed by P—Q5.

23 R—R7!

A fine sacrifice that is followed up by an attractive attack replete with quiet moves.

23 ....   QxR

Or 23 ... Q—Q1 24 PxP PxP 25 KRxP when 25 ... QxN loses to 26 QxP+ K—R1 27 R—N5+.

24 QxP+   K—N1
25 R—B3   KR—K1

Or 25 ... Q—R8+ 26 N—B1 B—N5 27 R—KN3 Q—Q8 or 27 ... P—R4 28 P—R3 winning. To move this rook further over to give K1 as a flight square would not help and would rob Black of a possible defensive resource. White merely plays 26 Q—R6 and wins quickly (26 ... K—R1 27 R—KN3 R—N1 28 Q—B6+).

26 R—KN3+!

26 Q—R6 looks crushing, but Black replies 26 ... Q—R8+ 27 N—B1 B—N5! 28 R—KN3 RxP! with a possible defence.

26 ....   K—B1
27 P—Q5   R—R1

Playing for a back row counterattack. 27 ... B—Q2 28 QxQP+ R—K2 29 Q—R6+ K—K1 30

R—N8 mate, while 27 ... B—B1 allows the same variation with White finishing off by 30 R—N8+ K—Q2 31 Q—QB6 mate.

28 P—R4

Played to safeguard his king. He does not want to capture the bishop yet, as that would release his queen's grip on the position (after 28 PxB RxP). Also Black was threatening 28 ... BxP! 29 QxP+ R—K2 and if 30 PxB? Q—R8+ 31 N—B1 QxN+ mating.

28 ....   Q—Q2
29 R—N7

The classic changing of the guard.

29 ....   Q—Q1
30 Q—R6

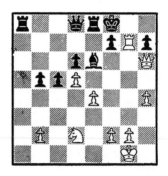

30 ....   K—K2?

Speeding the end, but 30 ... B—B1 also loses to 31 RxRP+ K—K2 32 P—K5! PxP 33 N—K4 QxP (33 ... R—R3 34 Q—N5+ K—Q2 35 RxP+ R—K2 36 Q—B5+ K—B2 37 QxP+ K—Q2 38 NxP+ K—K1 39 R—B8+! and 40 Q—R8+ winning the queen) 34 Q—KB6+ K—Q2 35 RxP+ QxR 36 NxP+ K—B2 37 QxQ+ K—Q1 38 Q—Q5+.

31 QxB   Resigns

1958-61 FAILURE AND SUCCESS

By 1958 Spassky was coming to the end of his Leningrad University course in the Faculty of Journalism, and was thus to become if effect a chess 'professional', though that word has derogatory connotations in Soviet semantics and when used nowadays to describe their own players is accompanied by the qualifying phrase 'in the best sense of the word'. (It is strange that though trained as a journalist Spassky has never been a prolific writer on the game and has annotated comparatively few of his games for the press.)

This period was marked by his failure on two separate occasions to qualify via the Soviet Championship for the World Championship Interzonal. The first failure came in the XXV event at Riga in 1958. Spassky, after having been among the leaders throughout lost his last two games — to Kotov by a blunder after having made a winning piece sacrifice, and to Tal in a game where Spassky had held the upper hand for a long time and missed a win as late as move 58 in a 73 move game.

The second failure came early in 1961 when a disastrous last round loss to Shtein left him just outside the four qualifying places. Spassky was severely criticised in the chess press for resigning the game at the adjournment, and Shtein himself had expected a tough fight in the second session to evaluate an extra pawn in a bishop ending.

Nevertheless this period also contains some of Spassky's finest and sharpest games such as the immortal Kings Gambit against Bronstein (No. 37) and the Albin Counter Gambit against Mikenas (No. 35) in which it is White and not Black who plays all the sacrifices.

The observant reader will have noticed that this section is called 'Failure and Success' with success coming at the end. In 1961 Spassky once again took up work with a new trainer, this time the experienced Bondarevsky, and under his guidance finally fulfilled the ambition of every Soviet grandmaster by winning the Soviet title — the only time Spassky has achieved this, though it must be pointed out that in the sixties he has played very rarely in this event.

25 XXV USSR Championship, Riga 1958
Black: Polugaevsky
Sicilian Defence

1 P—K4	P—QB4
2 N—KB3	P—Q3
3 P—Q4	PxP
4 NxP	N—KB3
5 N—QB3	P—QR3
6 B—KN5	QN—Q2

One of Black's many attempts at innovation in the Sicilian which look a little ugly, but have shown great resilience.

7 B—QB4   Q—R4

Not 7 ... P—K3 8 0—0 and the sacrifice 9 BxKP is threatened.

8 Q—Q2	P—K3
9 0—0—0	P—N4
10 B—N3	

The sacrifice on K6 doesn't work as long as Black has not played B—K2 leaving the KNP unguarded. Spassky himself once gave 10 B—Q5 as a strong move but Black answers not 10 ... PxB 11 N—B6! Q—N3 12 PxP with a win for White, but 10 ... P—N5! 11 BxR PxN 12 PxP N—N3 13 B—B6+ R—Q2 14 BxB+ KNxB threatening N—B5 or Q—R6+ and N—R5. In this 12 Q—K3 is no good because of 12 ... N—N5 13 Q—B4 QxP 14 PxP KN—K4 etc.

10 ....   B—N2

Now 10 ... P—N5 is met strongly by 11 N—Q5 PxN 12 N—B6 and 13 PxP.

11 KR—K1   B—K2

11 ... P—N5 was still bad e.g. 12 N—Q5 PxN 13 PxP+ K—Q1 14 N—B6+ BxN 15 PxB N—K4 16 Q—B4 while 12 ... NxP loses to 13 NxKP! NxQ 14 N—B7+. However, 11 ... R—QB1 may well

be Black's best.

12 P—B4	N—B4
13 P—K5	

The wrong order of moves. 13 BxN would practically force 13 ... BxB and then 14 P—K5! transposes back to the game.

13 ....   PxP

Once again 13 ... P—N5 is not good as 14 B—R4+ NxB 15 NxN QxN 16 PxN PxP 17 N—B5 or in this 14 ... K—Q1 15 PxN PxP 16 BxBP BxB 17 N—B6+ BxN 18 QxP+ are both wins for White.

14 BxN

Forced as 14 PxP KN—K5! 15 NxN QxQ+ would get Black out of all his difficulties.

14 ....   BxB?

Black's only way of keeping his head above water was 14 ... PxB 15 PxP 0—0—0.

15 PxP	B—R5
16 P—N3	B—K2
17 BxP!	0—0

White wins at once after 17 ... PxB 18 NxKP NxN 19 Q—Q7+ K—B2 20 R—B1+ or 17 ... NxB 18 NxN.

18 B—N3   QR—Q1

Black has removed his king into safety and with his two bishops has hopes of putting up a good resistance.

19 Q—B4	P—N5
20 N—R4!	

(See diagram next column.)

20 ....   P—R3

20 ... NxN loses to 21 N—B5 RxR+ (21 ... KR—K1 22 NxB+ RxN 23 RxR+ QxR 24 BxN) 22

RxR B—B4 (Or 22 ... B—Q1 23 BxN when 23 ... QxB loses to 24 RxB and 25 Q—N5) 23 Q—N5 P—N3 24 N—R6+ K—N2 25 N—N4 and wins.

21 NxN	QxN

Or 21 ... B—N4 22 NxB.

22 P—R4	B—Q4
23 N—B5	BxB
24 RPxB	RxR+
25 RxR	R—B1
26 Q—K4	

Black has apparently only a slight disadvantage, as White's extra pawn is doubled, but White's pieces are so well placed that the win is only a matter of time.

26	B—B1
27 P—K6	PxP
28 QxP+	K—R1
29 Q—K4	Q—B3

Black is eager to go into an ending because of the threat of 30 P—R5 and then 31 N—R4, but White prefers to retain his attacking chances.

30 Q—Q3	R—K1
31 P—R5	B—K2

31 N—R4 must be prevented.

32 NxB	RxN
33 Q—N6	Q—K1

Exchanging queens would lose quickly because the back row mate threat would tie down the rook.

34 P—N4	R—K8
35 QxQ+	RxQ
36 R—Q4	P—R4
37 K—Q2	R—K4
38 P—B3!	

With everything well guarded White now proceeds to force a passed pawn.

38	PxP+

Or 38 ... R—QN4 39 P—B4 R—KN4 40 K—K3 and 41 K—B4 followed by 42 R—Q5.

39 PxP	R—KN4
40 P—B4	K—N1
41 R—B4	

To cut off the king.

41	P—N3

This was Black's sealed move, but he resigned without playing on.

After 42 PxP K—N2 (42 ... RxP 43 P—B5 and 44 R—QB4) 43 R—B5 Rx either pawn 44 RxP the united passed pawns win

26 XXV USSR Championship, Riga 1958
White: Bronstein
Nimzoindian

1 P—Q4	N—KB3		3 N—QB3	B—N5
2 P—QB4	P—K3		4 P—K3	P—B4

5	B—Q3	0—0
6	N—B3	P—Q4
7	0—0	QPxP
8	BxBP	P—N3

With the option of developing his QN at Q2 or B3, while there is an immediate threat of 9 ... B—R3 exchanging White's good bishop.

9	Q—K2	B—N2
10	R—Q1	PxP
11	RxP	

Too ambitious an idea but the sort of unusual move that Bronstein specialises in. 11 PxP is correct.

11	....	Q—K2

Naturally he must guard the KB from a possible discovered attack.

12	B—Q2	QN—Q2!

12 ... N—B3 looks much more obvious but Black sees no need to drive away the rook which is badly placed anyway and prefers to leave his QB's diagonal unblocked.

13 B—K1

This passive move is already a confession that he does not have anything very promising to hand.

13	....	P—K4
14	R—R4	

Persisting in error. 14 KR—Q1 was essential.

14	....	P—K5
15	N—Q4	N—K4
16	N—B5	

The losing move. 16 B—N3 is correct when White's disadvantage is still not too great to overcome.

16	....	Q—B4!

With the double threat of 17 ... QxB and 17 ... N—B6+.

17	N—R4	Q—R4

17 ... QxB releases the pressure after 18 QxQ NxQ 19 BxB.

18 N—K7+

White also loses after 18 BxB QxB 19 B—N3 N—N3 20 R—R3 B—B1.

18	....	K—R1
19	B—N3	BxB
20	QxB	N—B6+!

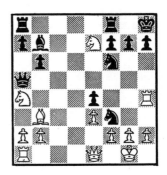

Wins the exchange and breaks up the King side.

21	PxN	Q—KN4+
22	K—R1	

Or 22 R—N4 NxR 23 PxN QxN.

22	....	QxR
23	Q—KN1	Q—R4
24	R—QB1	QxBP+
25	Q—N2	QR—Q1
26	QxQ	PxQ
27	R—B7	R—Q7!
28	RxB	RxBP
29	P—KR3	

Or 29 K—N1 N—N5 30 P—R3 R—N7+ and mates (31 K—B1 NxP+ 32 K—K1 R—K7).

29	....	N—K5
30	N—B5	R—N7

Resigns

A pleasant game to win on one's 21st birthday!

27 Semi-final XXVI USSR Championship, 1959
Black: Kopylov
Alekhine's Defence

1 P—K4	N—KB3
2 P—K5	N—Q4
3 P—Q4	P—Q3
4 P—QB4	N—N3
5 P—B4	

Only a bold player, or one who is very confident of his theoretical knowledge, plays such a committal move, especially against an opponent who, after Mikenas, was regarded at that time as the main Soviet authority on Alekhine's Defence.

5	B—B4

A finesse to tempt White into the "error" 6 B—Q3 when 6 ... BxB 7 QxB PxP 8 BPxP P—QB4 is considered strong (9 P—Q5 P—K3!) but White has a possible gambit answer in 9 N—KB3 or even 9 P—K6 followed by a quick N—KB3 and N—N5.

6 N—QB3	P—K3
7 B—K3	PxP
⌐ 8 BPxP	

Now we are back in the normal lines.

8	N—B3

Better is 8 ... B—QN5 which prevents the strong continuation 9 N—B3 B—K2 10 P—Q5.

9 B—K2	N—N5

The great parting of the ways. Boleslavsky favours the text as being more in line with Nimzovich's theory of attacking a pawn chain (in this case Q4/K5) at its base rather than at its head. However, I prefer 9 ... B—K2 followed by 0—0 and P—B3 which has been the main line in recent years. Black can also follow the risky course of 9 ... Q—Q2 intending 10 ... 0—0—0 or even 10 ... R—Q1.

10 R—B1	P—B4
11 N—B3	B—K2

Continuing development is better than opening the centre by 11 ... PxP when a famous game Bronstein-Mikenas, XVII USSR 1949 went 11 ... PxP 12 NxP N—B3 13 NxB QxQ+ 14 RxQ PxN 15 0—0 and with his strong threats of 16 RxP or 16 N—N5 White won quickly.

12 0—0	PxP

Here too the exchange comes too early and the unhurried 12 ... 0—0 is correct when White normally continues 13 P—QR3 with only very slight advantage.

13 NxP	B—N3

Playing to avoid the awkward consequences of the Bronstein-Mikenas game. However, White, with all his minor pieces in play and his king castled, can now start making direct threats with the black king still in the centre.

14 KN—N5

Earlier theory gave 14 P—QR3 N—B3 15 NxN and 16 QxQ+ with some Q side pressure for White, but the text is much stronger. The knight attacks QR7, QB7 and Q6 and after 14 ... QxQ 15 KRxQ there are threats of 16 N—B7+ and 16 NxP.

14	N—Q6?

Much too ambitious. 14 ... B—N4, which is also a typical Black move in this variation, playing for exchanges, would lose out of hand to 15 BxB QxB 16 Q—Q6 threatening to win a knight and also to mate by 17 N—B7.

Black must castle, though after 14 ... 0—0 15 QxQ he would be embarrassed for a good recapture (15 ... BxQ 16 B—B5 or 15 ... QRxQ 16 NxP or 15 ... KRxQ 16 NxP! likewise). The real error however, was to reach this position at all! (See move twelve).

15 BxN   BxB

Not 15 ... QxB? 16 N—B7+. Now presumably Black was hoping for some relief such as 16 P—QN3 or 16 N—B7+. White finds a much stronger reply.

16 R—B4

The threat of 17 R—Q4 now forces Black to safeguard his bishop.

16 ....   BxP

This loses quickly. As 16 ... B—N4? allows 17 N—Q6+ he had to admit the error of his ways and play 16 ... B—N3 though after 17 QxQ+ (not 17 R—Q4 Q—B1 and Black can hang on) he loses a pawn without any compensation.

17 QxQ+   RxQ

Not 17 ... BxQ 18 N—Q6+ nor 17 ... KxQ 18 BxN+ winning a piece in each case.

18 BxN

This wins material and Black's pieces are left on vulnerable squares.

18 ....   BxN
19 BxR   B—B4+

The spite check.

20 R—B2!

20 K—R1 B—K6! would let Black back into the game.

20 ....   B—B3

Or 20 ... BxR+ 21 KxB KxB 22 NxB.

21 B—B7   Resigns

28 XXVI USSR Championship, Tbilisi 1959
Black: Gurgenidze
King's Indian Defence

1 P—Q4	N—KB3
2 P—QB4	P—KN3
3 N—QB3	B—N2
4 P—K4	P—Q3
5 P—B3	0—0
6 B—K3	P—K4

This move represented the main line of the variation between 1958 and 1961. Recent theory also regards more hypermodern moves as playable e.g. 6 ... P—N3 or 6 ... N—B3 intending to undermine White's centre with moves less direct than .... P—K4.

7 P—Q5

7 KN—K2 was also extensively played but the text is positionally more promising, even though it removes tension from the centre for a short time.

7 ....   P—B3!

7 ... P—B4 is a great positional error since it cuts down Black's play on the queen side.

8 Q—Q2

Since White has not a great deal of development he cannot derive any benefit yet from pressure on the Q file e.g. 8 PxP PxP 9 Q—Q2 (9 P—B5 P—Q4) 9 ... Q—K2 10 0—0—0 R—Q1 11 P—B5 P—Q4 and Black even has some advantage (Ney-Boleslavsky, 1955).

8 ....   PxP
9 BPxP   P—QR3
10 P—KN4

In recent years White has preferred the quieter line of 10 0—0—0 intending K—N1, R—B1 etc. with piece pressure on the side of the board where he has more space.

10 ....   QN—Q2
11 KN—K2   P—KR4

A defensive manoeuvre first used by Gligoric in the Portorozh Interzonal of 1958. Black weakens his K side somewhat but reduces the mobility of his opponent's pawn mass.

12 P—N5

A straightforward plan. White is confident that once he has completed development he will be able to open lines on the K side. 12 P—KR3 and 12 B—N5 were extensively tried about this time without any appreciable advan-

tage to White, e.g. 12 P—KR3 N—R2! 13 0—0—0 P—R5! blockading the K side (Sherwin-Gligoric, Portorozh 1958). Or 12 B—N5 PxP 13 PxP N—B4 14 N—N3 BxP 15 P—KR3 B—B6! 16 R—KN1 QNxP 17 NBxN NxN 18 NxN P—B3 with advantage to Black (Gligoric).

12 ....   N—R2!

12 ... N—K1 is another possibility but the text is stronger.

13 P—KR4   P—N4?

13 ... P—B3! is rather favourable for Black and White's whole plan with P—KN4 in this variation is therefore dubious. Two possibilities after 13 ... P—B3! are: 14 PxP RxP 15 N—KN1 R—B5! 16 0—0—0 RxRP 17 B—KN5 B—R3 with advantage to Black (analysis by Tal); and 14 B—N2 PxP 15 PxP P—QN4 16 N—B1 N—B4 17 P—QN4 N—R5 18 NxN PxN 19 N—Q3 B—Q2 20 R—QB1 B—N4! 21 N—N2 R—B5! Avery-Gligoric, Sparks 1971. Gligoric comments: "Sacrificing the exchange Black solves all his strategic problems, brings his N and KB quickly into play and gets some material compensation on the way." The whole idea comes to Gurgenidze much too late in the game — see moves 19 and 25 — by when White is so well organised that it just boomerangs.

14 N—N3   N—N3
15 B—Q3

(See diagram next column.)

This position was reached in another game, Polugaevsky-Petrosian, played in the same round. The wily Armenian, with his highly developed sense for hidden dangers, thought for a long time

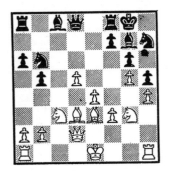

here and finally decided to complete his development by 15 ... B—Q2. Even then he had a long hard fight to draw. Gurgenidze with the carefree confidence of youth decided not to wait to see what his more senior colleague chose.

15 ....   N—B5?

This leaves Black with a further weakness, while White is quite happy to get rid of his inferior bishop.

16 BxN   PxB
17 0—0—0   R—N1
18 K—N1   B—Q2
19 R—QB1

Now Black realises that he has no real play on the QN file (it would be a different story if he did not have a pawn at his K4) and White can play to double rooks together with Q—K2 and N—B1—Q2 and then N—Q1 with a fourfold attack on the QBP. Hence Black decides he must activate his K side pieces and attack along the KB file — the very plan he rejected six moves ago!

19 ....   P—B3
20 NxP!

Played by White with hardly any thought.

20 ....   PxN
21 P—N6   P—B4
22 PxN+   KxP
23 PxP

Before Black can try to close it up by P—B5.

23 ....   BxP+
24 N—K4

Black now has a very difficult game: White can not only play to attack on the K side but also to put pressure on the QBP. Gurgenidze finds his best chance, removing the knight before it can play to K6 via KN5, and then offering the exchange to activate his remaining bishop.

24 ....   BxN+
25 PxB   R—B5!
26 RxP!

Much better than 26 ·BxR PxB 27 R—B2 Q—B3 and it is far from clear how White is to make use of his material advantage.

26 ....   RxRP
27 QR—B1!

While White has a sound extra pawn on the Q side the compensatory pawn on the other side of the board is very rickety so White plays to seize the KR file and thus put pressure on the weakness.

27 ....   R—B1

Otherwise 28 B—N5 is very strong (27 ... B—B3 28 RxR BxR 29 R—R1 and 30 Q—R2).

28 QR—K1   RxR

Not 28 ... RxP? 29 Q—Q3 R—B5 30 B—Q2 winning a rook.

29 RxR   Q—K1
30 Q—K2   Q—N3
31 QxP+

The simplest. The extra pawn is not so much the key factor in the ending as the fact that White's bishop is much the superior minor piece.

31 ....   QxQ

32	RxQ+	K—N3
33	R—N5+	K—B2
34	R—N4	

Better than 34 P—N3 as an answer to Black's threat of 34 ... R—B5. White wishes to advance his Q side pawns quickly so as to get a strong passed pawn, and also to keep his superior bishop, so he rules out a subsequent B—R3.

34	....	R—KR1

Or 34 ... R—QN1 35 B—Q2 followed by the advance of the pawns.

35	P—QR4	R—R6
36	B—Q2	B—B1
37	K—B2	R—R7
38	K—Q3	B—R3
39	B—B3	

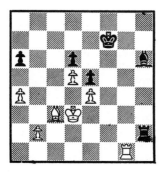

The most accurate. As the Russian chess proverb puts it "Vse ladeinye endshpily-nicheinye" (All rook endings are drawish).

39	....	B—B5
40	R—N1	R—R6+
41	K—B4	B—K6

Black is in a dilemma. 41 ... R—K6 is met by 42 R—K1 and he cannot bring his king to the Q side since 41 ... K—K1 is met by 42 R—N8+ K—Q2 43 R—QR8. Hence he plays to rob the white rook of QR7 and to attack the KP in another way.

42	R—K1	K—K2
43	P—N4!	B—N3

At last the bishop has reached a position to hold up White on the Q side.

44	R—K2	

White has no need to hurry and gives himself the option of going back to the KN file.

44	....	K—Q2
45	P—R5	B—Q1

Keeping the QRP under observation so as to meet 46 P—N5? PxP+ 47 K—N4 with 47 ... BxP+

46	B—Q2	R—R8

The sealed move. Black would dearly like to get behind the pawns at once, but after 46 ... R—R6 47 B—B3! his rook is trapped e.g. 47 ... B—N4 48 K—Q3 B—B8 49 R—KR2 and 50 R—R7 while the Black pieces are fully occupied in the corner of the board.

47	P—N5	R—R8

Or 47 ... PxP+ 48 KxP R—N8+ 49 B—N4 and then P—R6 followed by R—KR2—R7.

48	P—N6	R—KN8
49	R—KR2	R—N5
50	R—R7+	K—B1
51	B—N4!	RxP+
52	K—N3	RxB+

Forced, otherwise, after P—N7+ and BxP+, it is mate next move.

53	KxB	B—N4
54	K—B3	Resigns

White prevents 54 ... B—Q7+ tying his king down and now, after 54 ... K—N1, comes 55 R—R7 with two united passed pawns.

29 XXVI USSR Championship, Tbilisi 1959
Black: Lutikov
King's Indian Defence

1 P—Q4	N—KB3
2 P—QB4	P—Q3
3 N—QB3	QN—Q2
4 P—K4	P—K4

Black's order of moves has ruled out Spassky's favourite Saemisch variation (5 P—B3? PxP 6 QxP P—KN3 and B—N2, when the queen is subject to harrassment in the centre) so we get instead the most common variation of the King's Indian.

5 N—B3	P—KN3
6 B—K2	B—N2
7 0—0	0—0
8 R—K1	P—B3
9 B—B1	N—K1?

To play P—KB4 without having waited for the removal of central tension (by White's P—Q5) is bound to react against Black who lacks development. The text also has the tactical drawback of leaving Black's queen unguarded. Hence the usual moves 9 ... PxP or 9 ... Q—R4 are better, while 9 ... Q—N3 and 9 ... Q—K2 also have their points — pressure on the centre and particularly on the black squares.

10 B—N5

Another drawback to Black's last move is that White can develop his QB on this natural square with gain of time.

10 ....   P—B3

Black has little choice. Either knight to KB3 loses the KP, 10 ... Q—B2 allows 11 B—K7 and Black does not want to offer the exchange of his strong KB.

11 B—K3   P—KB4?

Black thus achieves his object but he would do better to adopt a strictly defensive attitude by 11 ... Q—K2 or 11 ... N—B2 unpinning his QP.

12 KPxP	NPxP
13 PxP	NxP

A sad necessity leaving him with a large number of weak squares and weak pawns. If 13 ... PxP then White wins material by 14 B—B5 R—B2 15 NxP as the QN is pinned.

14 NxN	BxN
15 Q—Q2	Q—B3
16 QR—Q1	

White now has a practically won game in the higher sense. The isolated KBP blocks Black's QB yet 16 ... P—B5 would give White still more control of the centre, (N—K4! at some stage) while 16 ... BxN? 17 PxB would enable White to invade on the black squares (B—N5 and R—K7 or B—K7). Black sensibly decides to complete his development and put the onus on White to take the initiative.

16	B—K3
17 B—N5	Q—N3
18 B—B4!	

The Black KB is his best placed piece and with its exchange White's advantage becomes more pronounced.

18 ....   Q—B3

This loses a pawn but it is hard to see any other reasonable move as after 18 ... BxB 19 QxB White plays R—K3 with great

pressure as the Black knight
remains tied to the defence of the
QP.

19	BxB	PxB
20	Q—K3	P—K5
21	P—B3!	N—N2

Black finally rectifies his mistake, but much too late to affect
the outcome of the game.

| 22 | PxP | PxP |

After this Black is conducting a
completely lost cause. 22 ...
P—B5 was a fighting chance,
though after 23 P—K5! to prevent
a blockade on a white square by
Q—K4 White should still win.

23 Q—Q4!

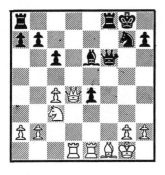

The Capablanca touch. White
gives Black the invidious choice
of going into an ending a pawn
down or conceding to White full
control of the centre and of the Q
file.

23	....	Q—N3
24	NxP	R—B5
25	R—Q3!	

Now White himself plays for
an attack based on piece pressure.

| 25 | .... | QR—KB1 |
| 26 | R—KN3 | Q—B2 |

27 B—Q3

Now the major pieces trebled
on the KB file find that they bite
on granite as KB8 and KB7 are
safely guarded by White's centralised minor pieces. White
threatens with his queen in all
directions.

| 27 | .... | K—R1 |
| 28 | Q—K5! | |

This further centralisation threatening 29 N—N5 or 29 N—Q6 is
much stronger than 28 QxP.

28 .... B—N5

Or 28 ... P—KR3 29 N—Q6!
winning two pieces for a rook.

29 P—KR3

It is useful to have a bolt hole
for the king at KR2.

| 29 | .... | B—R4 |
| 30 | N—N5 | |

Black could resign now but
decides to play on till the bitter
end.

30	....	Q—B3
31	NxP	QxQ
32	RxQ	R—Q1
33	N—N5	KR—Q5

Because of White's useful precaution at move 29 it will be of
little use for Black to penetrate
with his rook to Q8. However,
White's rooks are now so well
placed for the attack that White
need no longer worry about
having to take account of his
opponent's threats.

34 N—K6! RxB

Not 34 ....NxN 35 RxB mate.

| 35 | RxN | R—Q8+ |
| 36 | K—R2 | Resigns |

The only way to save his
bishop is by 36 ... B—K1 but
then 37 R—KB5 forces mate or
considerable material gain.

30 Semi-final XXVII USSR Champ., Tallinn 1959
Black: Furman
King's Gambit

1	P—K4	P—K4
2	P—KB4	PxP
3	N—QB3	

The very risky Steinitz gambit, based on the idea that the king is a strong piece over whose safety one need not have too much concern. The choice of opening was psychologically very shrewd as the move has hardly ever been played recently apart from the odd correspondence game, and Furman is well known as a solid player with a considerable knowledge of the lines which occur frequently in master chess. In fact Furman now thought for a very long time before replying.

3	....	Q—R5+
4	K—K2	P—Q4
5	NxP	B—Q3

This is quite playable. There is an attempt at outright refutation by 5 ... B—N5+ 6 N—B3 N—QB and if 7 NxP+ K—Q1 8 NxR N—K4 or 8 ... N—Q5+ with great complications. Spassky, however, intended 7 P—Q4 which in effect would transpose back into positions very similar to the game.

6	P—Q4	B—N5+
7	N—B3	N—QB3

Perhaps Furman in his long think over move 3 had finally remembered that there was a game Bronstein-Alatortsev, Moscow 1945, in which Black decided to get rid of the centralised knight by 7 ... N—KB3 but after 8 NxN+ PxN 9 P—B3 White has consolidated his central position and had a promising game.

8 P—K5

By analogy with the Bronstein game 8 P—B3 seems the right move here so as to prevent a Black minor piece coming to QN4. Then White can break the pin by moves like K—Q3, Q—N3 or Q—R4 and so achieve a fairly normal development. The text weakens the position of his centralised knight and should only have been played in answer to P—KB4. However, Spassky decides to win back the gambit pawn by force and dares his opponent to do his worst.

8	....	0—0—0!
9	BxP	

After 9 PxB RxP 10 P—B4 N—B3, Black, who has opened the centre files for his rooks, has a very strong attack.

9	....	KN—K2
10	P—B4	

He must try and maintain his centre.

10 .... N—B4?

Too engrossed in his idea of attacking the QP a second time. Black in fact thought for a very long time here but did not find the stronger moves 10 ... KR—K1 or 10 ... B—N5! While the former is fairly obvious it must be admitted that the latter is not easy to find. However, it would exploit White's inaccuracy at move eight and by preventing a possible Q—K1 or K—Q2 and by threatening 11 ... NxN 12 PxN RxP it would give Black much the better of it. Now, however, the white king has enough safe squares available to demonstrate the validity of Steinitz's axiom.

11 PxB   KNxP+
12 K—Q3!   Q—R4

12 ... B—B4+ 13 K—B3 is quite safe while 12 ... Q—B7 is met by 13 Q—Q2.

13 B—K2   N—K3
14 B—N3

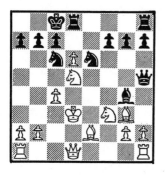

Now it is clear that Black is lost. The pin on the Q1 KR5 diagonal has been broken, the protected pawn at Q6 and the N at Q5 keep the Q file firmly closed and White has completed his development.

Moreover Furman was already in time trouble and he had to play the remaining moves just hoping for tactical tricks without having any clear plan.

14 ....   PxP
15 P—N4   KR—K1
16 KR—K1 N—B2

A terrible confession of failure to offer a piece exchange when a whole bishop down, but White's knight dominates the board and must be removed.

17 K—B3

Guarding the QNP and making for a haven at QN2.

17 ....   Q—R3
18 Q—B1   NxN+
19 PxN   R—K6+

The rest of the game is not very interesting. With more time, and cooler head, Furman would probably have resigned it but seeing a couple of checks feels honour bound to continue.

20 B—Q3   Q—B3+
21 K—B2   RxR

If 21 ... RxN hoping for a knight check at Q5, then 22 PxN. 21 ... NxP+ looks strong but the Steinitzian counter 22 K—N3 discovered check just wins a rook for nothing!

22 BxR   BxN
23 PxN   BxBP
24 B—B3   Q—B7+
25 Q—Q2   B—R5+

As long as he can see 'forcing' moves Black is reluctant to ring down the curtain!

26 K—N2   Q—R5
27 BxNP   K—N1
28 P—N3   Q—N5
29 B—B6   R—QB1
30 R—QB1 R—K1
31 P—N5

and Black lost on time with ten moves still to make.

31 Semi-final USSR Champ., Tallinn 1959
Black: Shishkin
Grunfeld

1 P—Q4	N—KB3
2 P—QB4	P—KN3
3 N—QB3	P—Q4
4 PxP	NxP
5 P—K4	NxN
6 PxN	B—N2
7 B—QB4	P—QB4
8 N—K2	0—0

In the fifties the main line was 8 ... PxP 9 PxP N—B3 10 B—K3 0—0 11 0—0 B—N5 12 P—B3 N—R4 as in the famous game of the Bronstein-Boleslavsky match 1950. However, little by little, attention was concentrated on keeping up the tension in the centre and attacking on the QB and Q files by Q—B2 followed by R—Q1. This game, one of the first in the new line, confirmed the old truism that the way of the innovator is hard!

9 0—0	N—B3
10 B—K3	Q—B2
11 R—B1	

To guard his tender spot at QB3 and to discourage Black from opening the Q file because of the vis-a-vis of rook and queen.

11 ....   R—Q1

Although this puts great pressure on the White centre it leaves his KB2 weak. However, Black probably has no better move as 11 ... P—N3 allows 12 B—B4 P—K4 13 B—N3 and Black has run out of good moves.

12 P—B4

The most energetic reply. White could try the prophylactic 12 P—KR3 as in the famous Olympiad win over Fischer (see game 98) while at Santa-Monica

in 1965 Spassky preferred 12 Q—K1 against the same redoubtable opponent (game 73).

12 ....   B—N5

The quieter 12 ... P—K3 or 12 ... N—R4 are also playable.

13 P—B5!

The game now rapidly boils up to a crisis.

13 ....   NPxP

Black asks to be shown. If he were more timid, then he could play to drive the bishop away by 13 ... N—R4 at the expense of reducing his central pressure.

14 BxP+!

This may well not be a forced win but over the board the attacker has many practical chances.

14 ....   KxB

14 ... K—R1 is not so good as after 15 KPxP PxP 16 PxP Black cannot safely play to regain the pawn (16 ... BxN 17 QxB BxP 18 BxB RxB 19 Q—R5 and White has a strong attack, e.g. 19 ... Q—K4 20 B—N6! Q—N2 21 R—B3 QR—Q1 22 R—KR3 R—Q7 23 P—B6! PxP 24 QxP+ QxQ+ 25 RxQ+ K—N1 26 RxP winning — analysis by Euwe).

15 Q—N3+   P—K3

Or 15 ... K—K1 16 N—B4 and the threats of 17 N—K6 or 17 Q—N8+ B—KB1 18 QxB+ or 17 P—KR3 are too strong to be met at one and the same time.

16 N—B4   Q—Q2
17 PxP

The opening of the KB file exposes the enemy king to manifold threats.

17 ....   N—R4

Or 17 ... BxBP 18 NxP! QxN (18 ... N—R4 19 NxR++ K—N3 20 Q—B7+! with the exchange up) 19 RxB+ B—B3 20 RxB+! KxR 21 B—N5+ K—B2 22 R—B1+ winning the queen.

18 QxKP+

18 PxP+ loses for White after 18 ... BxP e.g. 19 NxB+ K—N1! or 19 QxB+ QxQ 20 NxQ+ KxN 21 QR—K! K—Q4 22 R—B5+ K—B3 J. Littlewood-Hartston, English County match 1970.

18	QxQ
19 NxQ	N—B5?

The losing move as Black forces White to make a strong reply. Correct is 19 ... PxP! 20 NxR+ (or 20 PxP KR—QB1 21 N—N5+ K—N1 and Black is safe, e.g. 22 RxR+ RxR 23 P—B6 B—R3 24 P—B7+ K—N2 25 P—Q5 K—N3 and Black now stands better — analysis by Boleslavsky) 20 ... RxN 21 PxP N—B3 and Black's two bishops give him a defensible game in a position where White's rooks and extra pawns cannot easily be used. 19 ... B—B3 is also possible with the same idea of keeping his two bishops and inducing White to part with his powerful knight with 20 NxR+.

20 B—N5!	R—KN1
21 R—B4!	

(See diagram next column.)

Now Black's minor pieces on the fourth rank represent tactical weaknesses.

21	B—B3

A confession of defeat but, 21 ... B—R4 22 P—N4 or 21 ... B—K7 22 R—K1 B—Q6 23 NxP! win material for White, or 21 ... QBxP 22 NxB. Here as later White's knight is a dominating piece.

22 RxB	P—KR3
23 PxP	N—K4

Or 23 ... N—N7 24 R—N4 N—Q6 25 RxP+ K—K1 26 BxB winning (26 ... NxR? 27 R—K7 mate).

24 BxB!	NxR
25 B—Q4	

With three pawns for the exchange and his minor pieces 'anchored' on powerful squares White has an easy win. His plan is to advance the K side pawns driving the enemy forces back.

25	QR—K1
26 P—KR3	N—B3
27 P—N4	R—K2
28 K—N2	N—K5

Hoping to blockade the KNP before White gets in K—B3 and R—KN1, forcing P—KR4 and then P—N5.

29 K—B3	N—N4+
30 NxN	PxN

At last the brave steed has died but the bishop now proves an equally strong 'anti-blocker'.

31 P—KR4!	PxP
32 R—KR1	Resigns

Black's rooks have no scope for action and after RxP and R—R7+ the passed pawns will roll forward without meeting any real obstacle.

32 Leningrad Championship 1959
Black: Genin
Irregular Defence

1 P—K4	P—K4
2 N—KB3	N—QB3
3 B—B4	

Like the great majority of modern players, Spassky is keen on the Lopez, and this game is the only example I have been able to find, at least in the post 1952 period, of his adoption of the old 19th century favourite.

3 ....   P—KN3

A most unusual move which bears some resemblance to Steinitz's older defence to the Lopez. However, with White's bishop already directed against the weak spot at KB2 it can hardly be good.

4 P—Q3	B—N2
5 N—B3	KN—K2

It looks better to play 5 ... N—B3 controlling his KR4, so ruling out the early push of the KRP which White now adopts.

6 N—KN5	0—0
7 P—KR4!	N—R4

Trying to remove one of the attacking pieces. 7 ... P—KR3 is met by 8 P—R5! PxN 9 PxP NxP 10 Q—R5 R—K1 11 QxN while 7 ... P—KR4 8 P—KN4 is equally fragile a defence. Black must now have been bitterly regretting his 5th move.

8 P—R5	NxB
9 PxN	P—KR3
10 PxP!	

Here too this move gives a very powerful attack.

10 ....   PxP

Or 10 ... PxN 11 BxP PxP 12 N—Q5 R—B2 (12 ... R—K1 13

Q—B3 and 14 N—B6+) 13 Q—N4 P—B3 (13 ... P—Q3 14 Q—R4 K—B1 15 Q—R8+ BxQ 16 RxB+ K—N2 17 RxQ) 14 NxN+ RxN 15 Q—R4 K—B2 16 R—R3 P—Q3 17 R—B3+ K—K1 18 Q—R7. Black cannot improve the defence by 11 ... P—KB3 because of 12 B—R6 NxP (or 12 ... Q—K1 13 BxB KxB 14 R—R7+ K—N1 15 N—Q5! NxP 16 Q—R5 and wins) 13 Q—R5 N—B5 14 BxN PxB 15 0—0—0 with a won game.

11 N—B3	P—KN4

Not 11 ... K—R2 12 B—N5 Q—K1 13 Q—Q2 N—N1 14 N—Q5 etc.

12 NxNP!	PxN
13 Q—R5	Q—K1
14 Q—R7+	K—B2
15 R—R3!	P—N5

This loses quickly. The crucial line was 15 ... N—N3 16 R—B3+ (not 16 R—R6? Q—K3 and 17 ... R—R1) 16 ... N—B5 17 P—KN3 P—N5 18 BxN PxR 19 B—R6 R—KN1 20 Q—B5+ B—B3 (20 ... K—K2 21 N—Q5+ K—Q3 22 0—0—0 K—B3 23 N—N4+ etc.) 21 N—Q5 Q—K3 22 Q—R7+ B—N2 23 BxB RxB 24 Q—R5+ Q—N3 (24 ... K—N1 25 NxP QxP 26 0—0—0! QxN? 27 Q—K8+ mating) 25 QxP with a persistent attack despite his material deficit of a whole rook.

(See diagram next column.)

16 B—R6!	R—KN1

After 16 ... PxR 17 QxB+ K—K3 18 QxR QxQ 19 BxQ PxP 20 K—K2 and 21 R—KN1 White has a won ending.

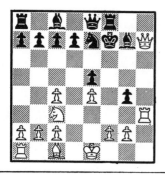

17 R—R5!   K—B1

The threat was 18 R—B5+ NxR 19 QxN+ K—K2 20 N—Q5+ K—Q3 21 P—B5+ K—B3 22 N—N4+ exposing the king to

grave dangers.

18 N—Q5   Q—N3

Black has relied on this move presumably missing White's fairly obvious reply. However, 18 ... NxN 19 R—B5+ loses material and 18 ... BxB 19 QxB+ is also a quick loss.

19	R—B5+!	K—K1
20	QxQ+	NxQ
21	B—N5!	P—Q3
22	NxP+	K—Q2
23	R—B7+	K—B3
24	NxR	P—Q4

The only way of giving the king a flight square.

25	BPxP+	K—Q3
26	B—Q2	K—B4
27	B—K3+	Resigns

33 Leningrad Championship 1959
Black: Reshko
Caro-Kann Defence

1	P—K4	P—QB3
2	N—QB3	P—Q4
3	N—B3	B—N5
4	P—KR3	BxN
5	QxB	N—B3
6	P—K5	

Playing to disrupt his opponent's development.

6	....	N—Q2
7	Q—N3	P—K3
8	B—K2	Q—B2

Spassky gave 8 ... P—QB4 as better, when he intended 9 P—B4 N—QB3 10 P—N3 and if 10 ... N—Q5 then 11 B—Q3.

| 9 | P—B4 | P—QR3 |
| 10 | P—N4 | |

A demonstration on the Q side. Black should probably try in

answer to seize the initiative with the pawn sacrifice 10 ... BxP 11 QxP R—B1 12 QxRP P—QB4 followed by N—QB3, and 0—0—0.

10	....	P—QB4
11	P—N5	P—B5
12	R—QN1	P—Q5
13	N—K4	PxP

Spassky's pawn sacrifice has led to a very unbalanced position in which he can soon break through on the K side with P—B5.

14 0—0

Not 14 RxP? Q—B3

14 ....   RxP

Pawn-grabbing is most inappropriate when he is so badly behind in development. 14 ... N—QB3 was a more solid move.

15 P—Q3   RxP
16 B—Q1!   R—R7

Black's last chance was 16 ... PxP e.g. 17 BxR PxB 18 RxP Q—B3 19 Q—Q3 N—B4 20 NxN BxN with a playable game, but White may do better with 18 R—N2 keeping up the tension.

17 P—B5!   NxP

Other defences are no better e.g. 17 ... QxP 18 PxP QxP 19 R—K1 or 17 ... PxP 18 RxBP threatening 19 RxP, 19 P—K6 or even 19 N—Q6+.

18 PxP   P—B3

Or 18 ... PxP 19 B—B4 QN—Q2 20 RxNP R—R4 21 PxP followed by 22 B—N4 or 22 N—N5.

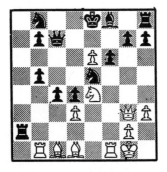

19 RxBP

The decisive breakthrough.

19 ....   PxR

He has to accept as otherwise comes 20 R—B7.

20 NxP+   K—Q1
21 N—Q5   Q—Q3

Or 21 ... Q—N2 22 P—K7+ K—Q2 23 B—N4+ K—K1 24 B—R5+ etc.

22 B—N5+   K—B1

Not 22 ... K—K1 23 B—R5+ N—N5 24 N—B7+ winning the queen.

23 B—N4

Now the threat of 24 P—K7+ is killing e.g. 23 ... B—N2 24 N—K7+ K—B2 25 N—B5 QxP 26 NxB Q—Q4 27 B—B6 and then 28 N—K6+ and 29 BxN+, or 23 ... QN—Q2 24 PxN+ NxP 25 R—K1 P—N3 (25 ... R—R8 26 B—B4 Q—R3 27 N—N6+ QxN RxR K—Q1 29 B—N5+) 26 Q—B3 B—N2 27 Q—B7 or finally 23 ... QxN 24 P—K7+ K—B2 25 P—K8(Q).

23 ....   NxB
24 P—K7

The winning move.

24 ....   BxP

Or 24 ... RxP+ 25 QxR B—N2 26 QxN+ N—Q2 but after 27 RxP the threat of 28 N—N6+ decides.

25 QxN+   N—Q2
26 NxB+   K—B2
27 B—B4   N—K4
28 Q—N7   K—N3
29 BxN   Q—K3
30 BxP+   Resigns

34 Riga 1959
Black: Witkowski
Grunfeld Defence

1 P—Q4   N—KB3
2 P—QB4   P—KN3

3 N—QB3   P—Q4
4 PxP   NxP

5	P—K4	NxN
6	PxN	B—N2
7	B—QB4	P—QB4
8	N—K2	PxP
9	PxP	N—B3
10	B—K3	P—QN4?

A "trappy" move the only justification for which lies in the variation 11 BxNP? Q—R4+ 12 N—B3 QxN+ 13 B—Q2 QxP 14 BxN+ B—Q2 15 BxR QxR.

11	B—Q5!	B—Q2
12	R—QB1	

The most energetic move, but 12 BxN BxB 13 P—Q5 B—Q2 14 B—Q4 was also sufficient to gain an advantage.

12	....	R—QB1
13	0—0	P—K3

Black should have played 13 ... 0—0 but was concerned about the variation: 14 BxN RxB 15 RxR BxR 16 P—Q5 B—Q2 17 BxP Q—R4 18 B—B5. However, 18 ... QxP 19 BxP R—B1 then gives Black compensation for the pawn and White does better to try 17 Q—Q2. The text delays Black's development and weakens his dark squares.

14	BxN	RxB

Or 14 ... BxB 15 P—Q5! PxP 16 PxP B—N2 17 B—B5 QxP 18 N—B4 QxQ 19 KRxQ with a powerful attack.

15	RxR	BxR
16	P—Q5	

Here too this breakthrough leads to a very strong attack.

16	....	PxP
17	Q—B2	Q—Q2
18	B—B5	PxP
19	R—Q1	Q—N2
20	N—Q4	

Now Black finds it very hard to defend as 20 ... B—Q2 is met by 21 N—N3 P—B4 22 Q—Q2 Q—B3 23 B—N4 B—K4 24 N—Q4! Q—B3 25 N—B3 while to give up his black squared bishop with 20 ... BxN would be a serious confession of failure (21 RxB P—B4 22 R—Q6 threatening 23 B—Q4 or 23 R—K6+).

20	....	B—K4
21	B—N4	BxN

Finally forced as 21 ... B—Q2 22 Q—B5 B—KB3 23 Q—Q6 Q—N3 24 Q—Q5 would leave Black with no useful move.

22	RxB	P—QR4
23	B—B5	

This steady move is the soundest way. The tempting 23 Q—B5 does not seem to work because of 23 ... P—B3 (23 ... PxB 24 Q—K5+) 24 R—Q6 0—0 25 R—Q7 R—B1!! and Black even has the better of it. After 25 RxB PxB 26 R—B7 R—Q1 27 P—KR4 Q—Q4 28 Q—R7 Q—Q8+ 29 K—R2 Q—Q3+ 30 P—N3 Q—B1 31 RxP R—R1, Black repels the attack. However, as Spassky pointed out afterwards, White would in fact win after 23 Q—B5 P—B3 with the simple 24 BxP K—B2 25 R—Q6 R—B1 26 B—B3.

23	....	Q—B1
24	P—KR3!	

A quiet move underlining the hopelessness of Black's position. Now Black has to face up to the threat of 25 RxP+ which, if played at once, would lose to the back-row mate threat after 25 ... BxR 26 QxB+ Q—K3 27 Q—R8+ K—Q2.

24 ....   P—B4

Or 24 ... P—B3 25 Q—N3 P—R5 26 Q—N2 P—R4 (to play his rook to R2) 27 R—Q1 K—B2 28 R—Q6 etc.

25 Q—N2   B—Q2
Or 25 ... R—N2 26 R—Q6.

26 RxP+   PxR

Now White forces mate in all variations.

27 QxR+   K—B2
28 QxP+   K—B3

Or 28 ... K—K3 29 Q—K7+ K—Q4 30 Q—Q6+ and 31 Q—Q4 mate.

29 Q—K7+   K—B4
30 P—N4+   K—B5
31 Q—Q6+   K—N4

Or 31 ... K—B6 31 Q—Q1+ K—B5 33 Q—Q2+ etc.

32 B—K3+   Resigns

35 Riga 1959
Black: Mikenas
Albin Counter Gambit

1 P—Q4   P—Q4
2 P—QB4   P—K4

In the previous round, against the Finnish player Niemala, Spassky himself had tried this gambit, so Mikenas decides that he too can allow himself this liberty.

3 QPxP   P—Q5
4 P—K4

A most unusual reply ignoring Black's centre pawn and taking up a more aggressive posture than White normally adopts in the first few moves of the Albin.

4 ....   N—QB3
5 P—B4

Only this double-edged response justifies his previous move. After 5 N—KB3 B—N5+ 6 B—Q2 Q—K2 to be followed by B—N5 and 0—0—0 Black has a fine free game.

5 ....   P—KN4

This is quite old 'book' deriving from games played in the first decade of this century. Nevertheless, as Lutikov demonstrated in a game against Spassky some four years later, Black has better equalising chances with the other gambit 5 ... P—B3! and if 6 PxP B—N5+ 7 B—Q2 NxP, or as in the actual game 6 N—KB3 PxP 7 B—Q3 B—N5+ 8 QN—Q2 PxP 9 0—0 N—B3+.

6 P—KB5

Not 6 B—Q3 PxP 7 BxP as Black stands well after ... N—N3.

6 ....   NxP
7 N—KB3   B—N5+

Black would do better to exchange knights and rely on his strong QP for counter chances after 8 QxN B—N2.

8 N—Q2

Also possible was 8 K—B2! and after, say, 8 ... N—N5+ 9 K—N1

B—B4 10 P—N4! White has the advantage. Perhaps this is objectively stronger than the text, but Spassky obviously wanted to try out his sacrifice.

    8 ....   N—QB3
    9 B—Q3

Spassky's improvement on 9 P—QR3 B—Q3 as played in a game between the Leningrad master A. Geller and Mikenas in 1951.

    9 ....   P—N5
    10 0—0!

A Muzio Gambit style sacrifice.

    10 ....   PxN
    11 NxP   B—Q3

Black's best defence was to defend his key K4 square with 11 ... P—B3, but after 12 P—QR3 B—Q3 13 P—QN4 N—K4 14 P—B5 NxN+ 15 RxN B—K4 16 B—QB4 to be followed by R—Q3 and B—N2 White has a strong attack along the Q file, while if 16 ... N—K2 then 17 R—R3 threatening 18 Q—R5 with or without check as the case may be. 11 ... Q—K2 is not so good; Spassky has already demonstrated in a game against Beliavsky (Leningrad 1955) that 12 P—K5! is then very strong. That game continued 12 ... P—QR4 13 P—QR3 B—B4 14 P—QN4 PxP 15 B—N5 P—B3 16 KPxP Q—B2 17 PxP RxR 18 QxR BxNP 19 Q—R8 K—Q1 20 B—K4 QxP 21 N—K5! and White soon won.

White of course plays to open lines.

    12 ....   NxP

Or 12 ... BxP 13 R—K1 P—B3 14 P—QN4 with good chances. After the text however, White has fewer problems.

    13 R—K1   P—B3

The only move as 12 ... Q—K2

13 P—B5! NxN+ 14 PxN B—K4 15 P—B4 lets White win the piece back at once.

    14 P—B5!   B—K2

Trying to close the K file. 14 ... KBxP 15 NxN PxN 16 RxP+ B—K2 would let White continue with the powerful 17 B—N5 or even with 17 Q—R5+ K—Q2 18 P—B6.

    15 NxN

The simplest. 15 RxN also came into consideration, but after 15 ... PxR 16 NxP N—B3 17 B—QB4 BxP the position is unclear.

    15 ....   PxN
    16 RxP   N—B3
    17 B—N5   0—0
    18 Q—N3+

Black has managed to castle, but White's pressure is quite undiminished.

    18 ....   K—R1

Or. 18 ... K—N2 19 QR—K1 R—K1 (19 ... KBxP 20 RxB or 19 ... R—B2 20 B—QB4) 20 B—N5 B—Q2 21 BxB QxB 22 Q—N3!

    19 QR—K1   KBxP

Or 19 ... R—K1 20 BxN+.

    20 RxB

Again the simplest. 20 R—K8 looks a more fitting end to the game, but after 20 ... Q—Q3 21 Q—B7 Black has 21 ... N—N1 22 Q—R5 N—B3. Hence the prosaic text.

    20 ....   Q—Q3
    21 KR—K5   N—N5
    22 B—KB4

Killing stone dead Black's hopes of a counterattack.

(See diagram next column.)

    22 ....   B—Q2
    23 B—N3   B—B3?

A blunder losing the knight but he was clearly lost in any event.

    24 KR—K4   Resigns

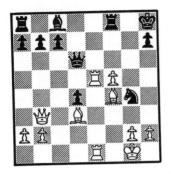

Spassky always seems to have tough tactical fights against the veteran Lithuanian International Master (see game 46 also). It is well known that certain opponents bring out the best in you, some the worst!

36 Riga 1959
White: Gipslis
Ruy Lopez

1 P—K4	P—K4
2 N—KB3	N—QB3
3 B—N5	N—B3
4 0—0	B—B4

Alekhine too in his day was not averse to trying this move which gets good results in practice despite the frowns of the theoreticians.

5 P—B3	0—0
6 P—Q4	B—N3
7 PxP	

The pin 7 B—N5 seems better calculated to give White the advantage.

7	KNxP
8 Q—Q5	N—B4
9 B—N5	

Or 9 N—R3 Gufeld-Spassky XXVI USSR, and now 9 ... P—QR3! gives a good game.

9	Q—K1
10 QN—Q2?	

This routine developing move puts White into trouble as it takes away a necessary flight square from his queen. 10 N—R3 is correct.

10	P—Q3!

With the powerful threat of 11 B—K3 winning at least the exchange.

11 PxP	B—K3
12 BxN	

Not 12 P—Q7 Q—N1 and Black wins.

12	PxB
13 Q—Q4	P—B3

The winning move. The tempting 13 ... N—N6 gets nowhere because of 14 Q—KR4 NxR 15 B—K7 N—B7 16 Q—K4 and White stands well.

14 QR—K1

If the bishop moves then 14 ... N—N6 becomes eminently playable.

14	Q—N3

The strongest. After 14 ... PxB 15 NxP White has some play e.g. 15 ... Q—N3 16 NxB NxN 117 Q—QB4 QR—K1 18 P—Q7 R—K2 19 N—B3! threatening 20 N—K5.

15 B—R4   B—Q4

A very strong attacking move as now both 16 N—K5 and N—Q6 are threatened.

16 R—K2   N—K5
17 Q—Q3   N—N6!

Yet another of the striking tactical moves that abound in this game.

18 Q—R6

To keep guarding the rook.

18 ....   NxR(8)

The right rook.

19 KxN   PxP
20 B—N3   KR—K1
21 BxP   RxR
22 QxR   R—K1
      Resigns

White cannot stop both 23 ... Q—B7 and 23 ... Q—Q6+.

A typical quick Spassky win on the Black side of the Lopez. Compare with game 40.

37 XXVII USSR Championship, Leningrad 1960
Black: Bronstein
King's Gambit

1 P—K4   P—K4
2 P—KB4   PxP
3 N—KB3   P—Q4
4 PxP   B—Q3

In this battle between two 20th century connoisseurs of the ancient 19th·centruy weapon, Bronstein is the first to produce a new move. However, the innovation suffers the fate of so many ingenious ideas. Its first trial proves unsuccessful and despite the verdict of the analysts that Black could have achieved a fairly level game it is never adopted again!

5 N—B3

First success though to Black. If the last move is to have a refutation then it probably lies in driving the bishop away from the defence of the KBP by moves like P—Q4 followed by P—QB4, although Black can react at the appropriate stage by P—QB3 or even P—QN4. Hence Spassky

decides to play safe and go for simple development.

5 ....   N—K2

Consistent play keeping the option of N—N3 with a further defence of the KBP. If 5 ... N—KB3 White can try a common method of play in the King's Gambit — force the exchange of queens so as to exploit the Q side majority of pawns in the ending e.g. 5 ... N—KB3 6 B—N5+ B—Q2 (6 ... P—QB3 may well be best) 7 Q—K2+ Q—K2 8 QxQ+ KxQ 9 B—B4! and Black's pieces are awkwardly placed. This method was of course well known to both players. See for example the opening of Bronstein-Lemoine in the 1958 Olympiad — 1 P—K4 P—K4 2 P—KB4 PxP 3 N—KB3 B—K2 4 B—B4 N—B3 5 P—K5 N—N5 6 N—B3 P—Q3 7 PxP BxP 8 Q—K2+! Q—K2 9 QxQ+ BxQ (9 ... KxQ is stronger) 10 P—Q4

B—Q3 11 N—K4 N—Q2 12 NxB+
PxN 13 QBxP with advantage.

    6 P—Q4   0—0
    7 B—Q3   N—Q2

Rather a timid move. It looks
more enterprising to exchange
White's attacking bishop by 7 ...
QB—B4 after which Black has less
fear of an attack on his king, while
he may also develop his QN at R3
intending N—N5.

    8 0—0   P—KR3?

Presumably intended to prevent
9 N—KN5 but the loss of tempo
and weakening of the K side are
more important factors. Black can
still equalise by 8 ... N—KB3 or
even 8 ... N—N3 e.g. 8 ... N—KB3 9
N—K5 KNxP 10 NxN NxN 11 BxP
NxB 12 RxN Q—N4! or 8 ...
N—N3 9 N—K4 N—B3 10 NxB
QxN 11 P—B4 B—N5 completing
development and pressing on
White's centre.

    9 N—K4!

Quite happy to give up his forward QP so as to achieve an
attacking position on the
QN1/KR7 diagonal.

    9 ....   NxP
   10 P—B4   N—K6

Or 10 ... N—N5 11 B—N1
followed by 12 P—B5 or P—QR3
according to circumstances.

   11 BxN   PxB
   12 P—B5

Already White visualises that
with his rook now active on the KB
file he will want to operate along
both white diagonals — QN1/
KR7 and QR2/KN8.

   12 ....   B—K2

Or 12 ... B—B5 13 P—KN3
B—N5 14 NxB PxN 15 Q—R5
with a strong attack.

   13 B—B2!

White could win the KP by 13
Q—K2 but then Black would

complete his development by 13 ...
N—B3 and after 14 NxN+ BxN 15
QxP˙ R—K1 or 14 QxP N—Q4
White has few attacking prospects.
After the text White achieves a
strong attacking formation and can
pick up the KP by QR—K1 concen-
trating all his forces on their best
squares.

   13 ....   R—K1

If 13 ... N—B3 14 Q—Q3 NxN
15 QxN P—B4 then 16 QxP
followed by N—K5 with a fine
position. The text prepares N—B1
to safeguard KR2 in a more
reliable way.

   14 Q—Q3   P—K7?

Black changes his mind or rather
decides to defer the defensive move
N—B1. Only defer, as White could
now play 15 R—B2 maintaining
all his threats. However, the fact
that Black had only twenty
minutes (!) left for his last twenty
five moves gave Spassky the idea of
playing a remarkable double
sacrifice.

   15 N—Q6!!

Now Black's KR2 and KB2 are
both under attack. Black was under-
standably shocked by the fact that
White was prepared to give up a
whole rook for the attack and must
have analysed the position with the
thought nagging at the back of his
mind that Spassky had found a
forced win in all variations.

   15 ....   N—B1?

Postponing a decision about
taking the rook and hoping White
will still be deterred by the cheeky
Black pawn in his midst. For Black
to go wrong in the circumstances
already described is far from surprising. His only good defence was
15 ... BxN (15 ... PxR(Q)+ transposes) so as to give his king a
flight square at K2. Then comes 16

Q—R7+ K—B1 17 PxB PxR(Q)+ (17 ... PxP 18 R—B2 N—B3 19 Q—R8+ N—N1 20 B—R7 or in this 19 ... K—K2 20 RxP+ B—K3 21 QxNP) 18 RxQ PxP 29 Q—R8+ K—K2 20 R—K1+ N—K4! 21 QxNP R—N1! to divert the queen from control of K5. 22 QxP Q—N3! 23 K—R1 B—K3 24 PxN P—Q4 and Black has finally managed to safeguard his king. The game would then probably end in a draw, as White has a pawn for the exchange and can still trouble Black by attacking the QP by B—N3 or R—Q1 combined with Q—B6+, while Black has Q—B7 in the offing to tie White down to the defence of KN2. It is hardly surprising that Bronstein opted to defend his king in the orthodox way rather than be driven about the board in this undignified manner.

16 NxBP!!   PxR(Q)+

"A dying man can eat anything".

17 RxQ   B—B4

If 17 ... KxN 18 N—K5+ K—N1 19 Q—R7+! NxQ 20 B—N3+ K—R1 21 N—N6 mate! or 17 ... Q—Q2 18 KN—K5. 17 ... Q—Q4 looks a good chance and most sources give White's correct continuation then as 18 KN—N5. This seems dubious. Thus a Bulgarian analysis runs 17 ... Q—Q4 18 KN—K5 BxP 19 NxP+ PxN 20 B—N3 etc., overlooking that Black can break the attack by 20 ... RxN! when I cannot find anything for White.

The players must have rejected 17 ... Q—Q4 because of the obvious 18 B—N3 which is in fact the correct winning line; only after 18 ... QxN(2)! 19 BxQ+ KxB White cannot win by immediate discovered checks. He must play 20

Q—B4+ K—N3 (20 ... B—K3 or N—K3 21 N—N5+ winning material) 21 Q—N8! and now if 21 ... B—K3 22 N—K5+ K—R4 23 QxP or 21 ... B—B3 22 N—K5+ BxN 23 Q—B7+ K—R2 24 QxR BxP+ 25 K—R1 N—N3 (to prevent Q—K4+) 26 R—Q1 BxBP 27 R—Q8 N—K2 28 P—KR4! and White wins. So Black gives back a bishop so as to be able to defend by Q—Q2 with gain of time.

18 QxB   Q—Q2
19 Q—B4   B—B3

Closing the KB file but White has more than enough pressure to force a win.

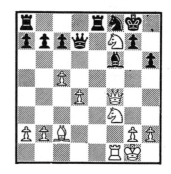

20 KN—K5   Q—K2

Or 20 ... BxN 21 NxB Q—K2 22 Q—K4 threatening 23 RxN+ to which 22 ... P—KN3 is no defence e.g. 23 ... P—KN3 24 RxN+ and now 24 ... KxR 25 NxP+ or 24 ... QxR 25 B—N3+ K—R2 26 QxP+ K—R1 27 N—B7+ or 24 ... RxR 25 B—N3+ K—R2 26 QxP+ K—R1 27 QxP+ Q—R2 28 N—N6 mate.

21 B—N3   BxN

Or 21 ... K—R2 22 Q—B5+ P—N3 23 QxB with decisive material advantage.

22 NxB+   K—R2

Or 22 ... K—R1 23 Q—K4 as in

the last note but one.

23 Q—K4+   Resigns

The fine finish of this game was adapted for use in the famous if implausible opening scene of the James Bond film "From Russia with Love". Strangely enough however, in the 'Kronsteen-McAdams game' the White pawns at Q4 and QB5 were omitted.

38 XXVII USSR Championship, Leningrad 1960
Black: Sakharov
King's Gambit

1 P—K4	P—K4
2 P—KB4	PxP
3 N—KB3	P—Q4
4 PxP	N—KB3

The most common defence. Spassky now chooses the favoured modern move, though 5 P—B4 or 5 N—B3 are quite feasible.

5 B—N5+   P—B3

Not 5 ... QN—2 6 0—0 NxP 7 P—B4 N—B3 8 P—Q4 B—K2 9 BxP when White has an undoubted advantage (Bronstein-Ragozin, 1948 Interzonal).

6 PxP   PxP

For a long time this was thought much superior to 6 ... NxP 7 P—Q4 when 7 ... Q—R4+ 8 N—B3 B—QN5 9 0—0 BxN 10 Q—K2+ B—K3 11 PxB is to White's advantage, in view of the threat of 12 P—Q5 and White's possession of the two bishops. However, Spassky himself found in a simultaneous game that Black obtains good play simply by continuing his development with 7 ... B—Q3, and used this discovery to good effect in his game against Hartston (Hastings, 1965-66) which went 6 ... NxP 7 P—Q4 B—Q3 8 Q—K2+ B—K3 9 N—K5 0—0! 10 BxN PxB 11 BxP N—Q4! and Black had excellent play for his pawn.

7 B—B4   N—Q4

Botvinnik's move which is designed to hang on to the gambit pawn.

8 0—0   B—Q3

9 N—B3

This is better than 9 P—Q4, when the stem game of the variation went 9 ... 0—0 10 N—B3 NxN 11 PxN B—KN5 12 Q—Q3 N—Q2 13 P—N3? N—N3 with a good game for Black, (Bronstein-Botvinnik, USSR Championship 1952).

9 ....   B—K3

10 N—K4   B—K2

Deciding to retain his bishop with gain of time due to the threat 11 ... N—K6! forcing favourable exchanges. If 10 ... B—B2 then 11 N—B5 Q—K2 12 P—Q4 with slight advantage to White.

11 B—N3	0—0
12 P—Q4	N—Q2
13 Q—K2	P—N4?

A serious error of judgement that would have been condemned in no uncertain fashion by old

Dr. Tarrasch as a *"Hara-Kiri"* move. Black obviously thought that with all his pieces developed he could afford to play this loosening move. Instead he should try 13 ... P—QB4 so as to open the game up. Then if 14 Q—N5 Q—N3! or 14 PxP NxP 15 NxN (15 R—Q1 Q—N3! 16 BxN BxB 17 RxB NxN+ 18 K—B1 P—B4 with great freedom for the lost pawn) 15 ... NxN+ 16 K—R1 Q—B2 with a reasonable game.

14 P—B4   KN—N3

From now on Black's minor pieces, developed though they are, get in each other's way. 14 ... KN—B2 was a better chance.

15 P—KR4!

The classic break-up move works well here, as it involves no risk to the White king.

15 ....   P—KR3

Not 15 ... P—N5 16 KN—N5 with advantage.

16 PxP   PxP
17 KNxP

A remarkable sacrifice based on dynamic positional judgement. At first sight one might assess the position as good for Black, whereas, after this move, it becomes clear that the Black king will be exposed to various awkward threats.

17 ....   BxN
18 BxP

White had a very strong alternative in the more forcing 18 Q—R5 and if 18 ... P—B3 (18 ... B—B3 19 P—Q5 wins a piece) then 19 Q—N6+ K—R1 20 NxN PxN 21 QxB+. However, the text enables White to concentrate his pieces so efficiently on the K side that from now till the end of the game he has a pronounced local

superiority where it really counts.

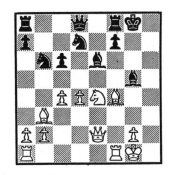

18 ....   B—B3

Not 18 ... BxB 19 RxB P—KB4 (The threat was 20 Q—R5 and 21 R—R4) 20 N—Q6 Q—K2 21 P—B5!.

19 QR—Q1

This quiet move underlines the fact that Black's minor pieces are too awkwardly placed to help in the defence.

19 ....   B—B4
20 B—K5!   BxN

20 ... BxB 21 PxB would give White the threat of 21 N—B6+ and so force transposition into the game.

21 QxB   BxB
22 PxB   Q—N4

The threat was 23 Q—N4+ K—R1 24 K—B2 and 25 R—R1+ mating. 22 ... R—K1 would give the king a flight square but after 23 B—B2 K—B1 24 RxP+! KxR 25 Q—N6+ K—K2 26 Q—Q6+ K—B2 27 R—B1+ White wins quickly.

23 R—B5   Q—N2
24 Q—B4

Black could now resign as he has no defence to 25 R—N5 e.g. 24 ... P—B3 25 P—B5+ N—Q4 26 RxN! PxR 27 BxP+ R—B2 28 P—K6 etc., or 24 ... Q—R2 25

Q—N4+ K—R1 26 R—R5.

24	....	KR—K1
25	R—N5	NxKP
26	RxQ+	KxR
27	R—Q6	

The attack continues unabated with the main threat 28 Q—R6+ K—N1 29 B—B2.

| 27 | .... | N—N3 |
| 28 | Q—B6+ | K—N1 |

| 29 | B—B2 | NxP |

If 29 ... N—KB1 30 R—Q4! R—K3 31 R—N4+ N—N3 32 RxN+!

| 30 | R—Q7 | Resigns |

After 30 ... N(5)—K4 comes 31 BxN, while 30 ... N(3)—K4 loses to 31 Q—N5+ K—R1 or B1 31 Q—R6+ K—N1 33 Q—R7+ and mate next move.

39 Mar del Plata, 1960
Black: Fischer
King's Gambit

This first meeting between the then two youngest grandmasters in the world is of great historical interest but is not a high quality game. The tension of the occasion was clearly too great.

1 P—K4   P—K4

The Sicilian is Fischer's almost automatic reaction to 1 P—K4, so clearly we have here an attempt to surprise the opponent and to get away from the consequences of opening preparation.

2 P—KB4

Spassky thinks the same way, though from him this move is not such a big surprise.

| 2 | .... | PxP |
| 3 | N—KB3 | P—KN4 |

It was only after this game (and possibly because of its result) that Fischer declared in a famous article that his analysis showed that Black should play 3 ... P—Q3 as a waiting move and then after 4 B—B4 try 4 ... P—KR3 followed by 5 ... P—KN4. This remarkable suggestion has not

been tried sufficiently for an opinion on its true worth to be given with confidence — but then such is the case too with the far older text move!

4 P—KR4

The sharpest counter at White's disposal.

4	....	P—N5
5	N—K5	N—KB3
6	P—Q4	

The modern line of the Kieseritzky gambit in which considerable interest has been shown ever since Rubenstein's advocacy of it. The older 6 B—B4 is hardly ever tried nowadays, while 6 NxNP leaves Black the advantage after the complicated variation 6 ... NxP 7 P—Q3 N—N6 8 BxP NxR 9 Q—K2+ Q—K2 10 N—B6+ K—Q1 11 BxP+ KxB 12 N—Q5+ K—Q1 13 NxQ BxN as the three Black pieces are worth more than the queen despite the cornered knight.

7 N—Q3   NxP

8 BxP	B—N2

The main alternative is 8 ... Q—K2 when White replies 9 Q—K2 as he does not fear the exchange of queens — Black's extra pawn on the King side is no great adornment of his position.

9 N—B3

A dubious innovation. The usual move is 9 P—B3 to safeguard his central bastion when Keres gives as a possible continuation 9 ... 0—0 10 N—Q2 R—K1 11 NxN RxN+ 12 K—B2 Q—B3 13 P—KN3 B—R3 14 B—N2 and White looks to stand better.

9	NxN
10 PxN	P—QB4

Now that he no longer has a QNP White finds this pressure on his centre much more awkward to meet than if he had played 9 P—B3. The text is an improvement on Keres' 10 ... 0—0 as now if 11 Q—K2+ trying to exploit Black's failure to castle then 11 ... B—K3! (not 11 ... Q—K2 12 BxP QxQ+ 13 BxQ PxP 14 0—0! with attacking chances on the central files) when 12 P—Q5 fails to 12 ... BxP+ 13 B—Q2 BxR and if 14 P—B3 trying to win both bishops then simply 14 ... Q—B3 and Black keeps his material advantage.

11 B—K2

So White decides to carry on in gambit style.

11	PxP
12 0—0	N—B3

In such situations it is known that moves like 12 ... P—KB4 or 12 ... P—KR4, to hang on to the pawn, weaken Black's king side further. White would then take over the initiative on the KB file with 13 B—N5 and his knight would subsequently be lodged on an ideal square at KB4. If 12 ... QxP

then 13 P—N3! and White wins back a pawn.

13 BxNP	0—0
14 BxB	RxB
15 Q—N4	

White has achieved the best he can and threatens mate with 14 B—R6, but once Black has put his king in safety it is hard to believe that White has enough compensation for the material sacrificed.

15	P—B4

A question of style. The text is an active defence giving more scope to his KR, but a Steinitz would have preferred 15 ... K—R1 as Fischer gave later.

16 Q—N3	PxP
17 QR—K1!	

It is certainly more important to keep the initiative than to hand it over to Black by 17 BxP R—B3! followed by 18 ... R—N3.

17	K—R1

Again an ambitious scheme intending to use the KN file for his rook. A more stereotyped, but possibly stronger, move was Aronin's 17 ... Q—Q2 to meet 18 BxP with 18 ... KR—K1 playing for an exchange of rooks and general simplification into a favourable ending.

18 K—R1

Fischer criticised this attempt to avoid a subsequent B—Q5 with check, and preferred 18 BxP at once, so that if 18 ... R—KN1 then 19 N—K5! as in the next note.

18	R—KN1
19 BxP!	

Now 19 ... B—Q5 20 Q—R2 R—N5 seems to win out of hand for Black, but then comes 21 B—K5+ NxB 22 NxN with the threat of 23 N—B7+ so gaining time to guard his KRP.

19	B—B1

20 B—K5+   NxB
21 QxN+   R—N2

Now 21 ... B—N2 22 Q—K7 and White should be able to win back a pawn with excellent drawing chances.

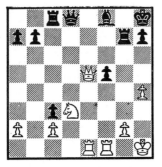

22 RxP

He cannot defend his KRP e.g. 22 R—B4? B—Q3 or 22 P—R5 Q—N4.

22 ....   QxP+
23 K—N1   Q—N5

Playing to attack the enemy king, but it was better to steer for the ending with 23 ... Q—N6 and Black has good winning chances.

24 R—B2   B—K2
25 R—K4

White now has all his pieces well centralised whereas the Black rooks are not too well placed. Fischer's 25 ... Q—Q8+ 26 R—B1 Q—N5 27 R—B2 Q—Q8+ with a draw by repetition is now the safest. (If 28 K—R2 then as Aronin gives 28 ... R—B3! forces a draw because of the threats of 29 ... B—Q3 and 29 ... R—R3+.) However, here as always the American grandmaster follows his universal (and admirable) practice of trying to avoid a draw when there

is still a reasonable amount of material left on the board.

25 ....   Q—N4
26 Q—Q4

Very strong, keeping up the pin on the rook. The pin cannot be broken by 26 ... R—Q1? because of 27 QxBP, nor does 26 ... B—B4 work because of the back row threats — 27 NxB QxN 28 R—K8+ winning. As Aronin pointed out Black must safeguard his position by 26 ... B—B1 when 27 QxRP is met by 27 ... B—B4 28 NxB QxN 29 R—K8+ R—N1 and 27 N—K5 by 27 ... B—B4! 28 N—B7+ K—N1 and after the exchange of queens it is a draw. Instead Black blunders.

26 ....   R—B1
27 R—K5!

This was White's real threat, to drive the queen away from the defence of the bishop when 28 RxB wins because of the pin on the rook. Black must now lose a piece in all variations, e.g. 28 ... Q—R5 29 RxR+. When the bishop is overloaded at 28 ... B—B3 28 Q—Q6! BxR 29 RxR+ R—N1 30 QxB+ QxQ 31 RxR+ and 32 NxB.

27 ....   R—Q1
28 Q—K4

The pin on the long black diagonal is gone but now the bishop is twice attacked.

28 ....   Q—R5
29 R—B4   Resigns

After 29 ... Q—R3 30 RxB RxR (30 ... RxN? 31 R—B8+ R—N1 31 Q—K5+ and mates) 31 QxR Black cannot regain material by 31 ... RxN because of 32 R—B8+ and mate next move.

40 'Trud' Championship, Kislovodsk 1960
White: Kuznetsov
Ruy Lopez

1 P—K4	P—K4
2 N—KB3	N—QB3
3 B—N5	N—B3
4 0—0	B—B4
5 NxP	

5 P—B3 gives better chances of an opening advantage for White (See game 62 Spassky-Zuidema).

5	NxP

Playing for complications right from the start. Spassky has played 5 ... NxN in several games e.g. 6 P—Q4 P—B3 7 PxN NxP 8 B—Q3 P—Q4 9 PxP e.p. N—B3! 10 Q—K2+ B—K3 11 B—KN5 QxP 12 BxN PxB 13 N—B3 Q—K4 14 N—K4 B—N3 15 K—R1 0—0—0 with play on the KN file (Krogius-Spassky, XXVI USSR 1959).

6 NxBP

Bold but unsound. White should play 6 Q—K2 NxN 7 P—Q4! Keres-Szabo, Candidates, Budapest 1950, but after the best reply 7 ... Q—K2! (Szabo played 7 ... B—K2) Black has equality.

6	KxN

Black could already demonstrate the drawback to White's psuedo-sacrifice of the knight by 6 ... Q—R5 and if 7 NxR BxP+ 8 RxB QxR+ 9 K—R1 Q—R5 10 P—KN3 NxP+ 11 K—N2 (11 K—N1 Q—Q5+) 11 ... Q—K5+ 12 KxN Q—K4+ 13 K—N2 Q—N4+ with perpetual check as 14 K—B1 QxB+ 15 Q—K2+ QxQ+ favours Black due to the trapped knight at KR1.

7 Q—R5+	P—KN3
8 Q—Q5+	K—N2
9 BxN	

Or 9 QxKN P—Q4 10 Q—QR4!

R—B1 and Black has ample compensation for the pawn minus even though he cannot get an immediate attack by Q—R5.

9	R—K1
10 B—R4	P—B3
11 Q—Q3	

Not 11 Q—N3 P—QN4. However the queen now blocks the QP and so makes it very difficult for White to complete his development.

11	Q—R5!

Threatening the KBP as well as (indirectly) the hanging bishop at QR4.

12 P—KN3	Q—R6
13 P—QN4!	

Inventive play which gives White a chance to embarrass Black's king for a few moves.

13	NxBP!
14 Q—QB3+	K—N1
15 QxB	N—N5
16 B—N3+	P—Q4
17 BxP+	

This is the position Kuznetsov had been playing for, thinking that after 17 ... PxB 18 QxP+ B—K3 19 Q—N2 he would beat off the attack and remain two pawns up.

(See diagram next column.)

17	B—K3!
18 R—B8+	K—N2!

Diamond cut diamond. After 18 ... RxR 29 BxB+ K—N2 20 Q—K7+ it is White who wins, while in this line 19 ... R—B2 20 BxR+ KxB 21 Q—B4+ and White wins as the king has not got a good square e.g. 21 ... K—B1 22 Q—B1+ or 21 ...

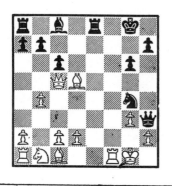

19 B—N2+   K—R3
20 RxR   RxR
21 B—B3

Hoping to block the K file.

21 ....   QxRP+
22 K—B1   QxNP
23 BxN

The threat was 23 ... N—R7+ as well as 23 ... B—B5+.

23 ....   B—B5+!
        Resigns

A hand to hand fight reminiscent of the 19th century encounters. Just look at White's inactive rook and knight in the final position!

K—N2 22 B—N2+ and 23 Q—K2.

41 XXVIII USSR Championship, Moscow 1961
Black Bronstein
King's Indian Defence

1 P—Q4   N—KB3
2 N—KB3   P—KN3
3 P—KN3   B—N2
4 B—N2   0—0
5 0—0   P—Q3
6 N—B3

6 P—B4 is almost *"de rigeur"* in modern chess, but since Black's last move shows a desire to make a fight of it (the symmetrical 6 ... P—Q4 leads to very drawish positions) White cannot be blamed for deciding to vary from the normal.

6 ....   P—Q4

A rather dogmatic move from Bronstein who sacrifices a tempo to prevent P—K4 and hopes to show that the old 'rule' applies — "In a Queen Pawn never block your QBP by playing N—QB3". A more modern concept would be 6

... N—B3 to meet 7 P—K4 by 7 ... B—N5 with pressure on the black squares in the centre and 7 P—Q5 by 7 ... N—R4 and then P—QB4 in conjunction with a Q side pawn advance.

7 B—N5

After this direct move Black is forced to take up a defensive position in the centre and White gets an ideal development.

7 ....   P—B3

7 ... B—B4 looks playable, but after 8 N—K5 White would have pressure in the centre.

8 R—K1

White could play 8 BxN and then 9 P—K4 but naturally prefers to retain his options, for once the K file is opened his rook and QB will exert awkward pressure against K7.

8 ....   N—K5?!

An ingenious way of preventing P—K4, but, as the sequel shows, Black is still left struggling for equality. 8 ... B—B4 looks better calculated to hold the balance.

9 NxN   PxN
10 N—Q2   P—K6

The point of his previous play hoping for further exchanges. 10 ... BxP is met by 11 P—QB3 and 12 NxP with a slightly better game (pressure on K7) and 10 ... QxP in the same way (11 P—QB3 Q—K4 12 NxP followed if necessary by B—B4). 10 ... P—KB4 looks an interesting double-edged idea and White has to be careful not to let his QB get into trouble (11 P—K3? P—KR3). However, after 11 P—QB3 followed by 12 P—B3 White should get the better of it, due to the weakness of Black's K2, K3 and K4 squares.

11 BxKP(3)

One of those cases where the descriptive notation player can easily go wrong by writing BxP or BxKP or even QBxP — all ambiguous moves! After 11 PxP the bishop is lost to 11 ... P—B3 12 B—B4 P—K4.

11 ....   BxP
12 BxB   QxB
13 P—B3   Q—B4?

Weak, as his queen is exposed to attack. He had to try 13 ... Q—Q1 or 13 ... Q—N3 14 N—B4 Q—B2 when he can complete development by B—K3 and then safeguard his king with N—Q2—B3.

14 N—K4   Q—N3

Perhaps his original intention was 14 ... Q—KR4 so as to follow-up with B—R6, but after the fine centralising move 15 Q—Q4! (threatening in some circumstances Q—K5) Black would still be in grave difficulties.

15 Q—Q2

Now that Q—Q4 is no longer any good, this move is a suitable substitute emphasising (by the threat of Q—R6 and N—N5) that the exchange of bishops has left Black with a chronic weakness on the dark squares.

15 ....   B—B4
16 N—N5

White's prospects lie in the middle game so he must avoid further minor piece exchanges.

16 ....   R—Q1?

The losing move as it weakens his KB2 and drives the enemy queen to a strong attacking position. 16 ... N—Q2 fails to 17 P—K4 so Black had to try either 17 ... Q—B2 or 17 ... P—B3 when the game would continue 18 P—K4 B—B1! 19 N—B3 P—K4 and now by 20 N—R4 White renews his pressure on the K side (20 ... N—Q2 21 Q—R6 or 20 ... K—N2 21 QR—Q1) but Black still has a defensible position.

17 Q—B4!

Now Black has no satisfactory move (17 ... QxNP 18 P—K4 B—K3 20 Q—KR4 P—KR4 21 NxB PxN 22 QxKP or 22 B—R3) so he tries to provoke a crisis.

17 ....   P—K4

Not 17 ... P—B3? 18 Q—B4+ K—N2 19 Q—B7+ K—R3 20 QxRP+ KxN 21 Q—R4 mate! nor 17 ... P—KR3 18 NxP KxN 19 P—K4 winning back the piece and opening the K file for his rook (19 ... P—K4 20 QxKP would then not transpose back into the game if Black chose 20 ... B—K3 but White still has a winning attack after 21 R—K3).

18 QxP   P—KR3
19 P—K4!   B—B1

20 NxBP!   KxN
21 R—K3!

Perhaps Bronstein had placed his hopes on the fact that White has the very tempting move 21 B—B1, but after 21 ... P—B4! 22 B—B4+ B—K3 White has no good continuation. The text is much stronger.

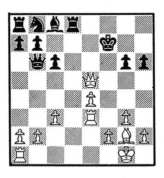

21 ....   K—N1

Another paradoxical defensive idea, doubtless hoping to induce White to play the wrong move e.g. 22 Q—B6? P—B4!. Obviously 21 ... QxNP loses quickly to 22 R—B3+ K—N1 23 Q—B6! QxR+ 24 B—B1 R—Q2 25 QxP+ R—N2 26 Q—K8+ K—R2 27 R—B8 and 28 R—R8+ with a mate, and 21 ... N—Q2 is no good either — 22 R—B3+

K—N1 23 Q—K6+ K—R1 24 Q—K7 and 25 R—B7 as the black queen is tied to the defence of the rook.

22 B—B1!

Now this move comes at the right time when Black has weakened his control of K3.

22 ....   R—Q2
23 Q—K8+   K—N2
24 R—B3

24 QxB also wins but White has much more to play for now than a won ending after the exchange of queens by 24 ... Q—Q1.

24 ....   Q—B4

Now 24 ... Q—Q1? loses to 25 R—B7+ and 24 ... N—R3 to 25 B—B4.

25 R—Q1

The rook at Q2 is now overloaded with defensive tasks.

25 ....   P—KR4

Or 25 ... Q—K2 26 RxR QxR 27 Q—B8+ K—R2 28 R—B7+ and White does not just win the queen, since after 28 ... QxR 29 QxQ+ K—R1 30 B—B4! mate is forced.

26 RxR+   NxR
27 R—B7+   K—R3
28 Q—R8+   K—N4
29 P—KR4+   Resigns

It is mate next move by 30 R—B4. A most pleasing attack.

42 XXVIII USSR Championship, Moscow 1961
Black: Vladimirov
Sicilian Defence

1 P—K4	P—QB4		4 NxP	N—KB3
2 N—KB3	P—Q3		5 N—QB3	P—QR3
3 P—Q4	PxP		6 B—KN5	QN—Q2

7 P—B4

7 B—QB4 at once is now considered to be more accurate.

7 ....   Q—B2

To prevent the most aggressive development of the bishop by 8 B—B4, but Black does better to seek counter-play on the dark squares with 7 ... Q—N3 aiming at QN7, Q5 and, if the KN moves, at K6.

8 Q—B3   P—KN3

An unusual way of developing his bishop in the Najdorf variation, but at least the move does have the merit of not weakening his Q3 by P—K3.

9 0—0—0   B—N2
10 B—K2   P—KR3

This move and his next introduce complications. Black should castle and then develop his QB by R—N1 and B—N2.

11 B—R4   P—K4

Here again he should castle. Note that 11 ... P—QN4 fails to 12 P—K5 PxP 13 PxP and if 13 ... B—N2 then 14 PxN! with three pieces for the queen, while 11 ... N—B4 12 BxN! BxB 12 N—Q5 is in White's favour.

12 KN—N5!

A typical Sicilian sacrifice that exploits Black's failure to castle and his unnecessary weakening of the QP.

12 ....   PxN
13 NxP   Q—R4
14 NxP+   K—B1
15 B—B4

Defending his QRP and winning the KBP.

15 ....   PxP

The best defence, opening the long black diagonal for a counter attack against QN7 and freeing K4 for his QN.

16 NxBP   Q—B2

Not 16 ... N—K4 17 NxN QxN 18 R—Q8+ K—K2 19 R—Q5! and 20 P—K5, nor 16 ... R—KN1 17 QxP threatening 18 Q—Q6+.

17 B—QN3   N—K4

A good alternative was 17 ... N—B4 to remove White's formidable KB. Then, after 18 R—Q8+, K—K2 fails to 19 RxR NxB+ 20 QxN (20 RPxN R—R8+) 20 ... B—K3! 21 Q—N4+ KxN 22 RxR and 18 ... N—K1 19 NxR NxB+ 20 QxN BxN 21 RxN+ gives a powerful attack.

18 NxN   QxN
19 R—Q8+   N—K1

Not 19 ... K—K2 20 R—Q5! and 21 P—K5 as before. Now we see the point of Black's defence. The threat of 20 ... QxP+ forces White to pause for a moment in his attack.

20 P—B3   P—KN4?

The losing move after which White's attack breaks through. Steinitz and Lasker taught that the defender should avoid weakening pawn moves and play to exchange pieces. 20 ... B—B3! is correct, and after 21 BxB QxB 22 KR—Q1 R—R2! (to prevent 23 R(1)—Q7) 23 R(1)—Q6 Q—N4 Black may be able to consolidate with R—K2.

21 Q—R5!·

Clearly Black overlooked that his last move allowed this powerful move, attacking both K8 and KB7.

21 ....   Q—K2
22 B—B2

Now White has a forced win.

(See diagram next column.)

22 ....   B—N5

If 22 ... P—N3 then 23 BxP making QB5 available again to his bishop.

23 RxN+

A strange oversight. The end of the game must have been played under conditions of great time pressure otherwise Spassky would

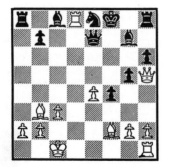

hardly have missed mate in two! (23 QxN+ QxQ 24 B—B5 mate).

As is well known the 'rule' for finding combinations is to play the various forcing moves in ones mind in every possible order. Spassky's last move obviously threatened 23 B—B5 and if 23 ... QxB 24 QxN mate. It is strange that he did not see the reverse order of moves. The explanation probably lies not only in time pressure but also in the fact that there were other mates by 24 RxN and 25 Q—B7 in the last variation.

| 23 .... | RxR |
| 24 QxB | |

With an easy win due to his powerful bishops.

| 24 .... | B—K4 |

Otherwise 25 Q—B5+ B—B3 26 B—B5.

| 25 R—Q1 | Resigns |

If 25 ... R—R2 then 26 B—B5 QxB 27 Q—B5+ K—N2 28 Q—B7+, while if 25 ... B—Q3 then 26 Q—B5+ K—N2 27 B—Q4+ forcing mate.

43 XXIX USSR Championship, Baku 1961
White: Kots
Ruy Lopez

1	P—K4	P—K4
2	N—KB3	N—QB3
3	B—N5	P—QR3
4	B—R4	N—B3
5	O—O	B—K2
6	R—K1	P—Q3

This game was played in the first round and Spassky naturally wished to exploit the nervousness of his opponent who was making his debut in the championship. Hence, instead of rattling off another ten moves or so of the ordinary closed defence he plays this slightly unusual move order which he had already tried in the previous Soviet Championship.

| 7 | P—B3 | B—N5 |
| 8 | P—KR3 | |

The experiment pays off! The text allows Black to exploit the old rule (normally seen in Guioco Piano positions) that a player should not weaken his K side by P—KR3 if he has castled on that side and his opponent hasn't. White should play either 8 P—Q3 or 8 BxN+ PxB 9 P—Q4. In mitigation of White's error it can be said that he was following a most powerful precedent — Emanuel Lasker made the same mistake against Janowski in the 1924 New York tournament!

8 ....   B—R4

9 P—Q3

White should still play 9 BxN+ PxB 10 P—Q4 e.g. 10 ... PxP 11 PxP 0—0 12 QN—Q2 R—K1 13 Q—B2, Shamkovich-Spassky, XXVIII USSR.

9 ....   Q—Q2

Preparing Q side castling to be followed by the advance of the KNP.

10 QN—Q2

Lasker realising the danger in time simplified here by 11 BxN QxB 12 B—N5 and so reduced Janowski's attacking chances. 10 B—K3 is also a reasonable move when Black may feel obliged to play 10 ... P—R3 since the offer of his KNP by 10 ... P—KN4 may not be quite sound (11 BxP R—KN1 12 BxN BxB — 12 ... QxP 13 N—N5 Q—R5 14 P—KN3 — 13 K—R2). The text allows Black to play the crucial attacking move straight away.

10 ....   P—KN4!

11 P—KN4

Thus White defers the opening of a file for move or two but 11 N—B1 was quite good e.g. 11 ... P—N5 12 PxP BxP 13 QN—R2 with a reasonable game, Evans-Sherwin, USA Championship 1962.

11 ....   B—N3

12 N—B1

12 NxNP P—KR4! is very risky for White as 13 ... PxP and 13 ... NxNP are both serious threats.

12 ....   P—KR4

13 KN—R2   PxP

14 PxP   0—0—0

White has defended his K side adequately for the moment by his 13th move, so Black must connect his rooks before he can safely prosecute the attack.

15 BxN

This wins a pawn but at too high a price. 15 N—K3 or 15 P—N4 look better moves aiming respectively at control of the white squares (KN4, KB5 and Q5) and at a counter attack (P—N5).

15 ....   QxB

16 BxP

This is now feasible as Black's last move left his KB undefended.

16 ....   Q—Q2

17 B—K3   NxNP?

Too headlong a move. Black has the two bishops and can build up pressure quietly by 17 ... QR—N1. However, fortune favours the brave.

18 QxN

White decides to be "shown". After 18 NxN R—R6 19 QN—R2 QR—R1 20 P—B3 B—R4 21 R—K2 BxN 22 PxB B—R5 followed by 23 ... B—N6 Black has a strong attack, though after the game, Spassky said that his actual intention was 18 ... P—KB4 19 PxP BxP and if 20 P—B3 the 20 ... QR—K1 hoping for a subsequent P—Q4 and P—K5. Though White is left with a purely passive position in that case the outcome would be far from clear.

18 ....   P—KB4

19 PxP?

White draws back. He should go all the way and insist on being "shown". In fact after 19 QxB! QR—N1 20 PxP QxP 21 QxR RxQ+ 22 N—N3 B—R5 23 K—N2 White has the better of it though the position is still complicated. Now, however, Black gets a decisive attack.

19 ....   BxP

20 Q—K2

To guard his QP, but as the next note shows the queen is thereby overloaded. Hence he should abandon it at once by 20 Q—B3 though after 20 QR—N1+

21 N—N3 (21 K—R1 R—R6 22 N—N3 B—N5 23 Q—N2 R—R1 24 N—B1 B—B6!) 21 ... B—R5 22 N—B1 R—N5! threatening 23 ... P—K5 White is completely tied up.

20 ....   QR—N1+
21 N—N3

Or 21 K—R1 BxP! and 22 QxB allows 22 ... Q—B3+ with mate in two.

(See diagram next column.)

21 ....   B—R5
22 Q—B3   BxP

Not so much to win a pawn as to rule out 23 K—B1.

23 B—Q2

Or 23 N—B1 B—QN4 followed by 24 ... B—QB3 and 25 ... Q—R6.

23 ....   BxN
24 QxQB

No matter how he plays, White

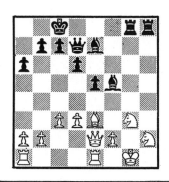

falls under a murderous attack e.g. 24 QxKB Q—R6! or 24 PxB Q—R6 25 QxB.QxN+ 26 K—B1 R—B1+ 27 B—B4 PxB.

24 ....   Q—R6
    Resigns

The finish could be 25 QxB RxQ+ 26 PxR QxP+ 27 K—B1 RxN and mate next move.

44 **XXIX** USSR Championship, Baku 1961
White: Savon
King's Indian Attack

1 N—KB3   P—Q4
2 P—KN3   P—QB4
3 B—N2   N—QB3

Black's first three moves form a rather risky set-up as White could now play 4 P—Q4 with a reversed Grunfeld Defence (i.e: with an extra tempo). In the type of sharp struggle that the Grunfeld normally produces a single tempo is worth a great deal. Moreover, even if Black took account of his exposed position and avoided the open variations he would risk (after White's

P—QB4) finishing up in a Catalan variation which is regarded as inferior for Black (e.g. if now 4 P—Q4 P—K3 then 5 0—0 N—B3 6 P—B4 producing a situation which could have arisen from the move order 1 P—Q4 P—Q4 2 P—QB4 P—K3 3 N—KB3 N—KB3 4 P—KN3 P—B4 5 B—N2 N—QB3 6 0—0.) Yet the move 4 ... P—B4 in this Catalan variation is generally considered as inferior to either 4 ... PxP or 4 ... B—K2.

4 0—0

White prefers to reach a reversed King's Indian in which, however, the extra tempo is of less value in view of the closed nature of the position.

4 ....   P—K4
5 P—Q3

Here 5 P—QB4 is better designed to sidestep a thoroughly closed position (5 ... P—K5 6 N—K1 or 5 ... P—Q5 6 P—Q3 and then 7 P—K3 opening either the K file or the KB file.)

5 ....   P—B3

Thus, in the end, a reversed Samisch variation!

6 P—K4   P—Q5
7 N—R4

By analogy with the Samisch 7 P—B3 is also quite good here. In a similar opening a game Botvinnik-Pomar, (Olympiad, 1962) went (there were some transpositions) 7 QN—Q2 B—Q3 8 P—B4 KN—K2 and only now, when he had made it more difficult for Black to open the game on the Q side, did Botvinnik play 9 N—R4 followed by 10 P—B4.

7 ....   B—K3
8 P—QB4 Q—Q2
9 N—Q2 0—0—0

A common plan in the ordinary Samisch. The king is quite safe on this side where it is hard for White to open the position (10 P—B3 now just loses the QP) and Black plans to continue K—N1, R—B1 and ultimately P—B5. Meanwhile, with the position so blocked, he can leave his minor pieces undeveloped for the moment.

10 P—R4 B—Q3
11 N—B4 B—QB2
12 B—Q2 KN—K2
13 P—B5?

Although in some variations the pawn storm P—B5, P—KN4—N5 and so on would be a sound plan,

White does not have time for it here. His only good plan is to tie Black down in the centre by attacking K5 with 13 N—B3.

13 ....   BxN!

Good concrete thinking. Black gives up his good bishop so as to force the exchange of his bad one; this was one of the points of his modest retreat at move 11. Had White found 13 N—B3!. however, this plan would not be feasible because of the loss of the KP.

14 PxB   B—R4
15 R—B2

If 15 B—B1 then 15 ... P—Q6! would be hard to meet. The threat of P—Q7 forces 16 PxP when Black can play either 16 ... QxP or 16 ... N—N5 with good play, as his knights will have fine squares at Q5 and QN5.

15 ....   BxB
16 RxB

White now has the slight, but permanent, disadvantage of a bishop hemmed in by the immovable pawns at K4 and QB4. Black now plans to improve his piece position generally, by manoeuvring his knight to Q3 where it attacks both fixed pawns, and then to open the KN file by P—KN3.

16 ....   K—N1
17 Q—B3 Q—B2

Black does well to have his queen on a black square as in some circumstance the attacking moves Q—N3 or Q—R4 would be good, (e.g. if now 18 R—K1 then 18 ... Q—R4 winning the QRP quite safely).

18 B—B1 N—B1
19 P—KN4

Putting another pawn on a white square is wrong in principle. At such points the commentator normally adds "and White weakens his KB4". The reader, I suspect, feels this comment is rather abstract. What significance can the weakening have here? Ah, just wait and see the position arising after the 33rd move!

| 19 .... | N—Q3 |
| 20 R—N2 | |

Apparently planning P—N5 but White would merely play into Black's hand by opening lines on the K side. Here, as on the previous move, I prefer N—N2 in order to manoeuvre the knight to the blockading square at Q3.

| 20 .... | Q—B2 |
| 21 Q—K2 | P—KN3 |

First part of the plan achieved.

| 22 PxP | |

Losing patience. As his rook was on the KN file already he should not fear the opening of that file. Now Black easily infiltrates the K side via the KR file.

| 22 .... | PxP |
| 23 N—B3 | P—KN4 |

Fixing the KNP on a white square so ruling out any possible White initiative based on P—N5.

| 24 R—B2 | Q—K3 |
| 25 N—K1 | R—R3 |

Attack along the KR file and defence of his own KBP.

| 26 P—N3 | |

Forced, if he is to get the knight to the blockade square, but now a number of black squares are weakened on the Q side.

| 26 .... | Q—K2 |

Freeing a square from which his knight will reach KB5.

27 N—Q3	N—K1
28 B—N2	N—B2
29 R—K1	N—K3
30 R—B5	

White has no active plan, he must just sit and wait, so why not console himself with occupying a most impressive post?

| 30 .... | QR—R1 |
| 31 P—R3 | |

In principle 31 R—B2 was better as his bishop is now even more a poor prelate.

| 31 .... | N—N5! |

So as to occupy KB5 with the other knight without fear of exchange.

| 32 QR—KB1 | NxN |
| 33 QxN | |

The alternative recapture 33 PxN rounds off his pawn structure and safeguards the KP, but then in an ending his QNP would be even wealer (the Black king must already be girding up his loins for a long trip to QN5 along the black squares.)

| 33 .... | N—B5 |

Mission achieved! (see note to move 19.)

| 34 QRxN | |

A counsel of despair, but with his KRP thrice attacked he had to do this or allow his king to be buffeted about by the Black rooks, after 35 Q moves NxP+.

| 34 .... | NPxN |
| 35 K—B2 | Q—QB2 |

Back to the black squares on the Q side.

| 36 Q—Q2 | R—N1 |

37 K—K2   R—N4
38 RxR

A final inaccuracy. He should give Black the chance to exchange rooks when, for the first time in the game, his bishop would see the light of day after KPxR.

38 ....   PxR
39 K—B3   Q—N3
40 B—B1   Q—N5

This finishes it, and normally White would resign here as the forty moves have been completed. However, he decides to be shown.

41 QxQ   PxQ
42 K—N2   P—Q6!

Before White can close it up completely by 43 B—Q3.

43 BxP   K—B2
44 B—B1   K—N3
   Resigns

The Black king penetrates to Q5 e.g. 45 K—B3 K—B4 46 K—K2 K—Q5 47 K—Q2 (to stop K—B6) 47 ... P—B6 with Zugzwang.

1962-65 THE ROAD BACK

By virtue of his victory in the Soviet Championship at the end of 1961 Spassky finally forced his way into the Soviet Olympiad team, and at Golden Sands (Varna) in Bulgaria in 1962 he made his debut on board three. Here he scored some fine wins marked by strong attacking play (Nos. 48-50 for which my favourite is 50). Then in 1963 came the start of the long road to become a world championship candidate again, beginning with the semi-final of the Soviet Championship. His best games of this period are probably the slow exploitation of a gambit position against Osnos (No. 54) and his two decisive wins against his main rivals Geller and Korchnoy in the USSR Zonal Tournament of Seven (Nos. 57 and 58) in which he had to overcome the consequences of a bad start (only half a point out of his first three games). The game against Korchnoy is probably the worst defeat suffered by the Leningrad grandmaster over the last twenty years.

The Candidates' Matches of 1965 were decisively won by Spassky once he had got over the hurdle of beating Keres in the closest of the matches, and at the end of 1965 British chess players got their first chance to see the candidate in action at Hastings. I can remember the prevailing impression amongst players and public that we were in the presence of the next world champion, and his quick win over Lee was carried out in a style reminiscent of Alekhine. (No. 71). Unfortunately our desires were soon to be shown up as wishful thinking.

45 Students' Olympiad, Marianske-Lazne 1962
Black: Ciric
Sicilian Defence

1 P—K4	P—QB4
2 N—KB3	N—KB3
3 P—K5	N—Q4
4 N—B3	P—K3

A reasonable alternative is to be found in 4 ... NxN 5 QPxN when Black may try either Zak's close defensive system 5 ... P—K3 6

B—KB4 N—B3 7 B—B4 Q—B2 8 0—0 P—QN3 with possible castling long, or 4 ... P—Q4 5 PxP e.p. QxP when Black may well lose his backward QP after 6 QxQ PxQ 7 B—KB4 and 8 0—0—0 but the resulting ending is hard to win for White as his extra pawn is doubled away from the centre.

5 NxN   PxN
6 P—Q4   N—B3

A move first played in 1924, but after its successful adoption by Larsen against Gligoric (Zurich 1959) it was analysed very intensively.

7 PxP   BxP
8 QxP   Q—N3

The point of the sacrifice; White can only defend his KB2 by retarding his development (9 Q—Q2), when Black castles, plays P—Q3 and has a promising lead in development. In accordance with modern ideas about the great value of the initiative, White has practically always left his KBP to its fate so as to gain the KB file for an attack.

9 B—QB4   BxP+
10 K—K2   0—0
11 R—KB1   B—B4
12 N—N5

All this is book, and it is held that White's pressure on the K side outweighs his exposed king. Black now plays a move specially prepared for this event by a team of Yugoslav analysts.

12 ....   NxP?

The normal course of events is 12 ... N—Q5+ 13 K—Q1 N—K3 to block White's attack on KB7, when after 14 P—B3! P—Q3! 15 P—QN4 BxP great complications arise. The text had been played in the previous year's Students' Olympiad, when a game Spiridonov-Miagmasuren

went: 13 QxN P—Q4 14 BxP B—N5+ 15 K—Q2 QR—Q1 16 NxBP Q—R4+ 17 K—Q3 Q—R3+ 18 P—B4 B—K3 19 NxR RxN 20 K—B3 BxB 21 P—QN3 BxP and White finally won. Clearly the Yugoslav team of analysts had found an improvement on this.

13 QxN

White could try 13 NxBP NxN 14 RxN but after 14 ... Q—K3! he has only a very slight advantage.

13 ....   P—Q4
14 QxQP!

Immediately after the game Spassky indicated that during his long think about this move he had discovered 14 BxP B—N5+ 15 K—K1 QR—K1! which is good for Black e.g. 16 BxP+ K—R1 17 BxR Q—R4+ 18 B—Q2 B—B7+ winning the queen with check. Hence his preference for the text, after which he can withstand the attack.

14 ....   R—K1+

After 14 ... B—N5+ 15 R—B3 B—N8 White plays either 16 K—B1 QR—Q1 17 Q—K4 or 16 Q—K4 at once and should win. The text at least has the merit of forcing White to go forward with his king.

15 K—B3   Q—B3+

To meet 16 B—B4 with 16 ... R—K6+ winning.

16 K—N3   B—Q3+

The attack looks dangerous for if 16 B—B4 then still 16 ... R—K6+. The correct reply, however, had been planned by Spassky several moves ago.

17 R—B4!

Black now thought for a long time, but could find nothing better than...

17 ....   B—K3

17 ... BxR+ would only improve White's development — the rook is pinned anyway.

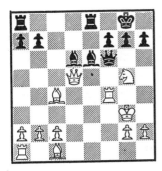

18 NxB	RxN

19 QxB!

A decisive liquidation.

19	Q—N3+
20 R—N4	R—K6+

Black finally manages to win the queen, but at too high a price, as White's inactive pieces now come into play.

21 BxR	QxQ+
22 K—B2	R—K1

Or 22 ... QxP 23 R—Q1 and White controls the board.

23 R—B4

Returning to his basic theme — the weakness of Black's KB2.

23	R—K2
24 B—N3	Q—K4
25 R—K1	P—KN4
26 R—B3	K—N2
27 R—Q1	P—B3
38 K—N1	P—N5
29 B—Q4	Resigns

46 USSR Team Championship, 1962
White: Mikenas
Nimzoindian

1 P—Q4	N—KB3
2 P—QB4	P—K3
3 N—QB3	B—N5
4 P—K3	P—QN3
5 Q—B3	

The veteran Mikenas is known for his ingenious play but this move has too much of the beginner's look about it to be good. He should have been warned about the inadvisability of early queen moves in this opening by his catastrophic twenty move loss to Keres in the 1944 USSR Championship, which went: 1 P—Q4 N—KB3 2 P—QB4 P—K3 3 N—QB3 B—N5 4 Q—Q3? P—B4 5 P—Q5 0—0 6 B—Q2 PxP 7 PxP P—Q3 8 P—KN3 P—QN3 9 B—N2 B—R3 10 Q—B2 QN—Q2

11 N—R3 R—K1 12 N—B4 BxN 13 PxB? P—KN4 14 N—Q3 RxP+ 15 K—K2 N—K4 16 K—Q1 BxN and White is hopelessly placed.

5	P—Q4

Best. After 5 ... N—B3 6 B—Q2 B—N2 7 Q—N3 (Alatortsev-Kan, 1939) White does not stand too badly.

6 B—Q3

If 6 B—K2 then 6 ... N—K5, while after 6 PxP PxP Black threatens both N—K5 and B—N5.

6	B—R3

Now the drawback to the queen position becomes clear.

7 B—Q2

Refusing to admit his error at move five. 7 Q—K2 guarding his

KB might let him complete his development and come out unscathed.

```
7 ....          P—B4
8 QPxP          QN—Q2
```

Now the threat of 9 ... N—K4 forces White, finally, to admit the error of his ways.

```
9 B—K2
```

Or 9 Q—K2 NxP and Black's advantage is clear.

```
9 ....           QBxP
10 PxP           0—0
```

Now White really is in danger of being routed before he can complete his development, so he refrains from such foolhardy adventures as 11 PxP N—K4 12 Q—N3 N—Q6+ when Black has a bind on the white squares, as in the afore-mentioned game with Keres.

```
11 BxB          N—K4
12 Q—K2          PxB
13 N—B3          N—Q6+
14 K—B1          PxP
```

White has been completely outplayed: Black has the open QR file, the threat of 15 ... NxNP and pressure against KB7.

```
15 B—K1          BxN
16 PxB
```

Or 16 BxB N—K5 17 B—K1 Q—B3 18 N—Q4 P—K4 and 19 ... KR—Q1 with complete domination.

```
16 ....          N—K5
17 N—Q4          P—K4
18 N—B2          Q—B3
19 P—B3          KR—Q1
```

Threatening 29 ... NxB and 21 ... R—Q7.

```
20 K—N1          NxB
21 NxN
```

Or 21 QxN R—Q7 22 N—N4 Q—N4 23 P—N3 QR—Q1 24 PxN Q—N5 with winning threats of 25 ... R—Q8 or 25 ... Q—B3. 21 PxN would remove the powerful central knight, but after 21 ... NxN 22 QxN R—Q6 White soon loses his weak isolated pawns (23 R—Q1? RxRP!).

```
21 ....          NxP
22 QxP           P—K5
         Resigns
```

The threat is 23 ... N—K7+ and if 23 K—B1 N—Q4 or 23 R—B1 QR—B1 24 Q—R6 N—K7+.

47 Havana 1962
Black: Gonzales
Queen's Indian Defence

```
1 P—Q4          N—KB3
2 P—QB4          P—K3
3 N—KB3          P—QN3
4 N—B3
```

A classical move first played in pre-Nimzovich days, but for a long time considered dubious in view of the strength of the Black pin B—N5.

```
4 ....          B—N2
5 B—N5          B—N5
6 P—K3          P—KR3
7 B—R4          P—KN4
```

A bold move to strengthen the effect of his pin.

```
8 B—N3          N—K5
9 Q—B2
```

White has to exert pressure on the key square K4 so that he can answer the aggressive 9 ... P—KR4 with 10 B—Q3 and if 10 ... P—KB4 then 11 P—Q5! leading to complications similar to those of the game.

9 ....   BxN+
10 PxB   P—Q3

10 ... NxB looks illogical after Black's efforts to establish his knight on its strong central square, but, as the course of the game shows, Black's many central pawn moves weaken his position, so 10 ... NxB 11 RPxN P—N5 is a good alternative, e.g. 12 N—K5 Q—N4 13 R—R4 P—B4 14 P—QR4 N—B3 and Black has a reasonable game (Uhlmann-Spassov, Zinnowitz 1965).

11 B—Q3   P—KB4

This looks quite natural, but White's next move casts doubt on it. Hence Black should prefer 11 ... NxB 12 RPxB N—Q2 13 P—QR4 P—QR4 followed by 14 ... Q—K2 and 15 ... 0—0—0.

12 P—Q5!

A dynamic move to gain control of the weak white squares at K6 and KB5. It was first played in Keres-Taimanov, XXII USSR 1955.

12 ....   PxP

The line of least resistance. Black's best chance is the sacrifice 12 ... N—Q2! to complete his development and speculate on exploiting White's weak pawns. If then 13 BxN PxB 14 QxP Q—B3 15 0—0 0—0—0 16 QxP QxQ 17 PxQ N—B4 18 N—Q4 QR—K1 and Black should equalise (Ree-Taimanov, Hamburg 1965). More crucial is Keres' suggestion 13 PxP QN—B4 14 N—Q4 Q—B3 15 P—B3 NxB+ 16 QxN N—B4 17 QxBP and White remains a pawn up.

13 N—Q4

The key move in White's attacking plan.

13 ....   Q—B3

Or 13 ... PxP·14 KBxP Q—B3 15 P—B3 NxB 16 RPxN with great pressure, e.g. 16 ... N—Q2 17 QxP 0—0—0 18 QxQ NxQ 19 P—N4! fixing the KRP with the better ending.

14 PxP   BxP
15 P—B3   NxB
16 RPxN   N—Q2

Black hurries to complete his development.

17 BxP   N—B4

If 17 ... 0—0—0 18 Q—R4 with strong pressure on the Q side. This was the way the original game of the variation (Keres-Taimanov, mentioned above) went. Black varies but leaves his king exposed in the centre.

18 0—0—0   P—R3

To prevent the awkward 19 N—N5. Black's position is so full of holes on the white squares that it is hard to suggest a reasonable move for him.

19 P—K4   B—B2
20 P—KB4

Naturally White plays to open lines in the centre.

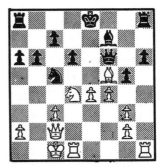

20 ....   K—B1

To achieve artificial castling by

21 ... K—N2 but White now harries him unmercifully.

21 P—K5!   QPxP

21 ... Q—K2 or 21 ... Q—N2 look better, but even then 22 KR—K1 would leave White with all his trumps intact and the awkward push P—K6 in the air.

22 PxKP   QxP

The boldness of the damned. 22 ... Q—N2 is still best. Now as the pictorial expression puts it: "All the doors and windows are open".

23 KR—B1   K—N2

Or 23 ... QR—K1 24 B—N6 R—K2 25 N—B6 Q—K6+ 26 K—N1 and wins material.

24 QR—K1   Q—Q3
25 B—K4   Resigns

There is the double threat of 26 BxR and the knight fork 26 N—B5+ e.g. 25 .... Q—B1 26 BxR QxB 27 RxB+! KxR 28 Q—B5+ K—N1 29 R—K7 with a swift mate.

48 Varna Olympiad, 1962
Black: Darga
Sicilian Defence

1 P—K4   P—QB4
2 N—KB3   N—QB3
3 P—Q4   PxP
4 NxP   P—K3
5 N—QB3   Q—B2

A modern opening finesse. After 6 KN—N5 Q—N1 7 B—K3 P—QR3 White has to retreat his knight to Q4, and his attempt to "punish" Black for his failure to play the usual P—QR3 has merely resulted in allowing Black that move with gain of time; Black's queen is quite well placed on QN1 where it is less exposed to the usual knight sacrifices N—Q5 or NxQNP.

6 B—K3   P—QR3

But Black feels he cannot do without this move in the long run, expecially since one of the main themes for Black in this system involves strengthening his pressure on the dark squares with ... B—Q3, which he cannot play until he has eliminated the possibility of N—QN5.

7 P—QR3

The theory of this line is still undergoing considerable changes. The text was then thought to be a very suitable prophylactic measure to prevent B—N5 and to take the sting out of P—QN4—N5. Two years later, however, in the Soviet Zonal ("The Tournament of Seven") Spassky preferred the sharper 7 P—B4 against Suetin, while if White does not want to play a non-developing move he can continue 7 B—K2 or 7 B—Q3.

7 ....   P—QN4
8 B—K2   B—N2
9 P—B4   N—B3

Black could try to exploit the slightly unusual move order by 9 ... NxN and if 10 QxN then 10 ... N—K2 11 0—0 N—B3 driving the queen from its centre post.

10 B—B3   P—Q3

Black has to return to normality

as 11 P—K5 was now a strong threat.

11 0—0　　　　N—QR4

This is not good. He could try to profit from the fact that he has reasonable control of his Q4 square by 11 ... NxN 12 QxN P—K4 when the White bishop at B3 is severely restricted by the blocked pawns in the centre. He could also play quite safely 11 ... B—K2 but he probably missed that after 12 P—K5 PxP 13 NxN BxN 14 PxP he could interpose 14 ... R—Q1! with a reasonable game on 15 BxB+ QxB•16 Q—K2 N—Q4. But not in this line, 14 ... N—Q2 15 BxB QxB 16 Q—R5! guarding the KP and threatening the KBP and preparing an attack e.g. 16 ... 0—0 17 R—B3 or 16 ... P—N3? 17 Q—R6 and 17 ... NxP fails to 18 Q—N7.

12 Q—K2　　　　N—B5
13 P—K5!

This is a typical Sicilian Defence breakthrough by White. It is particularly dangerous here, where Black is still two moves short of castling.

13 ....　　　　NxB

White's last move put Black's QB *en prise* as well as his KN, so 13 ... PxP would lose to 14 KNxQNP PxN 15 NxP and Black's queen cannot defend both bishop and knight.

14 QxN　　　　PxP

Once again if 14 ... N—Q2 Black has to take account of the overloading theme — 15 PxP BxP 16 KNxQNP PxN 17 NxP Q—B4 18 NxB+ QxN 19 BxB R—QN1 20 B—K4 RxP 21 KR—N1 and White's QRP will be strong enough to win the ending.

15 PxP　　　　N—Q2
Or 15 ... N—Q4 16 NxN BxN 17

BxB PxB 18 P—K6! with great advantage.

16 BxB　　　　QxB
17 Q—B4　　　　N—N3

Sokolsky suggests 17 ... 0—0—0 but it is not clear what compensation Black gets for his lost pawn after 18 QxP B—B4 (or 18 ... NxP 19 QxP+ N—Q2 20 N—K4 or even simpler 19 QxQ+ and 20 NxKP. If 18 ... Q—N3 then 19 N—K2 and White is again a sound pawn up) 19 QR—Q1 (not 19 N—K2 Q—K5!) NxP 20 QxP+ N—Q2 21 N—K4 KR—K1 22 NxB!

18 QR—Q1　　　　N—R5

A strange move, but Black must have realised that he would do well to remove the threat of N—K4 e.g. 18 ... B—B4 19 N—K4 BxN+ (19 ... QR—B1 20 Q—N4) 20 RxB 0—0 and now 21 N—B6+! is very strong. Even prettier, however, is 21 Q—N5 N—Q4 (21 ... P—KR3 22 N—B6+ K—R1 23 R—KR4 and mates by 24 RxP+) 22 N—B6+ K—R1 23 R—KR4 and mates quickly.

19 NxN　　　　PxN
20 K—R1

In some variations the pin along the black diagonal or a queen check at QN3 can be awkward for White, so he takes this useful precaution. Black now seems helpless.

20 ....　　　　B—B4

The only way to try and get castled, but now comes a winning sacrifice.

21 NxP!   PxN
22 QxP+   Q—N4

If 22 ... K—K2 then 23 Q—R4+ K—Kl and now White wins either by 24 Q—QB4 e.g. 24 ... Q—B3 25 R—Q6 or 24 ... Q—K2 25 Q—R4+ or 24 ... B—K2 25 QxKP R—KB1 26 RxR+ and 27 R—Q7, or by 24 Q—N4 e.g. 24 ... Q—N3 25 QxNP threatening the rook and 26 Q—Q7 mate or 24 ... Q—B3 25 QxNP as in the actual game.

23 Q—KN4   Q—B3

Or 23 ... R—KB1 24 QxP+ B—K2

25 RxR+ KxR 26 P—B4! Q—N2 27 R—B1+ K—Kl 28 Q—N8+ K—Q2 29 R—Ql+ K—B2 (29 ... K—B3 30 Q—K6+ K—B4 31 P—N4+) 30 Q—K6 and wins.

24 QxNP   R—KB1
25 RxR+   BxR
26 QxP   R—B1

Not 26 ... R—Ql 27 Q—N6+ and 28 Q—B6+ winning the rook, nor 26 ... B—B4 27 P—QN4!

27 Q—N6+   Resigns

After 27 ... K—K2 28 R—Q6 Q—B5 29 Q—R7+ Black must play 29 ... B—N2 to prevent immediate mate.

49 Varna Olympiad 1962
Black: Evans
King's Indian Defence

1 P—Q4   N—KB3
2 P—QB4   P—KN3
3 N—QB3   B—N2
4 P—K4   P—Q3
5 P—B3

This was Spassky's favourite move against the King's Indian in his early years and still is!

5 ....   P—B3

Experience has shown that this Q side build-up is too slow as it involves too many pawn moves. 5 ... 0—0 followed by 6 ... P—N3 aiming at P—B4, or by 6 ... N—B3 intending P—K4 (or even P—QR3, R—N1 and P—QN4) is better.

6 B—K3   P—QR3
7 Q—Q2

Also very strong here is 7 P—K5!

7 ....   P—QN4

8 0—0—0!

This is better than the more usual 8 B—Q3 when Black's play gains some point with the tempo gain 8 ... PxP 9 BxP P—Q4, (Botvinnik-Smyslov match 1958.)

8 ....   PxP

8 ... Q—R4 has been suggested, but after 9 K—N1 White still has good prospects as he threatens to meet 9 ... 0—0 with 10 N—Q5. If 8 ... QN—Q2 then P—Q5! is an advantageous opening of the game for White.

9 BxP   0—0

This seems inconsistent. Black should keep his king in the centre for as long as possible in order to deprive White of an obvious object of attack. Hence Black should try

9 ... P—Q4 10 B—N3 PxP 11 PxP N—N5! and Black has more play on the dark squares than in the game. Note that 9 ... QN—Q2 is met by 10 P—K5! exploiting the masked pin on the Q file.

10 P—KR4!   P—Q4

An obvious reaction from each side but White's move looks the more convincing as from now on right to the point where Black resigns it is difficult to improve on his play! Hence he would have better chances either with 10 ... P—KR4 to defer the opening of the KR file, or Petrosian's suggestion 10 ... B—K3 to reduce the influence of one of White's most aggressively placed pieces. Keep an eye on that QR2/KN8 diagonal from now on!

11 B—N3   PxP

If now 11 ... P—KR4 then 12 P—K5 N—K1 13 P—N4 PxP 14 P—R5 with a very strong attack, as is always the case in such positions when there is no defensive knight at KB3.

12 P—R5!

Possibly Evans had only expected 12 PxP when he could again try 12 ... N—N5 or even better 12 ... B—N5 13 N—B3 QN—Q2 completing his development.

12 ....   KPxP

Playing for the position that arises after his 15th move. If 12 ... NxP then White can play either 13 P—N4 N—B3 14 B—R6 (14 Q—R2 is also strong) or 13 B—R6 when the threats of 14 RxN or 14 NxP and then 15 N—N5 are too strong.

13 RPxP   RPxP
14 B—R6!   PxP
15 R—R4!

It's a real gambit now and a tempo lost in capturing a pawn slows down the attack, e.g. 15 QxP

B—N5! to force exchanges or to block the file by B—KR4. Now, however, there is a threat of 16 BxB KxB 17 Q—R6+ so Black has little choice.

15 ....   N—N5

Not 15 ... N—R4 16 RxN PxR 17 Q—N5.

16 BxB   KxB
17 QxP   N—R3

Black has several other possibilities e.g. (A) 17 ... N—K6? 18 Q—R2! R—R1 (18 ... NxR 19 R—R7+ K—B3 20 Q—K5 mate!) 19 RxR QxR 20 Q—K5+ winning the knight, or (B) 17 ... N—B3 18 N—B3 R—R1 (the threat was 19 QR—R1 or 19 N—K5 followed by 20 BxP!) 19 BxP! KxB 20 N—K5+ with a winning attack (20 ... K—K3 21 Q—R3+ K—Q3 22 N—B7+ K—B2 23 Q—N3+) or (C) 17 ... R—R1 18 RxN BxR 19 QxB N—Q2 20 N—B3 N—B3 21 Q—B4 followed by 22 N—K5 or (D) 17 ... P—KB4 18 N—B3 R—R1 19 RxR QxR 20 R—R1 Q—Q1 21 N—N5. In all these variations White's bishop is immensely powerful. Perhaps the best defensive chance was (E) 17 ... Q—Q3 18 RxN BxR 19 QxB P—KB4 20 Q—N5 Q—B3 but after 21 N—B3 White's active minor pieces should give him a win in the long run despite the exchange of queens.

18 N—B3   N—B4
19 R—R2

(See diagram next column.)

Here again Black has a wide choice e.g. 19 ... N—K6? 20 Q—N5! or 19 ... R—R1 20 BxP! or 19 ... P—K3 20 N—KN5 penetrating with a rook on R7 or best of all 19 ... N—Q2 when 20 QR—R1 N—B3 21 BxP! wins, e.g. 21 ... KxB 22

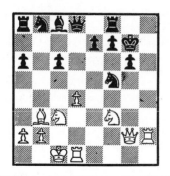

N—K5+ K—K3 21 QxP+ — a nice change of attacking direction!

| 19 .... | Q—Q3 |
| 20 N—K5 | N—Q2 |

Not 20 ... NxP 21 Q—N5 or even (yet again) 21 BxP! If instead 20 ... B—K3 then 21 N—K4 followed by 22 BxB wins. In all these variations it becomes clear that White has too much pressure along the KN and KR files as well as along the diagonal QR2/KN8.

| 21 N—K4 | Q—B2 |
| 22 QR—R1 | R—KN1 |

Or 22 ... N—B3 23 (You've guessed it!) BxP!

23 N—K4	Q—B2
24 R—R7+	K—B1
25 RxP+	K—K1

Evans decides to give the spectators a thrill and plays on.

| 26 QxP! | NxN |
| 27 R—B8+ | Resigns |

27 ... K—Q2 28 N—B5 mate would be an elegant final touch, but of course there is a dual by 28 Q—K6, and 28 Q—K8 or 28 B—K6 also come into consideration!

This game was generally considered to be the best of the Olympiad though Fischer's 24 move win over Najdorf ran it close.

50 Varna Olympiad 1962
Black: Schmid
Benoni

| 1 P—Q4 | P—QB4 |

A favourite opening of Schmid's, though in the previous Olympiad at Leipzig, 1960, he had lost with it when he employed it against Botvinnik.

2 P—Q5	P—Q3
3 P—K4	P—KN3
4 N—KB3	B—N2
5 B—K2	N—KB3
6 N—B3	N—R3

Inviting 6 BxN when the QN file will be very useful for Black (R—QN1 with intensification of pressure on QN2, then perhaps R—N5).

| 7 0—0 | N—B2 |
| 8 R—K1 | |

Spassky is the first to deviate from the Botvinnik game which went 8 P—QR4 P—QR3 9 N—Q2 B—Q2 10 N—B4 P—QN4 11 P—K5! and White punished Black's failure to castle. The text may well be an improvement as 8 ... P—QN4 does not work yet — 9 BxP+ NxB 10 NxN and the rook guards the KP.

| 8 .... | 0—0 |

Schmid has learned his lesson from Botvinnik! 9 ... P—QN4 is still not a direct threat but it is useful for White to restrain the possibility, so...

9 P—QR4   P—QR3
10 B—KN5!

White does well to play actively putting pressure on the KP and hoping to strengthen pressure on that square by P—K5 or Q—Q2—B4—R4. 10 P—R5 would not be so good for after 10 ... R—N1 Black gets in P—QN4 and on PxP e.p. his QRP is safely guarded by the QN.

10 ....   P—R3

Before White can play 11 Q—Q2.

11 B—KB4   B—Q2

If 11 ... N—R4 then 12 B—K3 and Black is still threatened with 13 P—K5 as well as with 13 N—Q2 forcing his knight to retreat to B3.

12 Q—Q2   P—QN4

Hoping for 13 BxRP? P—N5 and Black has fine game e.g. 14 BxB PxN! 15 Q—R6 N—N5 winning a piece or 14 N—Q1 NxKP. Naturally, Spassky has foreseen this eventuality and prepared a suitable counter in the centre, quite like the Botvinnik game. Black would therefore have done better to play 12 ... K—R2 or even 12 ... P—KN4.

13 P—K5!

The principle idea of this move is to gain the K4 square for his knight when it is forced to move from QB3.

13 ....   QPxP

This falls in with White's plan, but if 13 ... N—R4 then 14 PxQP while if 13 ... P—N5 then 14 PxN PxN 15 NPxP winning the KRP after which, as the game shows, White gets a strong attack against the king.

14 BxKP   P—N5
15 BxN   BxB

16 N—K4

Now the knight attacks the QBP, the KRP is *en prise* and White is ready in many variations to give up the QNP and then the exchange in order to achieve the attacking formation Q on R6, N on N5.

16 ....   B—N2

Black is not to be tempted. If 16 ... BxNP White can answer either 17 QR—Q1 adding P—Q6 to his choice of threats or else 17 QxRP B—N2 (17 ... BxR? 18 KN—N5 and mates) 18 Q—R4 P—B3 (18 ... NxP 19 KN—N5 R—K1 20 QR—Q1 with a powerful position) 19 NxQBP and as 19 ... NxP loses to 20 B—B4 P—K3 21 N—Q4 Black stands very badly.

17 NxP   BxNP

Now that a White knight has travelled slightly further away from the approaches to his king, Black decides he can safely re-establish material equality with prospects of winning the exchange or the QRP.

18 QR—Q1   B—B4

The losing move. 18 ... B—B6 was no good because of 19 QxRP and if 19 ... BxR? 20 N—N5 or 19 ... B—N2 20 Q—R4 as before. Hence Black had to safeguard his king by 18 ... B—N2 though he would be a pawn down after 19 QxNP.

19 QxRP   B—N2
20 Q—R4   Q—Q3

Black does not have time for 20 ... BxP because of 21 N—N5 R—K1 22 QN—K6!! PxN (22 ... NxN 23 PxN BxR 24 PxP+ K—B1 25 Q—R7 P—K4 26 Q—N8+ K—K2 27 PxR(Q)+ QxQ 28 QxB+ etc.) 23 PxP Q—B1 (23 ... BxR? 24 Q—R7+ K—B1 25 K—N1 26 RxB forcing the win of the queen by the threat of R—Q3—R3; or 23 ... N—Q4 24 B—Q3! P—N6 25 Q—R7+ K—B1

26 QxP K—N1 27 Q—B7+ K—R1 28 R—K4 and 29 R—R4+) 24 B—Q3 NxP 25 Q—R7+ K—B1 26 NxN+ QxN 27 RxQ BxR 28 RxNP and wins.

In this fine combination it is a knight which is sacrificed on K6. In the actual game it is a bishop that immolates itself on that square.

21 N—N5   KR—K1

The rook here takes a flight square away from the king. If Schmid had conceived the full force of the storm that was about to break over his head he would have played 21 ... KR—N1, though after 22 KN—K4 Q—Q1 his king would still be exposed to great pressure in view of the absence of defending pieces on the K side.

(See diagram next column.)

22 B—Q3!

A difficult move to find. Its point is that after 22 ... BxB 23 Q—R7+ K—B1 there comes the winning sacrifice 24 QN—K6+ PxN (24 ... NxN 25 PxN P—B3 26 RxB and 27 QxP) 25 PxP threatening 26 RxB Q

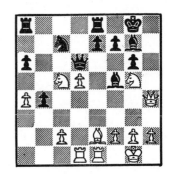

moves 17 R—B3+.

22 ....   QxN
23 BxB   NxP

Not 23 ... PxB 24 Q—R7+ K—B1 25 Q—R5 K—N1 26 QxP+ K—R1 27 R—Q3 mating.

24 B—K6!   Resigns

24 ... PxB 25 Q—R7+ and 26 NxP+ or 24 ... N—B3 25 BxP+ K—B1 26 N—K6+. Hence Black must try 24 ... QxQBP but after 25 BxP+ K—B1 26 BxN Black is a piece down and 27 Q—R7 will renew mating threats.

51 XXX USSR Championship, Erevan 1962
White: Savon
Sicilian Defence

1 P—K4   P—QB4
2 N—KB3   N—QB3
3 P—Q4   PxP
4 NxP   P—K3
5 N—QB3·   Q—B2
6 P—KN3

One of the favourite methods of combatting the Taimanov system.

White's last move has the tactical point that White can play B—KB4 in some variations e.g. as in the famous game Fischer-Tal, **Bled** 1961, which went 6 ... N—B3? 7 KN—N5 Q—N1 8 B—KB4 N—K4 9 B—K2! B—B4 10 BxN QxB 11 P—B4 Q—N1 12 P—K5 and

White is winning due to his grip
on the black squares.

6 ....   P—QR3
7 B—N2   N—B3
8 0—0   B—K2

Black's soundest line, as after 8
... P—Q3 9 R—K1 B—K2 10
NxN! PxN (10 ... BxN 11
N—Q5!) 11 N—R4 followed by
P—QB4 White has the Q side
pressure with P—B5 in the
offing. 8 ... NxN 9 QxN B—B4
10 B—B4 P—Q3 11 Q—Q2 is
slightly better for White as was
shown by the fourth game of the
Fischer-Taimanov match, 1971.

9 P—N3

Quite a good idea as the long
black diagonal cannot easily be
blocked by Black. 9 R—K1 hoping
to enforce P—K5 or to transpose
into the last note is also playable.

9 ....   0—0
10 QN—K2   P—QN4

Otherwise 11 P—QB4 will give
White a strong central position.

11 B—N2   B—N2
12 R—B1

Trying to open the QB file by
P—QB4 so Black is forced to
counter with 12 ... N—K4 as 12 ...
P—Q4 13 PxP PxP (13 ... NxP 14
N—B5!, or 13 ... NxN 14 NxN NxP
15 Q—N4!) 14 N—B5 is clearly
good for White.

12 ....   N—K4
13 P—KB4

White plays *va banque* as Black
now threatened P—Q4, and 13
P—KR3 is rather a tame move.
Spassky, striving to make up the
leeway caused by his bad start in
this event, is naturally equally
eager for complications.

13 ....   QN—N5
14 Q—Q3   P—K4?!

White threatened both 15
P—KR3 driving the knight to an
offside position, and 15 P—B4
P—N5 16 P—K5! Black's best
move seems to be 14 ... P—Q4
hoping that after 15 P—K5 N—K5
his centralised knight will hold his
game together.

15 N—B5!   B—B4+
16 K—R1   P—Q4!

Now we get a real melee! 16 ...
N—B7+ to win the exchange is not
good after 17 RxN BxR 18 BxP
and White has strong ·threats on
the black squares (BxN, N—K7+,
NxP, N—R6+).

17 KPxP   P—K5
18 Q—Q2

Not 18 BxP NxB 19 QxN
KR—K1 20 Q—B3 N—K6! 21 NxN
RxN 22 Q—N2 RxN! 23 QxP
BxP+ 24 B—B3 Q—B3 25 R—KB1
R—K1 followed by 26 ... R—K6 ex-
ploiting the killing pin.

18 ....   Q—Q2!

Putting the question to White's
best placed piece and preparing to
recapture the QP. Winning the exchange would again be bad as
White has the counter 18 N—B7+
19 RxN BxR 20 P—B4! and if 20 ...
P—K6 then 21 Q—B3 threatening
22 N—R6+ K—R1 23 QxN!
Accumulating threats is far more
important than slight win of
material.

19 N(2)—Q4?

Much too tame a move 19 N(5)—Q4 P—K6 and 20 ... BxP also leaves Black well placed. However after the game Spassky admitted that he was worried about the sacrifice 19 NxP! KxN 20 P—B4 with a very complicated position in which White has many chances due to his passed pawns and black square pressure.

19	BxP
20 P—KR3?	

In time trouble, Savon overlooks that Black mates first in the tactical line that now follows. 20 N—K3 and if necessary 21 P—B3 to hold his centre together and block the passed KP was called for. Then White would stand only slightly worse.

20	P—K6
21 Q—B3	N—B7+
22 RxN	

Or 22 K—R2 (or 22 K—N1) 22 ... BxB 23 KxB BxN 24 NxB QxP+ 25 K—B3 N—Q4! and 26 ... Q—N5+ with a winning attack.

22	BxN
23 QxB	

Continuing to cherish his hope of mating. After 23 NxB he would remain the exchange down for inadequate compensation.

23	PxR
24 N—R6+??	

After 24 BxB! QxN! 25 B—N2 QR—K1 26 QxP N—K5 Black would win in the long run, (27 Q—Q4? NxP+ 28 K—R2 N—R4 threatening to exchange queens by 29 ... QxP+). Savon played the text move quickly and then saw in a flash what Spassky had seen some moves ago. Hence White now resigned before Black could continue 24 ... PxN 25 QxN QxP mate! (First!).

52 Semi-final XXXI USSR Champ., Kharkov 1963
Black: Nikolaevsky
Queen's Gambit Accepted

1 P—Q4	P—Q4
2 P—QB4	PxP
3 N—KB3	N—KB3
4 P—K3	P—K3
5 BxP	P—B4
6 0—0	P—QR3
7 P—QR4	

Botvinnik's favourite move, weakening White's QN4 so as to keep Black's Q side expansion (P—QN4) under control.

7	PxP

The normal line is 7 ... N—B3 8

Q—K2 PxP 9 R—Q1 Q—K2 10 PxP as in the Botvinnik-Petrosian world championship match several months before this particular game. The point of the text is to isolate the White QP so that White cannot easily play Q—K2. However, White gets plenty of dynamic chances due to the freeing of his QB:

8 PxP	N—B3
9 N—B3	B—K2
10 B—K3	0—0

11 Q—K2

White has achieved the appropriate attacking move, but only after committing his QB to K3.

11 ....   N—N5
12 N—K5   P—QN3

Bad positional judgement. With the White KR at KB1 and not Q1, Black has to take account of a possible attack by P—KB4—B5. Hence the correct line was 12 ... B—Q2 keeping control of his KB4.

13 P—B4   KN—Q4
14 QR—Q1   B—B3

Black's moves give an impression of planlessness.

15 N—K4   B—N2
16 P—B5!

Thus White realises his plan and forces a decisive line opening.

16 ....   PxP

Playing for exchanges, but 16 ... B—B1 was a more reliable way of defending his position.

17 RxP   NxB

Missing White's fine combination and expecting only 18 QxN BxN 19 RxB B—Q4 with a safe position. The main threat was 18 NxB+ NxN 19 B—KN5 so Black should play either 17 ... P—KR3 or 17 ... B—B1.

18 NxB+   PxN
19 QxN

(See diagram next column.)

Now Black must accept the piece, otherwise his K side is

shattered without any compensation e.g. 19 ... N—Q4 20 Q—R6! or 19 ... B—Q4 20 N—N4!

19 ....   PxN
20 QxP   P—KR3

Otherwise 21 R—N5+.

21 R—B6

The best sort of attacking move — quite but deadly.

21 ....   K—R2

If 21 ... N—Q4 then 22 Q—N3+ K—R2 23 B—Q3+ mates, while if 21 ... B—Q4 then 22 RxRP P—B3 23 Q—N3+ K—B2 24 R—R7+ K—K3 25 R—K1+ K—B4 26 R—R5 mate.

22 QR—KB1   B—Q4
23 Q—B5+   K—N1
24 Q—N4+   K—R2

Perpetual check?

25 RxRP+

No! After 25 ... KxR 26 R—B5 is crushing.

25 ....   Resigns

53 XXXI USSR Championship, Leningrad 1963
White: Novopashin
Ruy Lopez

1 P—K4	P—K4
2 N—KB3	N—QB3
3 B—N5	P—QR3
4 B—R4	N—B3
5 0—0	B—K2
6 R—K1	P—QN4
7 B—N3	0—0
8 P—B3	P—Q4
9 PxP	NxP
10 NxP	NxN
11 RxN	P—QB3

Spassky had begun the tournament with a series of draws, so now he felt obliged to play a sharp line against one of the outsiders. This game was the first of a series in which he employed the evergreen Marshall Gambit, but with a new emphasis, not on burning bridges, but on steady play, so that the Marshall soon got the reputation of a drawing weapon!

12 P—Q4

The usual move, though in recent years White has tried other plans, such as 12 BxN, in order to retreat his rook to K3 instead of K1, or 12 P—KN3 so as to rule out Black's attacking thrust Q—R5.

12	B—Q3
13 R—K1	Q—R5
14 P—KN3	Q—R6
15 B—K3	B—N5
16 Q—Q3	QR—K1
17 N—Q2	R—K3
18 P—QR4	

Quite logical, White wishes to open a 'second front' along the QR file. In a game from the preliminaries of the 1966 Havanna Olympiad, Bushachter of Vene-

zuela, tried the old move 18 Q—B1 against Spassky, but even though he succeeded in driving away the queen and also forced an exchange of bishops, the impression remains that purely defensive measures are inadequate to stem the attack. (That game continued 18 ... Q—R4 19 B—Q1 BxB 20 QRxB P—KB4 21 Q—K2 Q—N3 22 K—R1 P—B5 23 PxP NxKBP 24 Q—B1 N—Q6 25 Q—N2 Q—R4 26 N—B1 RxB! 27 NxR RxP 28 RxN RxQ 29 KxR Q—N3+ 30 Resigns).

18 ....   PxP!

A paradoxical move that is much stronger than it appears. The point is to distract one of White's pieces from a vital field of activity; either the rook away from control of the back row or the bishop from the diagonal where it pins the central knight against the rook, KBP and Black king. It is not certain whether the right of authorship of the move belongs to Spassky alone, as a correspondence game played in 1963 in the Soviet Union followed the same course. White also replied 19 RxP in that game, and also lost quickly! The result of the two games even caused the move 19 RxP to be condemned as weak in the authoritative magazine "Shakhmaty v SSSR" but then Spassky's subsequent games with Shtein, USSR Zonal 1964 and Parma, Yugoslavia-USSR match 1965, cuased this initial impression to be revised.

19 RxP   P—KB4

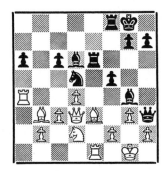

20 P—KB4?

The losing move. Shtein played 20 Q—B1! reinforcing his back rank and guarding his KR with gain of time. There followed 20 ... P—B5 21 QxQ BxQ 22 RxP! which is a very promising sacrifice of a piece for three pawns. Shtein and Parma only drew their games, but both had the better of it, and Parma even missed a clearly winning move. So the old impression was once again confirmed — the Marshall is a risky line!

20 ....   BxP!

A most disconcerting move to meet. You play a pawn on to a square where it seemingly forms an impregnable bulwark, and your opponent calmly takes it off.

21 B—KB2

This loses at once. He had to try 21 PxB R—N3 22 BxN+ hoping for 22 ... PxB 23 RxP B—K7+ 24 RxR BxQ 25 R—N3 with some compensation for the queen. Black however, can improve on this by 22 ... K—R1! with considerable advantage. If White tries to avoid the latter variation by 21 BxN then after 21 ... PxB 22 PxB Black can also vary with 22 ... KR—K1 which leaves him with a very strong attack.

21 ....   RxR+
22 BxR   R—K1
    Resigns

Now 23 Q—B1 loses to 23 ... B—K6+, 23 R—R1 to 23 ... BxN followed by 24 ... R—K7 and 23 B—B2 to 23 ... B—K7 followed by 24 ... BxN with the mate threat on B8.

After the game Bondarevsky revealed how far modern opening analysis goes. Spassky and he had examined this variation right down to the point where White resigned!

54 XXXI USSR Championship, Leningrad 1963
Black: Osnos
Torre Attack

1 P—Q4   N—KB3
2 N—KB3   P—K3
3 B—N5

The Torre attack which aims to meet Indian defensive systems with a classical build-up. It could be described as a Colle system with the QB outside the pawn chain.

3 ....   P—B4

The commonest reply, challenging in the centre and preparing to move the queen out of the pin with gain of time.

4 P—K3

White can also try the gambit 4 P—K4, but for the moment White sticks to the classical pattern.

4 ....   Q—N3

Now it is quite sound for White to guard the pawn with 5 Q—B1, as Alekhine·himself did in a game against L. Steiner, Dresden 1926. Spassky, however, decides that now is the right moment to turn the opening into a gambit.

5 QN—Q2   QxP
6 B—Q3

White can calmly develop, and he will soon gain more tempi by threatening the security of the enemy queen.

6 ....   PxP

A controversial decision, as White is soon able to make good use of the open K file. 6 ... Q—N3 to safeguard his queen, and to keep the position closed, looks best. If 6 ... N—B3 then White could profitably indulge in a further sacrifice by 7 0—0 and if 7 ... PxP then 8 R—N1 QxRP (8 ... Q—B6 9 N—B4 threatening 10 R—N3) 9 PxP with a promising position.

7 PxP   Q—B6
8 0—0   P—Q4

Black's last three moves have ensured that he can retreat his queen safely to QB2, but now White, who has already completed his development, starts making definite threats.

9 R—K1   B—K2

9 ... N—B3 would be illogical since after 10 R—N1 Black would again have to worry about his queen and the greedy 10 ... NxP

would be met by 11 NxN QxN 12 N—K4! threatening 13 B—N5+.

10 R—K3   Q—B2
11 N—K5   N—B3
12 P—QB3

A remarkably quiet consolidating move just when one would expect some fierce threat from White. However, closer examination of the position shows that Black is now in a dilemma as to how to continue. He should probably aim to castle long, despite the open QN file. Thus 12 ... B—Q2 intending 13 ... R—KB1 seems called for. 12 ... 0—0 is clearly bad because of 13 BxN followed by 14 BxP+ with a mating attack whether the bishop is accepted or not.

12 ....   NxN
13 PxN   N—N1

A disagreeable retreat, but after 13 ... N—Q2 14 BxB KxB 15 Q—N4 White has immediate threats e.g. 15 ... NxP 16 QxNP or 15 ... QxBP 16 Q—N5+ K—K1 17 R—Q1 threatening both 18 QxNP and a bishop move discovering an attack on the queen.

14 N—B3   P—KR3?

Steinitz would never have played a move like this. It weakens the pawn front near his king and robs the knight of a square on which it might re-emerge into the game. 14 ... B—Q2 was essential, when White would continue 15 R—N1 or P—QR4, but after 15 ... 0—0—0 Black's king would finally reach some sort of security.

15 B—KB4   B—Q2
16 N—Q4   B—KN4

Yet another weak move. He had to castle and try to solve the development of his knight later. White would have good attacking chances after 15 R—N1 or P—QR4 threatening 16 N—N5 but Black is far from lost.

17 BxB   PxB
18 Q—N4

Now the forward KNP provides an object of attack.

18 ....   QxBP

This is doubtless the position Black envisaged two moves ago. He threatens the rook in the corner and also 19 ... N—R3 driving the queen away from the defence of the knight. However, after Spassky's calm reply the threat of penetration by R—QB1 followed by N—B5 is too much when combined with White's pressure on the other side of the board.

19 N—N3!   N—R3
20 QxNP   Q—N5

The NP cannot be saved so the queen hurries back to the defence (21 QxP Q—B1).

21 R—N3

Leaving his queen at its post for the moment to prevent castling on either side, and ruling out the counter attack ... N—N5.

21 ....   Q—B1

A distinguished British chess author suggested 21 ... O—O—O here! Clearly he had the position set up wrongly. 21 ... Q—K2 is met by 22 Q—K3 followed by 23 R—QB1 with easy penetration on the black squares, while 21 ... P—KN3 is met by 22 R—R3 Q—B1 23 R—QB1 R—B1 24 RxR+ BxR 25 B—N5+ B—Q2 26 R—QB3! winning. Finally 21 ... R—KN1? is a blunder revealing yet another point of White's last move (**22 QxN! winning a piece**).

22 R—QB1

Threatening the decisive 23 R—B7 and 24 N—B5.

22 ....   P—B3

Not 22 ... R—B1 23 RxR+ BxR 24 B—N5+ B—Q2 25 R—QB3!

23 Q—K3   P—B4
24 N—B5

With the mortal threats of 25 NxNP or 25 NxB (after 24 ... R—QN1).

24 ....   P—B5

Winning material?

25 B—N6+

No!

25 ....   K—K2

Or 25 ... K—Q1 26 NxP+ and 27 Q—B5 mate.

26 Q—R3!   Resigns

If 26 ... B—B3 then 27 NxNP+ K—Q2 28 N—B5+ with a winning attack.

55 31st USSR Championship Play-off, Moscow 1964
Black: Holmov
King's Gambit

1 P—K4	P—K4
2 P—KB4	PxP
3 N—KB3	B—K2

One of the soundest defences to the King's Gambit. 4 ... B—R5+ is a definite threat and in the meantime Black hurries to castle, without as yet committing himself in the centre.

4 N—B3

A provocative move played quite a few times by Spassky, challenging Black to plunge into the complexities of 4 ... B—R5+ 5 K—K2 P—Q4! 6 NxP N—B3. Spassky's opponents have all preferred to avoid these complications!

4 .... N—KB3
5 P—K5

5 P—Q4 allows Black to equalise with 5 ... P—Q4 6 B—Q3 (or 6 PxP NxP 7 B—B4 B—K3 8 Q—K2 NxN with equality, Spassky-Liberson, XXVII USSR Championship 1960.) 6 ... PxP 7 NxP NxN 8 BxN B—Q3 9 0—0 Spassky-Najdorf, Olympiad 1962, when Black can equalise by 9 ... 0—0! (not 9 ... N—Q2 10 Q—Q3 as in the actual game.) Naturally Spassky plays a new move to pose new problems.

5 .... N—N5

5 ... N—R4 is probably better since Black would once again threaten 6 ... B—R5+ and thus make it more difficult for White to recover the gambit pawn. After the text the knight is rather left in the air.

6 P—Q4 N—K6

An ignominious end to three tempi! However, if 6 ... B—R5+ 7 K—K2 N—B7? 8 Q—K1, while 6 ... P—KN4? allows the simple 7 NxP.

7 BxN PxB
8 B—B4

With three pieces in play to Black's one, White has gained a clear opening advantage. This stems from Black's decision to avoid complications. Clearly bluff has a role in opening play!

8 .... P—Q3
9 0—0 0—0
10 Q—Q3 N—B3

Forcing White to exchange as 11 QxKP PxP 12 NxP NxN! leaves White with an isolated KP.

11 PxP PxP

A further concession. Black clearly feared that after 11 ... BxP 12 QxP the threat of 13 N—KN5 was very strong. However, 12 ... B—K2! would be an adequate defence, but not 12 ... B—KN5 13 N—KN5 B—R4 14 QN—K4! when 14 ... NxP fails to 15 Q—KR3! B—N3 16 RxP! winning.

12 QR—K1 B—N5
13 RxP K—R1

A confession of failure, 13 ... N—R4 to exchange the powerful bishop looks correct, though 14 N—Q5 would be a strong reply.

14 N—Q5 B—N4

He must not allow 15 NxB NxN 16 N—N5!

15 NxB QxN

16 R—N3

Now Black is hard put to find a reasonable move due to the pressure exerted by White's rooks.

16 ....   Q—R4

Not 16 ... Q—R5 17 R—B4.

17 N—K3   B—Q2

Not 17 ... B—K3 18 BxB PxB 19 RxR+ RxR 20 R—R3 and wins.

18 N—B5   BxN

19 RxB   Q—R5

Grasping his chance for a slight breathing space by threatening the exchange of queens. If 19 ... Q—R3 then 20 R—R3 Q—N3 (20 ... Q—B8+ 21 R—B1) 21 BxP! RxB 22 RxR wins at once.

20 P—B3   Q—K2

There was once again a threat to both his KBP and his KRP (by R—R3).

21 R—K3

From pillar to post!

21 ....   Q—Q2

22 R(3)—B3

Black's king is defenceless. If 22 ... P—B3 then 23 R—R5 P—KR3 24 Q—N6 followed by 25 B—Q3 or 25 R(3)—R3 and a sacrifice on KR6.

22 ....   N—Q1

23 Q—K4!

Now the bishop too is transferred to the attack on KR7.

23 ....   P—KN3

Or 23 .... R—K1 24 Q—R4. His best chance was 23 ... R—B1 24 B—Q3 P—KN3 but White would win by 25 R—B6 making it impossible for Black to defend his KRP by advancing his KBP.

24 Q—R4!

This wins at once.

24 ....   R—KN1

Or 24 ... PxR 25 Q—B6+ and 26 R—N3 mate. 24 ... QxR prolongs it by a move or two (25 RxQ PxR 26 Q—B6+ K—N1 27 QxP(5) followed by 28 B—Q3.)

25 RxP   Resigns

The final triumph of alternating attacks on KB7 and KR7.

56 Zonal Tournament of Seven, Moscow 1964
Black: Suetin
Sicilian Defence

1 P—K4	P—QB4	3 P—Q4	PxP
2 N—KB3	N—QB3	4 NxP	P—K3

5 N—QB3	Q—B2
6 P—B4?!	P—QR3
7 B—K3	P—QN4
8 NxN	QxN
9 B—K2	

Inviting Black to win the KP. 9 B—Q3 or 9 P—QR3 are playable, but seem unlikely to give White any advantage.

9	P—N5?

After this encounter the text has never been seen again in a serious master game! The crucial line is 9 ... B—R6! which (in the middle sixties) was thought to give Black a clear advantage. However, Suetin lost a game to Bogdanovic in the 1967 Yugoslavia-USSR match after 10 B—Q4! BxP 11 NxP BxR 12 BxB PxN 13 BxP QxP 14 0—0 RxP 15 B—Q3 Q—K6+ 16 K—R1 B—N2 17 BxR N—R3 18 BxP. White has strong bishops and the safer king. Moreover, Boleslavsky suggested that White could improve on his play by 16 R—B2. However, typically, an improvement in Black's play has also been found recently by Moiseev, namely 13 ... N—B3! 14 BxR NxP or 14 BxN R—KN1. Hence 6 P—B4 remains dubious but enterprising. and therefore it is marked above with the question mark given first!

10 B—B3!	PxN
11 P—K5	PxP
12 R—QN1	

Not 12 BxQ PxR(Q) and Black gets too much material for the queen.

12	B—N5+

Suetin improves on a game Ivkov-Szabo, Sarajevo 1963 which continued 12 ... Q—B6+ 13 B—Q2 Q—R6 14 BxR B—B4 15 Q—B3 QxP 16 K—K2 P—QR4 17 Q—KN3! B—R3+ 18 K—B3

QxQ+ 19 PxQ B—R6 20 BxP BxR 21 BxB with a won ending for White.

13. K—B2	Q—B6
14 BxR	P—B3

Black has the strong pawn at QN7 as compensation for the exchange, but unfortunately he cannot continue simple development with 14 ... N—K2. After 15 B—K4 White threatens 16 Q—Q4 (to exchange queens) followed up by KR—Q1 and B—Q4 winning the advanced pawn.

15 B—K4!	N—R3

Black's last chance of complicating the issue was the consistent 15 ... PxP, but after 16 Q—R5+ P—N3 (16 ... K—B1 17 PxP) 17 BxP+ PxB 18 QxR Black does not have perpetual check as is shown by Boleslavsky's line 18 ... QxP+ 19 K—N3 PxP+ 20 BxP Q—Q6+ 21 K—R4 B—K2+ 22 B—N5 BxB+ 23 KxB Q—B4+ 24 K—R4 P—N4+ 25 K—R5.

·16 PxP	QxKBP
17 Q—R5+!	

This move is equally strong now as it makes it more difficult for Black to castle.

17	N—B2
18 P—B4!	

Yet another strong move preventing P—Q4 and so making it harder for Black to get his QB into play.

18	P—N3
19 Q—K2	B—B6
20 B—B3	

A precaution against a possible P—N4.

20	0—0
21 KR—Q1	P—N4

The drawback to Black's position is that his pieces are not very active, so this violent attempt to open a line against the enemy king cannot really hope to succeed.

22 Q—Q3!	PxP
23 B—Q4	BxB+
24 QxB	

With the loss of the QNP Black is now faced with an uphill struggle to draw the game.

24	N—K4
25 RxP	NxP
26 QxQ	RxQ
27 R—N8	

The two pawns are not adequate compensation for the exchange as the chronically bad bishop is a mere spectator.

27	R—B1
28 R—QB1	P—Q4

Or 28 ... N—Q3 29 R—N6 N—B4 30 R—B7 with decisive advantage.

29 B—K2	N—Q3
30 R—B6	

An even stronger move was 30 B—N4 but, short of time, Spassky prefers to force an exchange of rooks which also wins a valuable pawn.

30	N—K5+
31 K—K1	B—Q2
32 RxR+	KxR
33 RxRP	K—K2
34 R—R8	

To make room for the advance of the pawn. Incidentally, Spassky avoids the blunder 34 P—QR4 N—B6 35 P—R5? NxB when recapturing loses the rook.

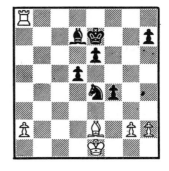

34	K—Q3
35 P—QR4	B—B3
36 R—R7	N—N4
37 P—R5	P—Q5
38 B—B3	P—K4

Suetin goes wrong in the last few minutes of the playing session. He could put up considerably more tenacious resistance in the variation 38 ... B—N4 39 RxP P—K4 40 R—R6+ K—B2 41 R—R5 K—Q3 but after 42 P—R4 White wins.

39 BxB	KxB
40 RxP	P—K5

Or 40 ... K—N4 41 R—R5 P—K5 42 R—B5 followed by 43 RxP combined with the advance of the KRP.

41 P—R6!	Resigns

After 41 ... NxP 42 R—R6+ K—N4 43 RxN! KxR 44 P—R4 and queens one move before the Black king can adequately support the united passed pawns.

57 Zonal Tournament of Seven, Moscow 1964.
White: Geller
Ruy Lopez

1 P—K4	P—K4
2 N—KB3	N—QB3
3 B—N5	P—QR3
4 B—R4	P—Q3
5 0—0	

After Fischer's fine victory over Geller at Bled 1961, this line became the most fashionable variation in the Steinitz Defence Deferred.

5	B—N5
6 P—KR3	B—R4

The piece sacrifice 6 ... P—KR4 is also playable, provided one has confidence and the right preparation!

7 P—B3   N—B3

Geller tried 7 ... Q—B3 against Fischer, but after 8 P—KN4! B—N3 9 P—Q4 White had a very strong initiative.

8 P—Q4	P—QN4
9 B—N3	B—K2

Accepting the pawn sacrifice by 9 ... BxN 10 QxB PxP 11 Q—Q3! PxP 12 NxP gives White a fine game, while 9 ... PxP 10 PxP BxN and now 11 PxB is certainly not good for Black as White has much more control of the centre. An alternative plan is 9 ... Q—Q2 intending P—KN4 (see game No. 43 with Kots).

10 B—K3	0—0
11 QN—Q2	

As if often the case in the Lopez, Black has a slight lead in development which he now exploits by offering a tricky pawn sacrifice.

11 ....   P—Q4!?

12 P—KN4

Geller thought for a total of an hour over this move and his next. Breaking the pin weakens his K side, but that is the correct line provided it is followed up properly.

12	B—N3
13 QPxP	

The soundness of Black's offer is most seriously tested in the variation 13 NxP NxN 14 PxN NxKP 15 P—KB4! NxN 16 QxN B—K5 17 QR—Q1 P—QB3 18 P—B5. Geller's actual choice is much inferior.

13 ....   KNxP

14 N—N1

This was the point of White's last move as the Black QP is now indefensible. However, Black can cheerfully sacrifice it for an attack.

14 ....   Q—B1!

15 N—Q4

White admits the failure of his idea, but changing horses in midstream is rarely good and from now on White (to change the metaphor) goes downhill quickly. If 15 BxP then the pin 15 ... R—Q1 is awkward as the sacrifice 16 BxN RxQ 17 RxR allows 17 ... P—KR4! breaking up the K side. 15 QxP is met by 15 ... N—R4 threatening to win the queen by 16 ... R—Q1. White must therefore retreat, and after 16 Q—Q1 R—Q1 17 QN—Q2 P—R4! Black has many threats.

15 ....   NxP

Black for his part can confidently accept the offer.

16 P—KB4   P—QB4!

17 PxN

Not 17 N—B2 P—B5, nor 17 N—K2 or B3 when Black sacrifices for a fierce attack by 17 ... NxP 18 PxN QxP+.

17 ....   PxN

18 PxP   Q—Q2

19 N—Q2   P—B3!

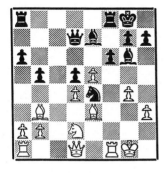

Black has a strong piece at K5 and if White exchanges knights then the bishop will be equally effective on that square. Hence Black plays to bring his rooks into play to intensify his piece pressure on the K side.

20 R—B1   K—R1

21 B—KB4

A tactical error missing Black's subsequent queen sacrifice. 21 N—B3 is met by 21 ... P—B4 and if 22 P—N5? then 22 ... P—B5 winning the KNP so White should try and weaken the force of the coming attack by ex-

changes and play 21 NxN BxN 22 B—KB4.

21 ....   PxP

22 BxP

Clearly not 22 PxP RxB! 23 RxR Q—R2+ 24 K moves Q—K6! with multiple threats.

22 ....   B—N4!

23 R—B7

White has no choice but to go on with his original intention. If 23 NxN BxR 24 N—B5 then Black remains the exchange ahead after 24 ... B—K6+.

23 ....   QxR!

24 BxQ   B—K6+

25 K—N2

Other moves are no better as the next note will show.

25 ....   NxN

26 RxR+   RxR

27 BxP

To eliminate one of the main dangers (B—K5+). If White's king were on R2, then R—B7+ would be the main threat while if it were on R1 Black simply plays R—B8+.

27 ....   R—B7+

28 K—N3   N—B8+

29 K—R4   P—R3

Now the king is threatened with mate in one.

30 B—Q8   R—B1

   Resigns

There is no defence to 31 ... B—B7 mate, e.g. 31 P—N5 B—B7+ 32 K—N4 N—K6 with an almost pure mate (only KB5 is controlled by more than one piece).

58 Zonal Tournament of Seven, Moscow 1964
Black: Korchnoy
Queen's Indian Defence

1	P—Q4	N—KB3
2	P—QB4	P—K3
3	N—KB3	P—QN3

Many leading players avoid the Queen's Indian nowadays as too drawish an opening, but Korchnoy has always shown a predilection for it even in those games such as this one where a draw was not in his interests.

4	P—KN3	B—N2
5	B—N2	B—K2
6	0—0	0—0
7	N—B3	P—Q4

Not a very common line as it goes against Black's expressed strategical concept of controlling the centre by pieces. In recent years Korchnoy has tried to make a fight of it, by the reintroduction of the old 7 ... N—K5 8 Q—B2 NxN 9 QxN and now P—QB4!?

8 PxP

This is a very old move. The popular continuation is 8 N—K5.

8 ....   PxP

Black gets an easier game from 8 ... NxP.

9 N—K5

This move shows the main drawback to Black's last two moves — his unguarded QB means there is a pin on the QP e.g. N—B4 is now possible for White, while if now 9 ... P—B4 then 10 PxP PxP 11 Q—N3 and 12 R—Q1 with great pressure.

9 ....   Q—B1

He guards the bishop. After 9 ... QN—Q2 10 Q—R4 White has

the better of it due to his many threats on the white squares (N—B6, or B—R3 or even NxQP).

10 B—N5   Q—K3

An artificial defence, but after 10 ... P—B3 White opens the centre with advantage by 11 P—K4 PxP 12 NxP and if 12 ... Q—K3 then 13 R—K1 — Bondarevsky-Plater, Moscow 1947.)

11 R—B1

It is a sign of White's advantage that every move he plays produces a new threat. Thus 12 N—N5 now has to be parried. Black must try 11 ... P—B3 when his QBP would come under attack after 12 Q—R4 or 12 P—K4. Instead he tries to force matters and loses quickly.

11	....	P—B4?
12	N—Q3	

Psychologists who have studied chess players' thought patterns point out that the most difficult moves to envisage are those which retreat a well placed piece. Forward towards the enemy is the obvious plan, but the real master is aware of all the possibilities in the position. Thus this modest retreat threatens the murderous 13 N—B4 and wins out of hand. Is it too far-fetched to conclude that Korchnoy did not think of this move at all?

12 .... PxP
13 BxN

Systematically weakening the support of Black's Q4. 13 N—B4 at once was also good e.g. 13 ... Q—K4 14 BxN etc., but not 14 QNxP NxN 15 BxB NxN! 16 BxB NxP+ and 16 ... QxB.

13 .... BxB

After 13 ... PxN 14 BxBP White has an easy technical win

14 NxP!

This forces matters as both 15 N—B7 and 15 NxB+ are threatened (that wretched hanging bishop at QN2 again!)

14 .... BxN

15 N—B4 Q—Q3

Giving up the queen is equally hopeless. (15 ... BxB 16 NxQ BxR 17 NxR B—R6 18 Q—Q3! KxN 19 Q—K4 and the weakness of the long white diagonal is seen all too clearly).

16 NxB

Now Black must lose a lot of material.

16 .... B—N4
Or 16 ... B—Q1 17 N—B4.
17 P—B4 B—Q1
18 N—B3!
The QP is pinned!
18 .... N—R3
Or 18 ... Q—B4 19 N—R4!
19 BxR Q—N1
20 N—Q5 QxB
21 QxP N—B4
22 P—QN4 N—K3
23 Q—Q3 R—K1
24 P—K4 Resigns

One of the most crushing ·wins ever played in games between world class players.

59 Amsterdam Interzonal 1964
Black: A. Foguelman
Caro-Kann

1 P—K4 P—QB3
2 P—Q4 P—Q4
3 N—QB3 PxP
4 NxP B—B4
5 N—N3 B—N3
6 B—QB4

Two rounds before, Tal had played 6 KN—K2 against Foguelman. Obviously Spassky does well to vary as after the post-

mortem with Tal, Foguelman would be well prepared to meet that line.

6 .... N—B3
7 KN—K2 P—K3
8 P—KR4 N—R4

An opening innovation, but a bad one. Black had to play 8 ... P—KR3 9 N—B4 B—R2 with an uncomfortable but tenable position which had already occured in the Tal-Botvinnik match in 1960.

9 NxN BxN
10 P—KB3

With the threat of 11 P—KN4 B—N3 12 P—R5, while if 10 ... B—K2 then 11 N—B4 is a strong counter e.g. 11 ... BxP+ 12 K—B1 B—N3 13 NxB forcing 13 ... BPxN as if 13 ... RPxN then 14 P—KN3! winning material.

10 .... P—KR3
11 N—B4 B—Q3
12 Q—K2!

12 NxB Q—R4+ would ease the tension, whereas the text threatens the bishop sacrifice 13 BxP! PxB (13 ... BxN 14 B—B8+) 14 NxP and if 14 ... Q—K2 to avoid a double check, then simply 15 NxP+ K moves 16 NxB.

12 .... BxN

A terrible concession to have to make as his black squares now remain very weak.

13 BxB N—Q2
Or 13 ... QxP 14 B—K5.
14 P—KN4 B—N3
15 0—0—0

This renews the threat of 16 BxP. Black would like to castle but then White can make use of his advanced K side pawns to open lines quickly for an attack, e.g. 15 ... 0—0 16 P—R5 B—R2 17 P—N5 and if 17 ... PxP then 18 P—R6 PxB 19 PxP KxP 20 RxB+ KxR 21 Q—R2+ and 22 R—N1+ and mates. 15 ... Q—K2 to prepare castling on the other side is met by 16 Q—Q2 when 16 ... 0—0—0? would lose at once to 17 Q—R5. Hence Black has to play his queen to an exposed square. 15 ... Q—R4 allows 16

BxP!

15 .... Q—B3
16 B—Q6 0—0—0
17 B—QN3

A useful waiting move to prevent 17 ... N—N3 attacking both bishops. Now Black has no useful move as moving his knight loses the KNP after 18 B—K5.

17 .... P—KR4
18 Q—K3

Now 18 ... PxP 19 PxP RxP? loses to 20 P—N5, while threats of 19 B—K5 or P—Q5 loom up due to the unprotected QRP.

18 .... KR—N1
19 B—KB4

The changing of the guard! 20 B—N5 has to be met.

19 .... Q—K2
20 P—Q5!

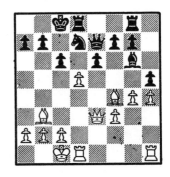

Now if 20 ... Q—B4 then 21 PxKP QxQ+ 22 BxQ PxP 23 BxRP with an easy win while the KP and QRP are both threatened.

20 .... N—B4
21 P—Q6 Resigns

After 21 ... NxB+ 22 RPxN Q moves 23 QxRP is decisive.

60 Amsterdam Interzonal 1964
Black: Tringov
Ruy Lopez

1 P—K4	P—K4
2 N—KB3	N—QB3
3 B—N5	P—QR3
4 B—R4	N—B3
5 0—0	B—K2
6 R—K1	P—QN4
7 B—N3	0—0
8 P—B3	P—Q3
9 P—KR3	N—QR4
10 B—B2	P—B4

Some chess players regard this sequence of moves as the quintessence of accuracy. One must remember that not everyone agrees. I personally like the jaundiced comment of Tarrasch, "One might say that both sides stand badly."

11 P—Q4	N—Q2

The Keres system, very popular in the early sixties, but little favoured nowadays. Black intends to capture twice in the centre and then to activate his KB by B—B3; then, as compensation for some weak points in the centre, he has QB4 and K4 as good squares for his knights.

12 QN—Q2	BPxP
13 PxP	N—QB3
14 P—Q5	

This cuts across Black's plan, but 14 N—N3 P—QR4 15 B—Q3 is a more fluid line.

14	N—N5
15 B—N1	P—QR4
16 P—QR3	N—R3
17 P—QN4!	

Using the pin on the QR file to rob Black's knights of QB4. The move also fixes the Black QNP on a square where it can be attacked by B—Q3, Q—K2 and then even by N—QN1—QB3.

17	PxP
18 PxP	N—N3

Black, however, gets in first and by unpinning his knight threatens the QNP. As 19 B—R3? is a self-pin allowing 19 ... NxP White has to guard with his queen. This means deferring any pressure by Q—K2 and White cannot be said to have achieved very much, which is either an argument for the alternative plan at move fourteen or else a confirmation of Tarrasch's comment of many years ago!

19 Q—N3	B—Q2
20 B—Q3	Q—N1
21 N—B1	N—B5!

Over half way to the time control and not much has happened yet. White cannot derive any advantage from 22 BxN as he thereby loses his own QNP and concedes the two bishops. Hence he decides to defend the QNP with his rook, giving up the QR file but freeing his queen.

22 R—N1	

There was also the tactical point that Black threatened 22 ... N—B4! 23 RxR NxQ 24 RxR RxR and Black has the initiative on the Q side.

22	R—B1
23 N—N3	P—N3

A standard defensive move in the Lopez, but there was no real call for it here. Black should carry on with his Q side play. Thus 23 ... N—B2, threatening R—R5 at a later stage, was quite feasible as 24 BxN PxB 25 QxP would give Black a fine position by 25 ... N—N4 followed by 26 ... N—B6.

24 Q—Q1   N—N3

A clear sign that he has "lost the thread". 24 ... N—B2 to play N—K1 and then R—R5 was still correct.

25 N—N5

At last White is able to make an aggressive gesture on the K side.

25 ....   R—B2
26 P—B4   Q—Q1

Falling back on the defensive, as to allow P—B5 would give White a formidable attack by transferring his rooks to the KB file.

27 N—B3   P—B3

Further hedgehog tactics, but 27 ... PxP 28 BxP would give White a very active position with his threat of P—K5.

28 K—R2   N—R5
29 Q—Q2   QR—B1
30 R—B1   B—B1
31 P—B5

A committal move but, as 30 ... B—R3 was a threat, the decision was partly forced.

31 ....   P—N4

Continuing his "Maginot Line" strategy.

32 R—R1

Before transferring all his forces to the K side White takes the opportunity to force Black into a more passive position on the other wing. The threat is 33 RxN so Black must either undouble his rooks by 32 ... R—R1 or retreat his awkwardly placed knight.

32 ....   N—N1
33 Q—K2   B—K1

To keep the queen out of R5. He always has N—B6 as a defence of his QNP.

34 B—K3

For the connoisseur of the "Guiness Book of Records" this is the first move by this bishop! Tringov was now in time trouble and instead of sticking to his waiting tactics by a move like 34 ... P—KR3 he plays an inaccurate move that allows White to make a very promising sacrifice.

34 ....   Q—Q2?
35 QBxP!   PxB
36 NxNP

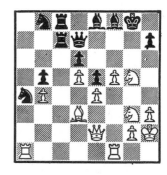

With Black's knights far away on the other side of the board White still has local superiority of material in the vicinity of the Black king and threatens N—K6 or N—R5 in conjunction with the advance of the KBP. Thus if now 36 ... B—B2 then 37 BxP N—B6 38 BxQ NxQ 39 BxR NxN 40 KxN RxB 41 KR—B1 wins.

36 ....   B—R3
37 N—K6   R—B6

Not 37 ... R—B8 38 Q—N4+ K—R1 39 Q—R4! nor 37 ... B—B5 38 NxB PxN 39 RxP.

38 Q—N4+   K—R1

Or 38 ... K—B2 39 Q—R5+ winning the bishop.

39 Q—R4   RxB

Or 39 ... B—N2 40 P—B6.

40 QxB   Q—B2

The only defence against mate on B8 (or on N7 after 40 ... B—B2?)

41 P—B6

41 N—R5 also wins e.g. 41 ... B—Q2 (41 ... QxN 42 Q—N7 mate) 42 N—N5 Q—K2 (the only square to prevent 43 Q—B6+ or 43 QxP mate) 43 P—B6 or 41 ... R—B2 42 P—B6 R—R2 43 Q—N7+ etc.

41 ....   RxN

Removing one of the potential attackers. If 41 ... K—N1 then 42 Q—N7+ QxQ 43 PxQ B—B2 44 RxB! KxR 45 R—B1+ K—K2 46 R—B8 etc.

42 KxR   Q—N3+

43 QxQ   BxQ

The mating threats have gone but the ending is lost because of the strong passed pawn.

44 P—B7   N—Q2

45 QR—B1!   R—B1

46 R—B6!   Resigns

Now the passed pawn dies and White reverts to mating threats based on his powerful knight which denies g7 as a flight square for the king e.g. 46 ... BxP 47 NxR or 46 ... RxP 47 R—B8+ and mates.

61 Amsterdam Interzonal 1964
Black: Benko
Caro-Kann

1 P—K4   P—QB3

2 P—Q4   P—Q4

3 N—QB3   PxP

4 NxP   N—Q2

The careful line of play intending KN—B3 without have to fear a doubled pawn. However, the assymetrical position resulting from 4 ... N—B3 5 NxN+ NPxN is not without counter-chances for Black, whereas the text generally leaves him with a passive position.

5 B—QB4   KN—B3

6 N—N5   P—K3

7 Q—K2   N—N3

8 B—N3

White's last move indicates that he is playing for tactical chances (such as sacrifices on KB7 or K6) especially if Black should play either knight to Q2 to challenge the White knight which will soon appear on K5. 8 B—Q3 is objectively better.

8 ....   P—KR3

A well known trap here is 8 ... QxP? 9 KN—B3 and 10 N—K5 winning the KBP, since Black cannot develop by 9 ... B—N5+ because of 10 P—QB3! BxP+ 11 K—B1 and material is lost.

9 QN—B3

Other knight moves would allow Black to capture the QP with impunity.

9 ....   P—B4

This is rather dubious. 9 ... P—QR4! gives Black good counterplay.

10 B—K3

Objectively this must be regarded as less accurate than 10 B—KB4 which should deny Black's queen the use of QB2 once the Q file becomes open (10 ... PxP 11 0—0—0 or 10 ... QN—Q4 11 B—K5 Q—R4+ 12 N—Q2! PxP 13 0—0—0 followed by 14 N—B4 and 15 N—B3). However, Spassky was following

10 ....   Q—B2

An improvement, on the game with Tal where, after 10 ... QN—Q4 11 0—0—0, White won in a complicated struggle.

11 N—K5   B—Q3
12 KN—B3   0—0
13 0—0

Castling long was quite feasible and was possibly stronger as the bayonet attack P—KN4—N5 would be very dangerous for Black. However, in view of the strong competition for places in the Candidates' event and the fact that only three of the five Soviet players (Bronstein, Shtein, Smyslov, Spassky himself and Tal) could qualify — there was an upper limit on the number of qualifiers from any one country — Spassky could not be blamed for choosing a more solid build-up.

13 ....   QN—Q4
14 P—B3   P—QN3
15 QR—Q1   B—N2

Perhaps 15 ... NxB first was better. The open KB file resulting from 16 PxB was not very threatening and White cannot play the natural attacking move N—KN5.

16 B—B1

Now Spassky keeps it tense by avoiding the exchange.

16 ....   QR—Q1
17 KR—K1   KR—K1
18 P—QR3

Apparently intending P—QB4 but in fact the follow-up is some-what different from the normal plan of P—QB4, PxP and P—QN3 intending B—N2.

18 ....   Q—B1
19 B—R4   R—B1
20 PxP

Giving up the support of his knight and opening the Q file along which Black can play for exchanges. By maintaining the tension with 20 B—B2 White could have increased Black's problems.

20 ....   PxP

There seems nothing wrong with 20 ... BxP but then in the ending White would be able to force a passed QBP, whereas experience has shown that the pawn formation Black now creates forms a more effective defence against a Q side majority. In the present case White will experience difficulties in forming a passed pawn unless he is pre-pared to exchange all the pawns on the Q side which would in-crease the prospects of a draw. Moreover, the text robs White's pieces of the use of Q4.

21 B—QN5

The next few moves do not pro-duce anything constructive for White, but with his strong cen-tralised position he can afford to await developments.

21 ....   N—N3
22 B—Q3   Q—B2

22 ... Q—B1 to play Q—R1 and then capture on his K4 looks

more promising.

| 23 P—KR3 | B—Q4 |
| 24 P—B4 | |

At last returning to the usual plan outlined in the note to move 18.

| 24 .... | B—R1 |
| 25 P—QN3 | QN—Q2 |

Hastening to exchange pieces before White plays B—N2 and then N—N4 (or first B—N1 and Q—B2) with attacking chances.

26 B—B2

White has to play this preparatory move, for if 26 B—N2 then 26 ... NxN 27 NxN Q—N2!

26	NxN
27 NxN	BxN
28 QxB	QxQ
29 RxQ	B—K5

Black has exchanged pieces so as to play this interesting tactical blow attacking the defender of Q1. However, White still keeps a better ending.

| 30 RxR | RxR |
| 31 BxB | |

Quite safe!

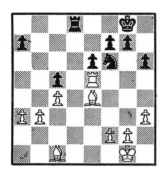

| 31 .... | R—Q8+ |
| 32 K—R2 | RxB |

Now Black realises that his intended 32 ... N—Q2 is met by 33

B—N2 NxR 34 BxN and White keeps his two bishops for the rook e.g. 34 ... R—K8 35 P—B3 P—B4 36 B—N3! R—K6 37 B—B6 RxP 38 P—QR4 and White wins the ending.

33 B—B6

This wins the QBP and so gives White a much superior ending.

33	R—QR8
34 RxBP	RxP
35 B—R4	

And his bishop is also a good mobile piece.

| 35 .... | N—K5 |
| 36 R—B7 | |

Not the most accurate play as the players hurry to get in the last few moves before the time control. White should play 36 R—B8+ K—R2 37 R—B7 N—B6 and now not 38 RxRP because of 38 ... NxB 39 PxN R—QB6 with good drawing chances, but the aggressive 38 B—K8 with play on both sides of the board — passed QBP and threats against the white squares on the K side as in the game.

36 .... N—Q7

Black too goes wrong. 36 ... K—B1 to rob the bishop of K8 is correct as 37 RxRP is met by 37 ... N—B4! (threat 38 ... NxP) 38 R—R8+ K—R2 39 B—B6 RxR 40 BxR NxP and White may not have a clear win. White of course has other possibilities such as 37 P—B3 or 37 P—B5! but at least Black would be able to put up a fight.

37 B—K8! NxNP

Not 37 ... P—B3 or 4 as White then mates or wins the rook by 38 B—N6 K—B1 39 R—B7+ K—N1 (39 ... K—K1 40 RxRP+) 40 R—K7.

38 BxP+   K—R2
39 P—R4

Threatening a new mating net by 40 P—R5 and 41 B—N6+. After a slow start the game has certainly shown some lively play later on!

39 ....   P—KR4
40 BxKP   N—Q5

The threat was 41 B—B5+ K—N1 (41 ... K—R3 42 R—R6+) 42 B—N6! etc.

41 B—Q5

The sealed move. White renews his threat of B—K4+ and wins without much trouble by urging forward his passed QBP.

41 ....   K—N3
42 R—Q7   N—B4

Or 42 ... K—B3 43 R—B7+ K—N3 (to save the KNP) 44 R—B4! threatening 45 B—B7+ or 45 B—K4+ as well as 45 RxN.

43 P—B5   K—B3
44 P—B6   N—K2
45 P—B7   R—B6

Black has succeeded in covering the queening square twice, but RxN will soon destroy a key defender.

46 B—N7

Not 46 R—Q6+? K—K4 47 R—B6 RxR 48 BxR K—Q3!

46 ....   P—R4
47 RxN   KxR
48 P—B8(Q)   RxQ
49 BxR   P—R5
50 B—R6   Resigns

62 Belgrade 1964
Black: Zuidema
Ruy Lopez

1 P—K4   P—K4
2 N—KB3   N—QB3
3 B—N5   B—B4
4 P—B3

This is better than 4 0—0 when 4 ... N—Q5 leaves Black with near equality, e.g. 5 NxN BxN 6 P—QB3 B—N3 7 P—Q4 P—QR3 8 B—R4 P—Q3 9 N—R3 (or 9 B—K3 N—B3 10 PxP PxP 11 QxQ+ BxQ, Tolush-Spassky, Leningrad 1956) 9 ... N—B3 10 B—B2 B—K3 11 B—N5 P—KR3 12 BxN QxB 13 P—Q5 B—Q2 14 N—B4 B—B2 (Portisch-Spassky, 1961).

4 ....   N—B3
5 P—Q4   B—N3

6 0—0   0—0
7 B—N5   P—KR3
8 B—KR4   P—Q3

After 8 ... P—N4 the sacrifice 9 NxNP is very strong as after 9 ... PxN (9 ... NxKP 10 N—B3) 10 BxP White already threatens 11 P—KB4.

9 P—R4

In a game against Smyslov played in 1958, Spassky successfully defended the position after 9 BxN PxB 10 PxP PxP 11 QN—Q2 B—N5 12 N—B4 P—N4! 13 B—N3 NxP when the further exchanges 14 QxQ KRxQ 15 KNxP B—K3 left it equal.

9 ....   P—QR4

Not 9 ... P—R3 10 KBxN PxB
11 P—R5! B—R2 12 PxP PxP 13
Q—R4! with advantage.

10 R—K1   PxP

If Black tries to hold the centre
by 10 ... Q—K2 then 11 N—R3
B—N5 12 N—B4 gives White
great pressure e.g. 12 ... P—N4 13
B—N3 N—Q2 14 N—K3 B—R4
15 N—Q5 (Spassky-Quinones,
Amsterdam 1964).

11 KBxN!

The many opening references
so far to Spassky's games show
that he has deep knowledge of
this variation. Now he forms a
concrete plan to give himself
pressure on both sides of the
board. After 11 PxP B—N5 12
KBxN PxB 13 N—B3 Black
might be able to equalise by 13 ....
P—N4 14 B—N3 N—R4! but not
by 13 ... BxN 14 QxB! BxP 15
P—K5! BxP 16 RxB! PxR 17
N—K4 with a powerful attack
(Kavalek-Zuidema, Tel-Aviv
Olympiad, 1964).

11 ....   PxB
12 NxP   R—K1
13 N—Q2

Not 13 NxP Q—Q2 14 BxN
QxN! winning back the pawn
and getting rid of his two main
weaknesses — the doubled QBP
and the pinned knight.

13 ....   P—N4

This weakening cannot be
avoided much longer as White
threatens to play Q—B3 followed
by P—K5 as in the Kavalek game.

14 B—N3   BxN
15 PxB   R—N1
16 P—B3!

At first sight Black has a fair
game with his pressure on the
QN file, but the text move
making White's bishop available
for action on the Q side shows

that the advantage is still clearly
with White.

16 ....   B—K3

Not 16 ... RxP 17 N—B4 and
18 NxRP when the QRP will advance quickly.

17 P—N3   R—N5
18 B—B2   Q—R1
19 R—QB1   KR—N1
20 R—B3   Q—N2

Black has concentrated his
forces in the most economical
manner on the enemy QNP, but
White's next two moves show
that this counter-play against one
weakness cannot adequately com-
pensate for the three weak points
in Black's position at QR4, QB3
and KN4.

21 Q—B1!   BxP
22 P—R4!

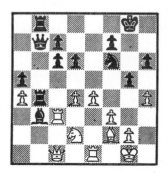

The crucial position. Black
cannot play 22 ... PxP 23 NxB
RxN 24 RxR QxR 25 QxRP
N—R2 26 P—K5! when the
threats of 27 P—K6 or 27 BxP
followed by 28 B—B6 give White
a winning attack, nor should he
try 22 ... BxP 23 PxP PxP 24
P—K5! N—Q4 (24 ... N—R2 25
N—K4 R—N8 26 Q—K3 RxR+
27 BxR with a strong attack) 25

N—K4! NxR 26 QxP+ K—B1 27
Q—R6+ K—K1 (27 ... K—K2 28
PxP+ and if 28 ... K—Q2 29
N—B5+ winning the queen) 28
N—B6+ K—Q1 29 Q—R8+
K—K2 30 PxP mate. 22 ... N—R2
looks the best defence, but after
23 PxP PxP 24 NxB RxN 25
RxR QxR 26 QxBP Q—N3
White can keep the advantage
either by 27 Q—Q7 or by 27
R—B1 QxQ 28 RxQ R—N5 (28...
R—N2 29 R—R6) 29 RxP RxP
30 R—B6 and the QP will prove
a more effective threat than the
QRP, because of the great scope
of White's bishop compared to
the offside knight.

22	B—K3
23 PxP	PxP
24 N—B4!	N—R2
25 NxRP	Q—N3
26 NxP	R—N8

Black had relied on this when
playing his 22nd move. However,

Spassky now has a neat reply that
forces a winning ending.

27 P—Q5!	RxQ
28 KRxR	Q—N7
29 NxR	BxP

A slightly better chance was 29
... QxN 30 PxB P—QB4 shutting
out the rooks. However, after 31
PxP+ KxP 32 R—Q1 and if
necessary 33 R(3)—Q3 White
wins the QP and ultimately the
game. However, now the QRP
decides matters much more
expeditiously.

| 30 PxB | QxN |
| 31 P—R5! | |

The QBP can wait. It is important to push the passed pawn so
as to reduce Black's chances of
blockading it.

| 31 .... | Q—R1 |
| 32 R—R1 | N—B3 |

Or 32 ... Q—R3 33 R—B6

| 33 P—R6 | NxP |
| 34 R—N3 | Resigns |

1966-69 SECOND TIME ROUND

The 1966 match with Petrosian was a great disappointment. It started very ominously with no, less than six draws and Spassky's main hope — that the champion's closed defences to the King Pawn would not work out too well — was not realised until as late as the 13th game when the challenger scored his first win. In the second half of the match however, Spassky did press very hard only to see the wily Armenian slip out of trouble time and again, often with the help of an exchange sacrifice. Spassky's own defences to the Queens Pawn creaked a little towards the end, and after levelling the score by winning the 19th game he went behind again in the 20th in a poorly handled Nimzoindian. This was a useful lesson to be borne in mind for the second chance in 1969.

1966 and 1967 were rather quiet years after the intense activity of the World Championship qualifying cycle, but all this time Bondarevsky and Krogius were preparing their charge for the next time round, and Spassky duly won the 1968 Candidates' Matches just as convincingly as three years before. He was particularly severe on Larsen and Geller.

Korchnoy's comment at the end of the final match seems worth quoting, "Spassky beat me decisively and my only consolation is that I held the advantage at various stages notably in the opening ... but Spassky's superiority in the middle game was so great that it simply cancelled out all my efforts. Spassky at the present time is superior to all his contemporaries and has proved this by his more than convincing victories over the strongest grandmasters in the world. I do not doubt for a minute that we are going to have a new world champion."

Shianovsky and Lazarev also gave a good description of Spassky's play when they wrote: "Spassky's decisive victories seem due to his greater consistency. Possibly he makes as many mistakes as his opponents — more in analysing variations, certainly fewer in assessing the position and in the choice of the correct plan. However he makes far fewer serious errors than his opponents."

Finally, as Bondarevsky pointed out, Spassky had overcome the deficiencies in his attitude to chess as a competitive sport. In the XXVIII Soviet Championship in 1961 Spassky offered a draw on eleven separate occasions and was refused every time. Nowadays he just plays on and says nothing whether he feels that he stands worse or not.

One other concrete indication of the new psychological attitude which helped in his second match with Petrosian was the fact that he did not analyse the game with his opponent when it was over. Obviously he felt that such post-mortems could unconsciously reveal too much to an opponent with whom he had to cross swords the following day.

63 5th match game, Candidates 1965
Black: Keres
Ruy Lopez

1	P—K4	P—K4
2	N—KB3	N—QB3
3	B—N5	P—QR3
4	B—R4	N—B3
5	0—0	B—K2
6	R—K1	P—QN4
7	B—N3	P—Q3
8	P—B3	0—0
9	P—KR3	N—QR4
10	B—B2	P—B4
11	P—Q4	Q—B2
12	QN—Q2	B—Q2
13	N—B1	BPxP
14	PxP	QR—B1
15	N—K3	KR—K1
16	P—QN3	

Restricting the mobility of the QN and preparing a strong fianchetto.

16 ....   PxP

A favourite scheme with Keres which introduces piece pressure on the centre.

17 NxP   B—B1

18 B—N2   Q—Q1

To threaten the KP as 18 ... NxP loses to 19 N—Q5 or even stronger 19 P—QN4 first to rob the Black queen of the QB4 square.

19 N(4)—B5   BxN

Nor is 19 ... NxP playable here. After 20 Q—N4 N—KB3 21 N—R6+ K—R1 22 NxP+ K—N1 23 BxN QxB 24 QxB P—N3 (24 ... QxN 25 BxP+!) White wins with 25 B—K4.

20 NxB

20 PxB can be met by 20 ... P—Q4 and if 21 BxN QxB 22 NxP (22 QxP RxN) 22 ... RxR+ 23 QxR Q—Q1 with good play on the black squares. Now however 20 ... P—Q4 is strongly met by 21 P—K5.

20 ....   P—N3
21 N—K3   B—N2

Not 21 ... NxP? 22 Q—Q4.

22 Q—Q2   N—N2

Not 22 ... NxP 23 BxN RxB (23 ... BxB 24 QxB RxB 25 N—N4!) 24 BxB KxB 25 N—N4 or 25 N—Q5 with a strong attack in which R—K8+ figures in many variations after 25 ... RxR 26 RxR. However, the text is the wrong way of redeploying his off-side knight. 22 ... N—B3 23 QR—Q1 R—K3! still refusing to swallow the poisoned bait on K5 was the line to give Black near equality.

23 P—QN4!

Now the knight is still badly placed.

23 ....   Q—K2

To give his knight Q1.

24 P—B3

Still not strictly forced, but a necessary preliminary to playing B—N3.

24 ....   Q—B1

Not 24 ... N—Q1 25 QR—Q1 R—B3 26 N—Q5. The weak QP and the weak squares in its vicinity cause Black to go into deep defence.

25 B—N3   N—Q1
26 QR—Q1   R—B3
27 R—QB1

27 K—R2 first was more accurate when 27 ... Q—K2 is met by 28 N—Q5 and 27 ... N—K3 by 28 N—Q5 N—Q2 29 R—QB1 KR—B1 30 BxB KxB 31 Q—N2+ K—N1 32 RxR RxR 33 R—QB1 penetrating Black's position along the QB file.

27 ....   Q—K2

Getting his queen back into play as 28 N—Q5 is met by 28 ... NxN 29 PxN RxR!

28 K—R2   Q—Q2
29 N—Q5

White allows simplification whereas 29 B—Q5 NxB 30 NxN

would keep up the pressure.

29 ....   NxN

30 BxN

30 BxB KxB 31 BxN would deny Black the chance indicated in the next note.

30 ....   RxR
31 RxR   Q—K2

31 ... BxB 32 QxB Q—K2 was slightly better.

32 BxB   KxB
33 Q—B3+

A second inaccuracy. 33 Q—Q4+ K—N1 34 R—B8 N—K3 35 BxN and 36 RxR wins the QP and should give a win in the long run as White's king is not open to checks in the resulting queen ending.

33 ....   K—N1

34 P—B4   N—K3
35 P—N3   N—N2

Now that the knight has finally reached a reasonable square Black can put up stiff resistance by 35 ... Q—R2 threatening 36 ... Q—B7+. Instead Keres, in time trouble, moves the knight to a poorer square where it no longer prevents an entry by the enemy queen.

36 Q—B7   Q—B3

Or 36 ... N—R4 37 Q—N6
Q—B3 (37 ... N—B3? 38 R—B7)
38 R—B2 and the Black pawns
begin to fall.

37 R—B2	R—KB1
38 Q—N6	

With decisive effect.

38	P—N4
39 PxP	QxP
40 QxRP	Q—K4

41 QxNP	N—K3

Or 41 ... N—R4 42 Q—Q3.

42 Q—B1	K—N2
43 Q—B5	QxQ

This was the sealed move but
Keres resigned during the
adjournment.

One of those games that gives
the impression that the Lopez is
well nigh a forced win for White!

64 10th match game, Candidates 1965
White: Keres
King's Indian Defence

This was the last game of the
match and with Spassky leading
by five points to four, Keres had
to play for a win. He had had
little success in the Lopez,
whereas in the eigth game he had
won in a Nimzoindian in only 25
moves! Hence the choice of
opening move. Spassky in turn
puts a bold front on it and
instead of the Queen's Gambit in
which he has scored many
creditable draws against leading
grandmasters, chooses an
aggressive reply.

1 P—Q4	N—KB3
2 P—QB4	P—KN3
3 N—QB3	B—N2
4 P—K4	P—Q3
5 P—B4	

The double-edged Four Pawns
Attack in which Keres has a
sharp line prepared.

5	P—B4
6 P—Q5	0—0
7 N—B3	P—K3
8 B—K2	PxP
9 BPxP	

An unusual reply. 9 KPxP is
usual as now Black has a powerful move outflanking White's
centre.

9	P—QN4!
10 P—K5!	PxP
11 PxP	N—N5
12 B—KB4	

Keres' new move. 12 B—N5 is a
complicated alternative whose
main disadvantage from White's
point of view is that it has been
analysed a lot and so has no surprise value. 12 BxP NxP 13 0—0
leaves White with a slight advantage, but is much too tame for
the present circumstances.

12	N—Q2

Still inviting White to come at him. 12 ... P—N5 is given as better by Boleslavsky but the position remains very complicated after 13 N—K4 N—Q2 15 P—K6.

13 P—K6   PxP

13 ... QN—K4 was the safe move but Spassky's attitude throughout the game is not to fear complications. The drawback to the text is that it frees White's Q5 square.

14 PxP   RxB

Spassky thought for 35 minutes here. The text is certainly best as after 14 ... N—N3 15 QxQ RxQ White has either 16 P—K7 R—K1 17 B—Q6 or 16 P—KR3 P—N5 17 N—QN5 and Black has a struggle to equalise.

15 Q—Q5

Winning the exchange at the cost of the initiative.

15 ....   K—R1

16 QxR

Or 16 0—0—0 R—N1 17 Q—Q6 B—KR3! and White's threat of 18 QxR has been scotched by the discovered check 18 ... R—Q5. Nor, in this, does White achieve anything by 17 PxN B—N2 18 QxP because of 18 ... P—N5 19 N—Q5 R—B4.

16 ....   N—N3

17 QxP

White could retain the KP by 17 Q—N8 or 17 Q—B6 but after 17 ... N—K6! White could not castle and his king is exposed.

17 ....   BxP

18 0—0

Not 18 R—Q1 B—Q5!

18 ....   N—K6

19 R—B2

Another crucial decision. If 19 QR—Q1, which Keres long considered, there comes 19 ... NxQR 20 RxN B—Q5+ 21 K—R1 P—N5

22 N—N5 B—Q4! with a counter attack e.g. 23 QNxB PxN 24 NxP RxN 25 RxR BxP+ 26 KxB QxR 27 Q—K7 P—R4 or in this 24 Q—R5 .Q—Q3 and Black is quite safe. 19 BxP would leave White a pawn up but after 19 ... NxR 20 RxN R—B2 21 Q—R5 Q—N1 Black's black square control gives him adequate counter play.

19 ....   P—N5

20 N—QN5

Or 20 N—Q1 hoping for 20 ... N—N5 21 N—N5! as actually occured in an Argentinian club game, Bartis-Smetan 1970. Now the threat of 22 QxB+! is very strong and White won after 21 ... RxR 22 NxR QxN 23 BxN N—B1 24 Q—R4! BxP 25 BxB BxR 26 Q—K8+ K—N2 27 Q—B7+. However Spassky's second Bondarevsky had already anticipated this turn of events and gives 20 N—Q1 R—B2! 21 Q—R5 N—N5 22 R—KB1 B—Q5+ 23 K—R1 (23 NxB QxN+ 24 K—R1 RxR+ 25 BxR Q—KB5!? 23 ... Q—Q3 24 P—KN3 B—Q4 with a decisive attack. If instead 20 N—QR4 then 20 ... NxN 21 QxN BxNP with a strong passed QBP.

20 ....   R—B2

Here too the harrassment of the queen enables Black to keep the initiative.

21 Q—R5

Or 21 Q—R6 BxNP 22 R—K1 N—N5 23 R—Q1 B—Q4 with good prospects.

21 ....   Q—QN1

Unpinning the knight and threatening mate by 22 ... N—N5 23 R(2)—KB1 RxN. 21 ... BxNP was playable but Black prefers to build up threats in all directions (N(3)—B5).

22 QR—K1   B—Q4

Not 22 ... N—N5 23 B—B1 NxR 24 RxB attacking two pieces or 23 ... RxN 24 PxR.

23 B—B1

His best chance was 23 B—Q3 and after 23 ... N(3)—B5 24 BxN (24 Q—R6 NxKNP! 25 KxN Q—B5 26 R—K8+ B—B1 27 B—K2 Q—N4+ with perpetual check as 28 K—R1 Q—B8+ 29 R—B1? loses to 29 ... RxN) 24 ... NxB 25 Q—R6 R—B3 26 Q—R4 (26 Q—R7 QxN 27 R—K7 N—Q3! 28 RxB N—B2 winning) 26 ... R—B1 when the threats of 27 ... NxP or 27 ... B—QB3 give Black a good game.

23 ....   NxB
24 KRxN   N—B5
25 Q—R6   R—B3
26 Q—R4

Not 26 Q—R7 QxN 27 N—N5 RxR+ 28 RxR when Black wins by the sacrifice 28 ... B—Q5+ 29

K—R1 BxP+! 30 KxB N—K6+ 31 K—N3 NxR+ 32 K—R4 B—B7+ etc.

26 ....   NxP
27 Q—B2?

The losing move. One can understand that Keres was eager to get his queen away from the QR file where she is exposed to regular attack, but he misses a simple point. He should play 27 Q—R5 when Black still has to be careful (27 ... N—B5 28 Q—B7! QxN 29 Q—Q8+ B—N1 30 R—K8). Black would in fact continue 27 ... N—Q6 with some advantage due to his passed QBP, but White is not yet lost and the position remains tense.

27 ....   QxN
28 R—K7

Alas, 28 QxN merely loses a piece to 28 ... RxN discovering an attack on the queen. Keres was now very short of time.

28 ....   N—Q6
29 Q—K2   P—B5

Decisive.

30 R—K8+   R—B1
31 RxR+   BxR
32 N—N5

Or 32 N—Q4 Q—B4 33 Q—K3 B—N2 34 Q—K8+ B—N1.

32 ....   B—B4+
34 K—R1   Q—Q2
35 Q—Q2   Q—K2
36 N—B3

The threat was 36 ... B—K6

36 ....   Q—K6

White lost on time, while Spassky still had over ten minutes left on his clock.

65 6th match game, Candidates 1965
Black: Geller
Ruy Lopez

1 P—K4	P—K4
2 N—KB3	N—QB3
3 B—N5	P—QR3
4 B—R4	N—B3
5 0—0	B—K2
6 R—K1	P—QN4
7 B—N3	0—0
8 P—B3	P—Q3
9 P—KR3	N—Q2

An artificial looking move, but White's slow development gives Black a wide choice of manoeuvring lines.

10 P—Q4	N—N3
11 QN—Q2	B—B3
12 N—B1	R—K1
13 N(1)—R2	

In the 4th game, Spassky had sacrificed a pawn by 13 N—K3 PxP 14 PxP RxP 15 Q—B2 but after 15 ... Q—K1 Black had a satisfactory game which was drawn in 32 moves.

13	PxP
14 PxP	N—R4
15 B—B2	P—B4
16 N—N4	BxN
17 PxB	PxP

Playable, but 17 ... P—N3 would eliminate White's immediate threats and after 18 P—N5 B—N2 Black is quite all right. 17 ... N—B3 18 P—K5 QPxP 19 PxBP QxQ 20 RxQ N—R5 would not leave White with much either.

18 P—N5	B—K2

A bad move whose motivation it is hard to find. 18 ... B—K4 19 NxP R—QB1 would keep it fairly level.

19 P—K5!

It is hard to believe that Geller had not taken this into account. The explanation for his lack of vigilance must be that he regarded 20 BxP+ as out of the question in vies of the fact that the KNP on N5 blocked White's normal attacking follow-up N—KN5+ in the Greek gift sacrifice.

19	B—B1?

He had to play 19 ... PxP 20 NxKP P—N3 (to prevent BxP+) when White would continue 21 N—N4 and then 22 Q—B3 with a strong attack, exploiting if necessary the KR file by P—KN3 and K—N2.

20 BxP+	KxB

Or 20 ... K—R1 21 B—B2 P—N3 22 P—K6! and the KNP becomes too weak.

21 P—N6+	K—N1

Not 21 ... KxP 22 Q—Q3+, while 21 ... PxP transposes into the game after 22 N—N5+.

22 N—N5	BPxP
23 Q—B3!	QxN

Or 23 ... Q—Q2 (23 ... Q—B2 24 Q—R3) 24 P—K6. Black also loses his queen after 23 ... B—K2 24 Q—B7+ K—R1 25 N—K6.

24 BxQ	PxP

(See diagram next column.)

Black has only a slight material deficit with two knights and two pawns for the queen, but his knights are not very actively placed, so White should win

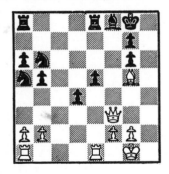

without too much difficulty.

25 QR—B1	R—R2
26 Q—Q3	R—K3
27 P—B4	

Opening the game so as to increase still more the mobility of the queen.

27	N(4)—B5
28 PxP	NxKP
29 QxQP	R—Q2
30 Q—K4	B—K2
31 B—K3	

31 BxB was a simpler way of tackling the technical problem. After 31 ... R(3)xB 32 KR—Q1 or 31 ... R(2)xB 32 R—KB1 Black has little to play for.

| 31 .... | N(3)—B5 |
| 32 QR—Q1 | |

Not strictly necessary as 32 P—N3 N—N7 (32 ... N—Q3 33 Q—Q5) 33 R—B8+ would force further piece exchanges.

32	RxR
33 RxR	NxP
34 Q—Q5	

A more accurate follow-up to the pawn sacrifice was 34 R—Q7.

| 34 .... | K—B2 |
| 35 R—N1 | |

Time trouble uncertainty. The obvious 35 R—KB1+ B—B3 36 P—N4 is a quicker win as 36 ... NxP 37 B—Q4 N—B5 38 Q—Q7+ wins a piece.

35	N(7)—B5
36 B—B2	P—N4
37 R—K1	B—B3

Black too does not find the way to create difficulties. 37 ... P—KN5 would give his tangled pieces more room.

38 K—R1	N—N7
39 R—K3	N(7)—B5
40 R—K2	N—Q3
41 B—Q4	N(3)—B5
42 P—N4	

Spassky sealed this move which creates a Zugzwang position.

| 42 .... | K—K2 |

Or 42 ... P—N3 43 K—N2.

| 43 B—B5+ | K—B2 |
| 44 Q—N7+ | Resigns |

If 44 ... B—K2 then 45 R—KB2+ K—K1 46 Q—B8+, or 44 ... K—N3 45 Q—B8 K—B2 46 Q—B8+ K—N3 47 Q—KN8 R—B3 48 Q—K8+.

Rather a prosaic second half after the exciting 20 BxP+.

66 8th match game, Candidates 1965
Black: Geller
Sicilian Defence

| 1 P—K4 | P—QB4 |

Having scored only half a point in three Lopez games, Geller tries his luck in a more complicated line, especially as he needed a win to keep himself in the match.

2 N—KB3	N—QB3
3 P—Q4	PxP
4 NxP	P—KN3
5 N—QB3	B—N2
6 B—K3	N—B3
7 B—QB4	P—Q3

Now the threat of 8 ... N—KN5 induces White to make the following move that leaves his bishop unguarded.

8 P—B3   N—QR4

An unusual move which has not found any supporters. The appropriate response to White's last move is the complicated 8 ... Q—N3 though after 9 B—QN5 or 9 N—B5 White is generally thought to have the better prospects.

9 B—N3   NxB
10 RPxN

Black has 'won' the two bishops but White's open QR file and strong central knight represent more than adequate compensation.

10 ....   0—0

This gives White an object of attack and 10 ... P—QR3 deferring a decision seems preferable.

11 Q—Q2   P—QR3
12 Q—R4! B—Q2

Too complaisant. 12 ... P—KR4 would hold up White's attack for a few moves.

13 P—R5

Although in such positions the preparatory P—KN4 is often played (perhaps to switch the queen from Q2 to KR2 or to facilitate a sacrifice by N—KB5 followed by NPxP opening the KN file towards Black's king) Spassky correctly realises that in the present situation it is superfluous. Here the direct pawn sacrifice, without preparation, is already very good.

13 ....   R—B1

Or 13 ... NxRP 14 P—KN4, N—B3 15 B—R6 and if 15 ... B—R1 then 16 N—B5! with Q—R2 and N—Q5 in the offing.

14 B—R6   P—K4

The only active plan at Black's disposal, challenging the centralised knight that he could have exchanged off at move 8.

15 KN—K2 B—K3
16 P—KN4 Q—B2

Black has hardly any prospects on the QB file as 16 ... P—Q4 fails to 17 BxB KxB 18 PxP BPxP 19 P—N5 winning a pawn safely Black should try 16 ... BxB 17 QxB Q—K2 18 0—0—0 P—QN4 with a playable game.

17 N—N3   P—QN4
18 P—N4!

Very strong as Black now lacks counter play and will have to defend his weaknesses at QR3 and Q3.

18 ....   Q—N2

Not 18 ... Q—B3 because of 19 BxB KxB 20 PxP BPxP 21 Q—R6+ K—B2 22 P—N5 winning. 18 ... KR—Q1 19 RxP or 18 ... R—R1 19 0—0—0 KR—Q1 20 QR—N1 with the threat of 21 N—B5 look equally hopeless.

19 BxB   KxB
20 PxP   BPxP
21 QxP

Perfectly sound as Black still lacks aggressive moves and the threats to two pawns and a bishop leave Black no choice.

21 ....   R—B3
22 QxP   K—N1
23 KN—K2 B—B1

24 N—Q4   R—QB2

White dominates the whole board and now castles at his leisure with an easy win.

25 0—0—0   R—K2
26 Q—N5   R—N2

Otherwise 27 N—B5 or 27 N—Q5.

27 KR—K1   N—K1

At last a semi-threat from Black but it lets White exchange queens.

28 Q—Q5+   Q—KB2
29 QxQ+   R(2)xQ
30 N—Q5   N—B2
31 NxN   RxN
32 K—Q2   P—KR4
33 PxP   PxP
34 R—KR1   R—KR2
35 QR—KN1+   K—B2
36 R—R4

This blockade kills Black's last hope of achieving something with his passed pawn.

36 ....   R(1)—R1
37 K—K3   R—N2
38 R(1)—KR1 R(2)—R2
39 N—K2

At last the knight that held such a successful watching brief leaves his post to force the win of the KRP.

Black reigns. The two bishops were a completely irrelevant factor.

67 Trade Union Spartakiad, Moscow 1965
Black: Arutiunian
Ruy Lopez

1 P—K4   P—K4
2 N—KB3   N—QB3
3 B—N5   P—QR3
4 B—R4   N—B3
5 0—0   B—K2
6 R—K1   P—QN4
7 B—N3   P—Q3
8 P—B3   0—0
9 P—KR3   P—KR3

The Smyslov system which Spassky himself employed frequently in the sixties.

10 P—Q4   R—K1

11 QN—Q2   B—B1
12 N—B1

In the Keres-Spassky match a game went 12 P—QR3 B—Q2 13 B—R2 P—QR4 14 Q—N3 Q—K2 15 N—B1 P—R5 16 Q—B2 P—N3! and after fianchettoing the bishop, Black had a safe position.

12 ....   B—Q2

Not 12 ... PxP 13 PxP RxP? or 13 ... NxP? because of White's fork B—Q5. It is still a moot point whether the text or 12 ... B—N2 is better.

13 N—N3

In another game from the Keres-Spassky match Keres tried 13 PxP but after 13 ... QNxP Black had a perfectly satisfactory position.

13 ....   P—QR4

The normal move is 13 ... N—QR4 followed by P—B4 and the fianchetto of the KB, but the text is quite playable too.

14 B—Q2   P—R5
15 B—B2   N—QR4
16 P—N3

To prevent the knight coming to B5.

16 ....   RPxP
17 RPxP   P—B3

Simply 17 ... P—B4 at once would leave Black with a good game.

18 B—K3   Q—B2
19 N—Q2   P—B4
20 P—Q5   P—N5

This rigidifies the position and allows White to obtain some play on the Q side as his QB has its diagonal opened from K3 to QR7. 20 ... N—N2 was sufficient to maintain equality.

21 PxP   PxP
22 B—Q3   KR—B1
23 Q—K2

Now White is ready to double rooks on the QR file combined with B—R6. Black hurries to stop B—R6.

23 ....   Q—N2
24 R—R2   B—K2
25 KR—R1   B—Q1
26 N—R5!   N—R2

Obviously he had to avoid the doubled pawn that would result from 27 NxN+, but the text is the wrong way of going about it, as the White knight now constitues a genuine menace. 26 ... NxN is

correct and after 27 QxN there is no immedaite threat of a sacrifice on KR6.

27 Q—B3   N—B1

Presumably Spassky's inexperienced Armenian opponent (all Armenian surnames end in the stressed syllable 'yan' — Petrosian, Mikoyan, Khachaturian, Grigorian) thought he had consolidated and could meet 28 Q—N3 by 28 ... N—N3. However, he is now swept off the board by a hurricane of sacrifices.

28 RxN!!

To remove the defensive KB from the board.

28 ....   BxR

If 28 ... RxR to retain his KB, then 29 RxR BxR 30 BxP B—Q1 31 BxP with two pawns for the exchange and strong threats such as 32 B—B6 or 32 B—KR6 followed by N—B6+.

29 RxB!   RxR
30 BxP   N—R2

Not 30 ... PxB 31 Q—B6 and mate on KN7. Meanwhile there was a threat of 31 N—B6+ K—R1 32 Q—R5 as well as the simple capture of the KNP.

31 NxP   P—B4

The threat was 32 Q—N3 and king moves are no better e.g. 31 ... K—R1 32 N—R5 R—KN1 33 QxP B—B3 34 Q—K6 B—K1 35 QxQP! BxN 36 QxKP+ R—N2 37 BxR+ and 38 QxB with four pawns for the exchange, or 31 ... K—B1 32 N—B5+ K—K1 33 NxP+ winning the queen.

32 PxP

Not 32 Q—N3 P—B5!

(See diagram next column.)

32 ....   K—R1
33 N—R5   R—KN1
34 P—B6!   Resigns

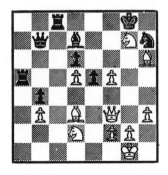

Both 35 B—N7+ and 35 P—B7 are murderous threats, e.g. 34 ... R(4)—R1 35 B—N7+ RxB 36 PxR+ K—N1 37 Q—K4! N—N4 Q—N6 and 29 N—B6 mate.

68 Trade Union Spartakiad, Moscow 1965
White: Mukhitdinov
Sicilian Defence

1 P—K4	P—QB4		
2 N—KB3	P—Q3		
3 B—N5+	N—B3		

Probably the most accurate answer to Sokolsky's favourtie move as after 3 ... B—Q2 4 BxB+ QxB the late Soviet master suggested the ingenious 5 P—B4 followed by 6 P—Q3 putting his central pawns on the white squares after his white square bishop has been exchanged. Then White has a good grip on the centre without conceding much counter play to Black.

4 P—Q4	PxP
5 QxP	B—Q2
6 BxN	BxB
7 N—B3	

A straightforward developing system that gives White good piece play at the expense of conceding the two bishops.

7	N—B3
8 B—N5	P—K3
9 0—0—0	B—K2

10 KR—K1	0—0
11 BxN	

Too precipitate a move. White does better to keep this bishop and aim for a gradual K side attack, e.g. 11 K—N1 Q—R4 12 Q—Q2 Q—N3 13 N—Q4! followed by P—B3 and P—KR4 (Gipslis-Polugaevsky XXXVI USSR 1969).

11	BxB!
12 QxQP	

Or 12 P—K5 BxN and Black wins a pawn or the exchange.

12	Q—N3
13 P—K5	

White has only a choice of evils as 13 R—B1 BxN 14 PxB KR—Q1 15 Q—N4 RxR+ 16 KxR BxP leaves him with a bad ending, and 13 R—K2 BxN 14 PxB Q—R3! gives Black a strong attack with level material.

13	KR—Q1
14 Q—R3	BxN

An example of the rule that the

advantage of the two bishops lies partly in the chance to exchange one of them at a suitable moment.

| 15 NPxB | B—N4+ |
| 16 K—N1 | B—Q7! |

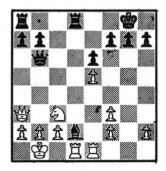

For the first time in the game (but it will not be the last.) Black indicates to his opponent that his back row is weak.

17 R—R1

Not 17 R—K2? BxN! winning a piece, while 17 R—KB1 does not save his KBP (17 ... BxN 18 QxN QxBP!)

| 17 .... | B—B5 |

Not 17 ... QxBP 18 N—K4!

18 N—K2

Now the bishop becomes a dominating piece, but 18 QR—K1 QxBP leaves White with a very un-coordinated set of pieces.

| 18 .... | BxKP |
| 19 N—B1 | |

White decides to let the KBP go so that he can exchange the powerful bishop after 19 ... QxBP 20 N—Q3 when he will also win the QRP. Spassky however, finds a simple way to gain a decisive advantage.

| 19 .... | RxR |
| 20 RxR | BxRP! |

The KRP is now a serious threat in the ending and White cannot make use of the open KR and KN files.

| 21 R—Q7 | B—K4! |
| 22 N—Q3 | B—B3 |

To stop 23 Q—K7 now that White has eased the pressure on his QN2.

| 23 N—B5 | R—Q1! |

Another reminder of the weak back rank.

| 24 P—QB4 | P—KR4 |
| 25 RxNP | Q—Q3 |

And another!

26 Q—K3

This is a losing move but 26 N—N3 QxQ 27 PxQ P—R5 is also a quick loss. Mukhitdinov in fact now resigned without waiting for Spassky to reply. After 26 ... Q—Q8+ 27 Q—B1 QxP White has no defence to the threats of 28 ... R—Q8 and 28 ... Q—B4+.

69 Sochi 1965
White: Kotkov
Ruy Lopez

| 1 P—K4 | P—K4 | 3 B—N5 | P—QR3 |
| 2 N—KB3 | N—QB3 | 4 B—R4 | N—B3 |

5	0—0	B—K2
6	R—K1	P—QN4
7	B—N3	0—0
8	P—B3	P—Q3

Not revealing his hand. Only a few weeks after the Sochi event Spassky met Tal in the Candidates matches and achieved great success with the Marshall gambit.

9	P—KR3	P—KR3

The Smyslov system playing the rook to K1 so as to exert central pressure. However N—KN5 has first to be prevented.

10	P—Q4	R—K1
11	B—K3	

In the match with Keres earlier in the year, the Estonian grandmaster played 11 QN—Q2 which is still considered the main line. The text looks stronger as White has no problem over harmonious development (his QB is not blocked).

11	....	B—B1
12	QN—Q2	B—Q2

Now White has to decide what plan he is to follow. The early release of tension by 13 PxP QNxP 14 NxN PxN 15 Q—B3 only gave equality in an early game played in this line — Tal-Smyslov, 1961. 13 B—B2 anticipates N—QR4 but then comes 13 ... PxP 14 PxP N—QN5! with a threefold attack on the KP. White therefore decides to close the centre and try to get pressure on the Q side.

13	P—Q5	N—K2
14	N—R2	N—N3

The freeing 14 ... P—B3 would reveal the point of the last move, namely 14 ... P—B3 15 PxP BxBP 16 N—N4! N—N3 17 Q—B3 when White will exchange knights and have control over his Q5. (Ivkov-van den Berg, Bever-

wijk 1963).

15	P—QR4	B—K2

All this manoeuvring with the minor pieces looks tortuous, but Black will soon show how active his men become once he has exchanged his bad bishop and achieved P—KB4.

16	P—QB4	

Too ambitious a plan. True, White ultimately wins the QRP but allows his minor pieces to be committed to one side of the board. The standard 16 PxP PxP 17 Q—K2 or 16 Q—K2 at once, intending B—B2—Q3 with pressure on the QNP, was better.

16	....	PxBP
17	BxBP	N—R2
18	N—N3	B—KN4!

Although the position is not completely blocked Black does well to get rid of his less mobile bishop so as to guarantee a good square for his knight at KB5.

19	N—R5	BxB
20	RxB	

20 PxB is an interesting idea to cross Black's plan and to reduce the strength of the coming P—KB4. However, Black continues 20 ... Q—R5 followed by 21 ... N—N4 and presses on the KP as well as threatening sacrifices on KR6 while Q—N6 is also a strong post for his queen.

20	....	P—KB4
21	PxP	

Otherwise P—B5 and this pawn can play a part in the attack.

21	....	BxBP
22	P—QN4	

White temporises. 22 Q—KB1 to attack the QRP is more logical as his queen would also guard his KR3 indirectly from possible sacrifices. Then after 22 ... Q—B1 (the distant opposition?) White can try 23 N—B6 to tie the Black pieces to the defence of K7 and follow up with a later N—QN4, perhaps preceded by P—R5. The text also forces a passed QRP but the White knight remains something of a spectator, whereas on QB6 or QN4 it would be better placed for return to the centre or the K side.

22 ....   N—B5
23 R—B1

Toying with the idea of doubling rooks on the QB file to attack QB7 but 23 P—N5 was a more logical sequel to his last move.

23 ....   R—KB1
24 B—B1   K—R1

A useful preparatory move. If 24 ... N—B3 then 25 P—N5! puts a spanner in the works, e.g. 26 B—B4 B—K3 27 R—Q3 winning material.

25 N—B6

Further inconsistency. He should play 25 KR—QB3 R—B2 26 N—N4 and bring the N to the strong square at K3 where it guards the QP and the K side generally.

25 ....   Q—B3

Now the QP is threatened by 26 ... Q—B2 followed by 27 ... N—B3 so White brings his bishop back to the Q side.

26 P—N5   PxP
27 BxP

If 27 PxP then 27 ... R—R7 is strong. Now, however, KN2 is temporarily weakened.

27 ....   Q—N3
28 R—KN3   Q—B2

A nice alteration.

29 N—QN4   N—B3
30 N—N4

He need not guard the QP

because of the B—B6 possibility, forking rook and minor piece, but there was a formidable concentration of forces aimed at his king, so he tries to exchange minor pieces hoping to eliminate one attacker of the QP.

30 ....   BxN
31 PxB   N—K5!

Black's last move cleared a unit away from the KB file along which there is now winning pressure.

32 R—K3

Or 32 R—KB3 N—N4 33 R—KN3 N(5)—R6+ 34 RxN NxR+ 35 PxN QxP+ 36 K—R1 R—B6 37 B—B1 R—KN6 and 37 ... R—N8 mate. Or in this 33 KR—QB3 NxNP! with winning attacks e.g. 34 KxN QxP+ 35 K—R1 N—B6 36 RxN RxR 37 B—B1 R—KN6 as before.

32 ....   NxNP!
33 R—K2

33 RxN QxP+ 34 K—R1 R—B6 etc. or 33 KxN QxBP+ and 34 ... QxR.

36 R(1)—B2   QxP
37 RxN   Q—N8+
38 K—K2   Q—K8 mate

70 11th match game, Candidates 1965
White: Tal
Ruy Lopez

1	P—K4	P—K4	
2	N—KB3	N—QB3	
3	B—N5	P—QR3	
4	B—R4	N—B3	
5	0—0	B—K2	
6	R—K1	P—QN4	
7	B—N3	0—0	
8	P—KR3		

In earlier games of this match Spassky had been successful with the Marshall Counter Attack which Tal now seeks to avoid.

8 ....   B—N2

Not 8 ... P—Q4 9 PxP NxP 10 NxP NxN 11 RxN P—QB3 by analogy with the Marshall as after 12 BxN PxB 13 P—Q3 B—Q3 14 R—K1 Q—R5 15 N—Q2 Black has none of the immediate threats that arise in the ordinary Marshall and 16 N—B3 will force a retreat.

9 P—Q3

If 9 P—B3 then 9 ... P—Q4 is feasible due to the weakening of White's Q3 square, (10 PxP NxP 11 NxP NxN 12 RxN N—B5!)

9	....	P—Q3	
10	P—B3	N—N1	

Opening the line of his QB which, as the game proceeds, develops into his most effective piece despite the impression that at the moment it is 'biting on granite'.

11	QN—Q2	QN—Q2	
12	N—B1	N—B4	
13	B—B2	R—K1	
14	N—N3	B—KB1	
15	P—N4		

A common move in this posi-

tion hoping for 15 ... N—K3 16 P—Q4 threatening 16 P—Q5. However, as the move allows Black to open lines on the Q side quite soon White would do better to play 15 N—R2 P—Q4 16 Q—B3 N—K3 17 N—B5 P—B4 18 N—N4 with considerable attacking chances.

15	....	QN—Q2	
16	B—N3	P—QR4	

To meet 17 N—N5 by 17 ... P—Q4 18 PxQP P—R5!

17 P—R3   PxP

In Tal-Tukmakov, Sochi 1970 the young master went wrong by 17 ... P—B4? and Tal set in motion a fine attack by 18 N—N5! P—Q4 19 PxQP N—N3 (19 ... NxP 20 Q—R5 or 19 ... P—R3 20 N—K6!) 20 PxBP QNxP 21 P—Q4 P—R3 22 NxP! KxN 23 PxP.

18 BPxP

Or 18 N—N5 P—Q4 19 KPxP N—B4 and if 20 B—R2 P—N6! finally scotching all the threats on the QR2/KN8 diagonal.

18 ....   P—R3

A concession that prevents N—N5 but weakens his K side. For the first time in the match Tal gets an attacking position but, as the course of the game shows, Spassky's defensive skill is equal to the task.

19 N—B5

19 P—Q4 may be better, but it is really a matter of taste.

19	....	P—Q4	
20	N(3)—R4	P—B4!	

20 ... PxP or 20 ... BxP would win a pawn but give White attacking chances which naturally does not suit Spassky at all.

21 R—K3   P—B5!
22 R—N3   K—R2!

Spassky played this after only a few seconds thought. 22 ... PxB 23 NxP+ K—R2 24 NxP gives White a fine attack and with material equality as the third Black pawn is always there for the taking.

23 B—B2

23 B—R2 striving to keep the bishop on its potentially most aggressive diagonal looks better, but then comes 23 ... PxKP 24 PxBP PxP 25 KBxP N—N3! forcing the exchange of queens or the removal of the bishop.

23 ....   P—Q5

Now the bishop has been neutralised as 24 PxP PxP 25 NxQP? PxN 26 P—K5+ fails to 26 ... P—Q6.

24 Q—B3

After the game Tal thought that a better justification of his 23rd move would have been 24 P—R4 attempting to break-up Black's compact pawn mass. The sacrifice 24 NxRP PxN 25 N—B5 R—R3 23 NxRP BxN 27 BxB fails to 27 ... R—N1 28 B—N5 Q—KB1.

24 ....   R—R3!

Further reinforcements for his hard pressed K-side.

25 NxRP

The sacrifice is unsound and White should try 25 B—Q2 followed by 26 R—K1 bringing up the reserves. 25 PxP PxP 26 NxQP PxN 27 P—K5+ P—Q6 28 QxB R—N3 is clearly good for Black.

25 ....   PxN

26 N—B5   Q—R1!

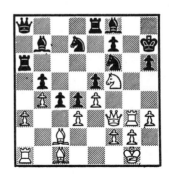

Psychologically a difficult move to see as the queen moves away from the threatened K side. The point is to keep a grip on the QR file (26 ... R(1)—K3 27 P—QR4! N—K1 28 N—Q6! R—KB3 29 Q—N4 R—KN3 30 Q—B5! with winning threats) and to force decisive exchanges in the centre by 27 ... PxP followed by 28 ... BxKP. In view of this, White has to throw more wood on the fire, without, however, managing to raise many sparks.

27 NxRP   BxN
28 Q—B5+   K—R1
29 BxB   R—KN1
30 B—N5   Q—K1

Accurate defence to the end. 30 ... PxP 31 BxP BxP? loses to 32 BxB QxB 33 BxN+ NxB 34 RxR+ KxR 35 Q—B8+ picking up the QR.

31 P—B4   N—R2

Now White is forced to retreat and Black gradually evaluates his extra piece.

32 B—KR4   RxR
33 BxR   R—KB3
34 Q—N4   R—KN3
35 Q—R4   KPxP!

Preparing useful outposts for the knights.

36 QxP	P—B3!
37 B—B2	PxP
38 BxP(3)	N—K4
39 B—B1	N—N4
40 K—R1	NxKP
41 R—B1	

Spassky was now about to consider his sealed move but Tal resigned the game and thereby

the match. Balck does best to play not 41 ... NxB+ but 41 ... N—B5! to close the QB file as 42 BxN' leaves White's KN2 ultimately indefensible, while 42 BxN N—N6+ is decisive for the same reason. (43 K—R2 NxB‡ 44 RxN(1) RxP+ or 43 K—N1 BxP! 44 BxP+ K—N1 45 Q—R4 N—K7+!' 46 BxN BxP+ and mates).

71 Hastings 1965/66
Black: Lee
Nimzoindian

1 P—Q4	N—KB3
2 P—QB4	P—K3
3 N—QB3	B—N5
4 B—N5	P—KR3
5 B—R4	P—B4
6 P—Q5	BxN+

In recent years preference has been given to the quieter 6 ... PxP 7 PxP and now not 7 ... P—Q3 but 7 ... 0—0 getting the king into safety and retaining options over when and whether to play P—QN4 and P—Q3. Bagirov-Sakharov, **XXXI USSR** 1969, now went 8 P—K3 R—K1! 9 R—B1 P—Q3 and after the standard, but inaccurate, 10 B—QN5 Black has a good game either by 10 ... QN—Q2, as actually played, or by 10 ... B—Q2!. However, at the time this game was played the text and the subsequent move were considered quite correct.

7 PxB	P—K4
8 P—Q6!	

An improvement on 8 Q—B2

which Spassky has played before. Black can then, however, reach the blocked position which he is aiming for by 8 ... P—Q3 e.g. 9 P—K4 P—KN4 10 B—N3 N—R4! 11 N—B3 N—Q2 with full equality (Spassky-Sliwa, Riga 1959.) The course of this game suggests that Black should have played 7 ... P—Q3.

8	N—B3

The best, exploiting the one drawback of White's last move — the loss of control over QB6. If 8 ... Q—R4 9 R—B1 and Black has to face the threat of 9 BxN, while if 8 ... 0—0 an analysis by Spassky's former trainer Zak gives 9 P—K3 R—K1 10 B—K2 N—B3 11 N—R3! intending 12 0—0 and then P—B4! with a strong position in view of the intensifying pressure in the centre and on the pinned knight (PxP or N—B2—K4 or N4).

9 Q—B2	P—KN4

The pin is too strong and has to be broken.

10 B—N3 Q—R4?

The wrong follow-up to his last move. His next few moves are all played with queen and knight and leave his game badly behind in development and thoroughly disorganised. He should try either Barden's suggestion of 10 ... P—N3 so as to develop on the Q side where his king may find safety or Taimanov's 10 ... N—KR4 e.g. 11 P—K3 Q—B3 12 R—Q1 Q—K3 13 B—K2 N—N2 and Black has a reasonable game as he has protected all his weak points and can try to tie White down to the defence of the QP by N—B4 or even better P—B4 followed by 0—0 and N—K1.

11 R—B1

To remove the threat of 11 ... N—K5.

11 .... Q—R6

Black persists in his error renewing the threat of N—K5 but leaving his queen thoroughly "offside" The same drawback would arise from 11 ... P—N3 as White can start to make threats himself by Q—B5 with the defence Q—Q1 ruled out. The conclusion must be that Black is already lost.

12 N—B3 N—K5

Spassky suggested 12 ... P—K5 13 N—Q2 0—0 as a better chance, but after 14 P—R4 and 15 P—K3 White stands much better.

12 .... N—K5

13 BxP NxB

After 13 ... P—B3 White replies 14 BxP! and if view of the threats 15 BxR and 15 QxN with check, Black has nothing better than 14 ... 0—0 (14 ... NxB 15 Q—N6+ K—B1 16 QxN+ K—N1 17 R—Q1! as his queen now guards QB3 — a point we shall see again and again in the actual game.) 15 B—K7! NxB 16 PxN R—K1 and now comes 17 N—Q2! with a quick win (17 ... P—Q4 best — 17 ... RxP 18 N—N1! and 19 P—B3 followed by Q—N6+ — 18 PxP B—B4 19 N—N1! Q—R4 20 P—B3 N—Q3 21 P—K4 RxP 22 B—K2 with two sound pawns up.

14 NxN NxQP

An achievement by Black? Yes, but at too high a price!

15 P—KR4

With his knight so strongly placed (15 ... P—B3? 16 Q—N6+ K—K2 17 Q—N7+ K—K3 18 N—Q3 followed by 19 PxP or 19 P—N3 and 20 B—R3+.) White naturally prefers to open lines at once on the King side rather than play for banal development by 15 P—K3 or N3.

15 .... PxP

Final capitulation; the herioc 15 ... R—KN1 was called for though White clearly wins after 16 PxP PxP 17 P—K3 and 18 R—Q1.

16 P—K3

Not just development but also giving his king a flight square as after the premature 16 R—Q1 Black has 16 ... N—K5 threatening to exchange queens.

16 .... P—N3

17 R—Q1 N—N2

Now if 17 ... N—K5 then 18 QxN and Black can no longer give perpetual check as he would in the last note. If 17 ... K—K2 then 18 RxN!

18 NxBP

(See diagram next column.)

The complete exposure of the

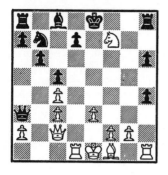

Black king.

18	KxN
19 Q—B5+	K—N2

To go to the K file allows 20 Q—K5+ and 21 QxR, while if 19 ... K—N1 then 20 Q—N6+ K—B1

21 Q—B6+ (guarding QB3) 21 ... K—N1 22 RxRP and 23 R—N4+ or 23 R—B4 with a quick mate.

20 Q—K5+	K—N1
21 RxP	P—Q3

To prevent R—N4+ but the abundance of open lines on the K side gives White a wide choice of attacking moves.

22 Q—N3+	K—B1
23 R—B4+	K—K1
24 Q—N7	

Back to the defence of QB3 again, but also with other threats, to put it mildly!

Black resigns. With four men still on their original squares the final position gives the impression that it arose from a game between two players in the lower echelons of the grading list!

72 19th game, World Championship, 1966
Black: Petrosian
French Defence

1 P—K4 .	P—K3
2 P—Q4	P—Q4
3 N—QB3	N—KB3
4 P—K5	

The Steinitz variation, but followed up next move by Tarrasch's suggested improvement on Steinitz's 5 P—B4.

4	KN—Q2
5 N—B3	P—QB4
6 PxP	N—QB3
7 B—KB4	BxP
8 B—Q3	

Tarrasch concluded that White had a good game here, but Black's next move seems to equalise.

8	P—B3

Not 8 ... 0—0 allowing the elementary 9 BxP+

9 PxP	NxP
10 0—0	0—0
11 N—K5	

A more natural move is 11 B—N3 but the text suggested by Bondarevsky is quite playable as Black cannot make use of the unguarded position of the QB

11	B—Q2

Not 11 ... N—K5 12 BxN RxB 13 N—Q3 with advantage.

12 NxN	BxN

Or 12 ... PxN 13 N—R4 and 14 P—B4 with central pressure.

13 Q—K2	Q—K2
14 QR—K1	

Now White has firm control of his K5, but Black's position is quite sound.

14	QR—K1
15 B—N3	P—QR3

An unnecessary move putting another pawn on a white square. 15 ... Q—KB2 looks better.

16 P—QR3	Q—KB2
17 P—QN4	

A crucial choice leading to the exchange of the black square bishops but at the cost of losing control of K5. 17 Q—Q2 seems a better chance of ultimately pressing hard along the K file by doubling rooks.

17	B—Q5
18 B—K5	BxB
19 QxB	N—Q2
20 Q—N3	P—K4
21 P—B3	

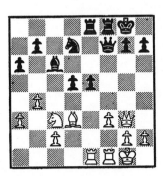

A difficult position to assess. The Black centre pawns are impressive where they stand, but ultimately come under pressure on the open centre files. The decisive role is probably played by the presence of a potentially bad

bishop which makes White welcome an ending.

21	Q—B5?

Black should avoid exchanges by 21 ... R—K2 intending to double on the K file or by 21 ... Q—B3 safeguarding his centre.

22 QxQ	RxQ
23 R—B2	

Inaugurating pressure on the centre pawns.

23	P—KN3
24 R—Q2	N—N3
25 R(2)—K2	N—Q2
26 N—Q1	P—QN4

Ruling out an ultimate P—QB4 but making his bishop even worse.

27 P—B3	R—B2

Petrosian offered a draw here but Spassky naturally refused and with his next move reveals his plan to break through by combining the breakthrough P—QR4 with pressure on the Q file by B—N3.

28 B—B2	K—N2
29 B—N3	P—KR4

To prevent N—K3—N4.

30 N—K3	N—N3
31 N—B2!	

The knight too begins to improve his position, preparing to go to Q4 while leaving the rooks a chance to alternate between the two centre files.

31	N—Q2

This makes it more difficult to defend by blocking his bishop and making P—QR4 possible again. After the better 31 ... R(2)—K2 32 P—KB4 P—K5 33 N—Q4 Black would defend all his weak points by 33 ... B—Q2.

32 R—K3	P—R5
33 P—R3	R—B3
34 N—Q4	B—N2
35 P—R4	

In the last few minutes of the session, Spassky finally makes it clear that he now has a strong initiative.

| 35 .... | R—Q1 |
| 36 N—K2 | PxP? |

A further concession. His last move correctly drove the White knight away from Q4 so as to reduce pressure on the QNP. Now 36 ... P—N4 37 R—Q1 R—Q3 was the correct way to defend.

| 37 BxRP | N—N3 |
| 38 B—N3 | P—K5 |

One evil follows logically upon another. 38 ... R—K3? 39 N—Q4 loses a pawn, and 38 ... R—K1 39 N—Q4 N—Q2 40 B—R4 leads to the same result.

| 39 N—Q4 | K—R3 |
| 40 R—Q1 | R—QB1? |

Probably the losing error. After 40 ... R—Q2! Black can probably still draw. In any event White cannot continue as in the game as after 41 PxP PxP his knight is pinned.

41 PxP!

The sealed move preparing to enter Black's position with his knight and rook.

| 41 .... | PxP |
| 42 N—K6! | |

With the very strong threat of 43 N—B5. 42 ... B—Q4? is no defence because of 43 BxB NxB 44 RxP threatening 45 RxP mate as well as the knight. 42 ... N—R5 is met by 43 N—Q7 B—B3 44 R—Q6. The assembled mass of grandmaster analysts in the press room thought 42 ... P—R4 was the best defensive chance, as the ending after 43 PxP N—B5 44 BxN RxB 45 N—Q4 R—R5 is probably drawn. Similarly 43 N—B5 B—R1 44 NxKP BxN 45 RxB RxP 46 RxP+ K—N2 is not enough to win. However, after 42 ... P—R4 43 R—Q6! N—B5 44 BxN RxB 45 N—Q8! White wins e.g. 45 ... RxR 46 N—B7+ K—R4 47 NxR R—B2 48 PxP followed by 49 NxB or 49 NxP according to circumstances, or 45 ... R—B2 46 NxB PxP! 47 R—Q4!

42	N—B5
43 BxN	RxB
44 N—B5	R—B2

Guarding the 2nd rank.

| 45 R—R1 | K—N4 |
| 46 R—R5! | |

Not 46 NxB RxN 47 RxRP R(2)—QB2 or R—Q2 with drawing chances. The text tries to construct a mating net.

| 46 .... | K—B5 |
| 47 K—B2 | B—Q4 |

Otherwise 48 N—K6 mate.

48 N—N3!

The QRP can wait. Now 48 ... B—N2 loses to 49 N—Q4 threatening mate by either N—K6 or N—K2.

48	K—K4+
49 K—K2	R—QB3
50 N—Q2!	K—K3

Otherwise 51 P—B4.

51 NxP   B—B5+

Or 51 ... BxN 52 RxB+ K—Q3

53 P—B4 and Black cannot activate his rooks. The text aims at maintaining a blockade on the Q side.

52 .K—Q2	R—Q2+
53 K—B2	K—B2
54 R—K5	K—N2
55 N—Q2	B—N4
56 N—B3	

The blockade is achieved but the weakness of the K side pawns now comes into the reckoning.

56	B—R5+
57 K—N2	R—Q8
58 R(5)—K4!	

The knight must guard Q2 for the moment.

58	R—KB8

59 R—K1!
Forcing the exchange of the cheeky invader.

59	RxR
60 RxR	R—B3
61 R—K4	P—N4

Despair, but 61 ... B—B3 62 RxP BxN 63 PxB RxP 64 K—N3 was also a steady loss.

62 NxNP	R—B7+
63 K—R3	B—B3
64 RxP	BxP
65 N—K4	R—K7
66 N—B5	

Back to the last weakness.

66	B—B8
67 R—KB4	R—K8
68 P—R4	Resigns

73 Santa Monica 1966
Black: Fischer
Grunfeld Defence

1 P—Q4	N—KB3
2 P—QB4	P—KN3
3 N—QB3	P—Q4
4 PxP	NxP
5 P—K4	NxN
6 PxN	B—N2
7 B—QB4	P—QB4
8 N—K2	N—B3
9 B—K3	0—0
10 0—0	Q—B2

A good alternative is 10 ... N—R4 11 B—Q3 P—N3! as 12 PxP PxP 13 QBxP Q—B2 gives Black a lot of play.

11 R—B1	R—Q1
12 Q—K1	

A more careful move than 13 P—KB4 as he played against Shishkin in 1959 (see game 32).

12	P—K3

Panov recommends 12 ... Q—R4 hoping to force the exchange of queens.

13 P—B4!	N—R4

Not 13 ... PxP etc. snatching the QP because of the eventual discovered attack on the queen by 16 BxP.

14 B—Q3	P—B4

Now Black has successfully blocked White's K side push.

15 R—Q1
Preparing a retreat square for his bishop in the event of 15 ... KBPxP 16 BxP N—B5.

15	P—N3
16 Q—B2	PxQP

Black shoult try to keep the

position closed by 16 ... B—B1.

17 BxP

The exchange of bishops will weaken the Black K side. Black should extract a price for this by 17 ... B—N2 18 BxB QxB and if 19 N—Q4 then 19 ... Q—KB2 and White's QBP is a potential weakness.

17	BxB
18 PxB	B—N2
19 N—N3	Q—B2

Or 19 ... PxP 20 BxP and the further exchange leaves Black some K side weaknesses to watch. Hence the text or 19 ... Q—N2 seem called for.

20 P—Q5!

The only way to get at the enemy K side.

| 20 .... | BPxP |

Not 20 ... KPxP 21 PxBP.

| 21 PxP | QxKP |

Or 21 ... Q—B3 22 NxP QxKP 23 N—N5.

22 P—B5

The complement of his break two moves earlier.

| 22 .... | Q—B2 |

Not 22 ... PxP 23 NxBP and now if 23 ... PxB? 24 Q—N3+ K—B1 25 N—N7+ or 23 ... R—K1 24 Q—Q4 and the threats (25 Q—N7 mate, 25 B—B4 accumulate.)

23 BxP

Not 23 NxP RxB 24 N—N5 Q—Q2.

| 23 .... | RxR |

The correct defence diverting the rook from the KB file. 23 ... BxB 24 NxB QxBP? allows 25 RxR+ RxR 26 Q—R4 P—KN4 (26 ... Q—QB1 27 N—B6+) 27 NxP Q—B4+ 28 K—R1 and Black's K side is bare.

24 RxR   R—KB1!

Again the right defence. 24 ...

BxB 25 NxB QxBP 26 N—B6+ K—N2 27 R—Q7+ KxN 28 Q—R4+ gives White a winning attack as does 25 ... PxP 26 R—Q7! Q—N3 27 R—Q6 Q—N2 28 N—B6+ K—R1 29 QxBP (29 ... R—KB1 30 R—Q7! RxN 31 R—Q8+ or 29 ... Q—N3 30 QxQ PxQ 31 R—Q7). If however, 24 ... BxB 25 NxB R—KB1 then 26 P—B6 with a very strong passed pawn. In all these variations the absence of Black's knight from the main scene of battle counts against him.

25 B—N1

White has to retain his bishop to keep up his threats.

25	Q—B3
26 Q—B2	K—R1
27 PxP	PxP
28 Q—Q2	

Not 29 QxP? without check due to Black's threat of 29 ... Q—B7+ mating.

| 28 .... | K—N2 |
| 29 R—KB1 | Q—K2 |

He cannot stop both Q—Q4+ and an exchange of rooks followed by Q—R6+.

| 30 Q—Q4+ | R—B3 |

30 ... K—R3 seems a better chance, e.g. 31 RxR QxR 32 Q—R4+ K—N2 33 Q—N5 Q—QB4+ with a tenable ending, while in this 33 N—K4 BxN 34 QxB Q—Q3 also holds.

| 31 N—K4 | BxN |
| 32 BxB | |

Keeping the knight at the edge of the board and threatening to exploit the pin by 33 P—N4, while if 33 ... K—B2 34 B—Q5+ and the king is driven back into the pin.

| 32 .... | Q—B4 |
| 33 QxQ | RxR+ |

A crucial decision. After 33 ...

PxQ 34 RxR KxR 35 P—KR4
N—B5 and 36 ... N—Q3 Black
has a defensible ending, but he
had also to weigh up the ending
with rooks on (34 R—B1 P—B5
35 R—B3 threatening 36
R—QR3) in which he is under
severe pressure just as much as in
the purely minor piece ending.

34 KxR   PxQ
35 P—KR4!

Fixing the pawn on a square
where it remains under fire by
the bishop. Despite the slight
material left, the advantage of the
long ranging bishop and un-
symmetrical pawns gives White
winning chances.

35 ....   N—B5
36 K—K2   N—K4
37 K—K3   K—B3
38 K—B4

Getting the last few moves in
quickly. 38 B—B2 freeing K4 for
the king was more accurate.

38 ....   N—B2
39 K—K3

White can afford to wait as 39
... P—N4+ was not too much to
be feared.

39 ....   P—N4

A second crucial decision just

before the time control. 39 ...
N—K4 40 B—B2! (repairing his
original inaccuracy) 40 ... P—R3
41 K—K4 K—K3 42 K—B4 K—B3
43 P—N4 would let White force a
passed pawn (not that he has the
queenable RP left after this
passed pawn diverts the enemy
king or wins the knight.)

The correct defence pointed out
by Gligoric is 39 ... N—R3! 40
K—Q3 N—B4 41 K—B4 NxP (exchanging minor pieces by 41 ...
N—Q3+ leaves White with a distant passed pawn) 42 KxP K—K4
and with the pawn formation
now symmetrical Black has
drawing chances by going for the
KNP with his king.

40 P—R5

Now this pawn has to be
watched very carefully and
Black's defensive resources are
taxed to the limit and beyond by
the play on both extremities of
the board.

40 ....   N—R3
41 K—Q3   K—K4
42 B—R8   K—Q3

Or 42 ... K—B5 43 K—B4
K—N5 44 B—B3+ K—R5 45 KxP
P—N5 56 B—K4 KxP 47 P—R4
etc.

43 K—B4   P—N5
44 P—R4   N—N1
45 P—R5   N—R3

Or 45 ... N—B3? 46 P—KR6
threatening 47 B—K4.

46 B—K4   P—N6

Or 46 ... N—N1 47 P—N3
N—R3 48 B—Q3 N—N1 49
B—K2 N—R3 50 K—N5 with
Zugzwang. 46 ... K—K4 47
B—Q3 would force the same varia-
tion unless Black gave up his
QBP at once, which leaves him
no chances if the Black king goes
to KN6 to attack the pawn, White

can always get his bishop to the long white diagonal in time to guard it.

| 47 | K—N5 | N—N1 |
| 48 | B—N1 | |

Now the task of the bishop is no longer to keep the king from QB6 but to blockade the QBP from a square where it is not easily subject to attack.

48	....	N—R3
49	K—R6	K—B3
50	B—R2	

Not the precipitate 50 KxP P—B5 51 P—R6? K—B2 and Black draws. The QRP can wait until White has completed his blockade.

Black resigned.

74 Havana, 1966
Black: Weiss (Monaco)
Centre Counter Gambit

I must apologise for the inclusion of this particular game, but a little light relief does not seem out of place amidst all the other fairly heavy subject matter. Moreover the comments on the game do include some interesting psychological observations. My final justification for its inclusion must be the fact that Spassky himself chose to demonstrate it in that holy of holies the Central Chess Club in Moscow and I translate his comments verbatim.

| 1 | P—K4 | P—Q4 |
| 2 | PxP | N—KB3 |

"Apparently my opponent knows the opening. The text is still the best move."

3	B—N5+	B—Q2
4	B—B4	B—B4
5	N—QB3	QN—Q2
6	P—Q3	N—N3
7	Q—B3	NxB
8	PxN	BxP
9	B—B4	

"From this point I stopped trying to guess my opponent's

moves and I probably behaved somewhat tactlessly — I tried to sit at the board for as little time as possible."

| 9 | .... | P—QR3? |
| 10 | KN—K2 | P—R3?? |

"Now I remembered a game I once had with master Kopylov. Then too I could not guess a single move of my opponent for a long period. My first reaction was one of annoyance, but then I merely started playing 'my own' developing moves and eight moves later, he resigned."

| 11 | 0—0 | Q—B1 |
| 12 | N—Q4 | |

"My own move."

| 12 | .... | B—R2 |
| 13 | KR—K1 | R—QN1? |

"Here I remembered how Bronstein had once confided to Keres, who in his turn had chortled for an hour over it, his 'theory' that you shouldn't refute a weak move by the opponent as it is merely the introduction to an even weaker one, and so I played Bronstein's way."

14 P—KR3   P—KN4??
"Bronstein is right!"

15 BxBP   QxB
16 QxN   R—N1
17 P—Q6   Q—Q2
18 RxP+   BxR
19 R—K1

"My opponent amazed me by his imperturbable appearance."

19 ....   B—N3
20 RxB+

Now Petrosian added his comment to the audience in Moscow "Boris got up and walked away leaving me to sit right next to all this." Then Spassky again, "When I came back Weiss had resigned, but I learned that before this, he had calmly written down on his score sheet, and then played 20 ... R—Q1."

The incident reminds me of the story that Leonard Barden told of an Olympiad in the fifties when an Irishman was White against Bronstein. The game opened 1 P—K4 P—QB3 and after his demise the Irishman asked Bronstein "What was the name of that opening?"

75 Havana Olympiad 1966
Black: Bobotsov
Queen's Gambit Declined

1 P—Q4   P—Q4
2 P—QB4   P—K3
3 N—QB3   B—K2

A little finesse. 3 ... N—KB3 allows the immediate pin 4 B—N5, whereas after the text White has either to play the exchange variation 4 PxP PxP 5 B—B4 or develop his KN at B3 thereby losing the option of a less rigid development by KN—K2 (or even KN—R3).

4 N—KB3   N—KB3
5 B—N5   0—0
6 Q—B2

And now a finesse from White instead of the usual 6 P—K3. By leaving his KP unmoved White intends to meet 6 ... P—KR3 by the sharp 7 BxN BxB 8 0—0—0 followed by P—K4! with a strong position in the centre, and attacking chances against the king whose castle has been slightly weakened by 6 ... P—KR3. (White can play for the line-opening manoeuvre P—KR4, P—KN4 and then P—N5.)

6 ....   P—QN3
7 P—K3

White could still try for the line indicated in the previous note by 7 0—0—0 B—N2 8 BxN BxB 9 P—K4, but Black could then play 7 ... QN—Q2 so as to retake on f6 with a knight.

7 ....   B—N2
8 0—0—0

A bold decision as Black will obtain considerable counter-play against the king, while White's attack takes longer to build-up than if he had managed to play P—K4.

8 ....   QN—Q2

8 ... N—K5 was also playable and if 9 P—KR4 then 9 ... NxN 10 QxN with a sound position, as White's attack is not easy to play and Black has obvious counter play along the QB file where the White monarch and his consort stand in a straight line.

9 B—Q3   P—B4

This looks logical but 9 ... PxP 10 BxP N—Q4 was better as Black's QB would then play a less passive role than is the case in the actual game continuation.

10 BPxP!   KPxP

Forced (10 ... NxP? 11 BxP+ or 10 ... BxP? 11 P—K4, 12 P—K5 and 13 BxP+).

11 P—KR4   P—QR3

Planning a general Q side pawn advance, but 11 ... R—B1 to open the QB file looks a less long-winded method of obtaining counter play.

12 P—KN4   P—B5
13 B—B5   P—N3

Giving White a 'target' which enables him to force line-opening on the K side, but the threat of 14 QBxN NxB 15 P—N5 winning a pawn obliges either the text or 13 ... P—R3.

14 QBxN   BxB?

14 ... NxB 15 P—N5 N—K1 16 B—N4 P—N4 was better as Black gets definite chances on the Q side, whereas after the text he is left with a purely passive position.

15 P—N5   B—N2

Not 15 ... PxB 16 PxB QxP when 17 QR—N1+ and 18 R+N5 gives White immediate threats.

16 BxN

Winning for his knight a good central square and producing the

state of affairs we have already seen in Spassky's games — the two knights against two bishops.

16 ....   QxB
17 N—K5   Q—K2

After 17 ... BxN 18 PxB Q—K3 19 P—B4! Black could win the exchange for a pawn and eliminate his rather feeble bishop by 19 ... P—Q5, but after 20 PxP BxR 21 RxB White's centre pawns and attacking chances (P—R5 and Q—R2 or N—K4 and N—B6+) give him the advantage.

18 P—B4   P—N4
19 P—R3   QR—Q1

Protecting his QP again so as to activate his QB. After 19 ... P—N5 20 PxP QxQNP 21 P—R5 White breaks through without any difficulty.

20 P—R5

Rather too sharp. Simply 20 Q—N2 followed by P—R5 was the correct way of conducting the attack.

20 ....   BxN
21 BPxB

Now 21 QPxB doesn't work because of 21 ... P—Q5 22 N—K4 (22 PxP BxR 23 RxB RxP 24 N—K4 RxN! 25 QxR Q—K3 with counter chances) 22 ... P—Q6 23 Q—N2 (23 N—B6+ QxN!) 23 ... BxN! 24 QxN P—N5 renewing his counter attack.

21 ....   QxNP

This looks risky, but Black hardly had anything more constructive. If 21 ... B—B1 then 22 Q—N2! followed by doubling rooks on the KR file before opening it.

22 Q—B2   B—B1
23 QR—N1   Q—K2

Best. If 23 ... B—N5 then 24 Q—N3! PxP 25 N—K2 and Black has no good counter to the threat of 26 N—B4 followed by 27 NxRP.

24 Q—B4

White could try the more complex and less obvious attacking line 24 P—K4 as 24 ... PxP? 25 NxKP brings the knight into the assault with decisive effect. Black's best defence is 24 ... B—N2 25 Q—K3 PxP but after 26 Q—R6 White has a very good attack e.g. 26 ... RxP 27 N—K2! R—Q6 28 N—B4 P—K6 29 PxP R—B6+ (not 29 ... BPxP 30 RxP+! K—R1 31 R—K6! Q—N2 32 QxQ+ and 33 R—K7+ winning) 30 K—N1 B—K5+ 31 K—R2 BPxP 32 PxR BxR 33 RxB with advantage. Another strong possibility was 24 Q—B3 to combine threats in the centre with those on the K side. After 24 ... B—K3 25 P—K4 comes with practically decisive effect while 24 ... B—N2 25 Q—B4 gives White the same attack as in the game with the bishop no longer available for defence of the king. Black's best seems 24 Q—B3 K—R1! 25 NxQP RxN! 26 QxR B—N2 27 Q—Q6 QxQ 28 PxQ

BxR though after 29 RxB R—Q1 30 PxP BPxP 31 P—K4 RxP 32 P—Q5 White has a favourable ending.

    24 ....   K—R1!
    25 P—K4

If 25 Q—R6 then 25 ... B—B4 and White has no good continuation.

    25 ....   QPxP

Not 25 ... B—K3 26 KPxP BxP 27 NxB RxN 28 Q—K4 followed by 30 RxNP winning.

    26 P—Q5

Now thanks to his 24th move, Black can meet 26 NxKP by RxP.

    26 ....   QR—K1!

Not 26 ... KR—K1 when White wins by 27 PxP PxP 28 NxP (threat 29 N—B6 or N5) 28 ... QxP 29 RxP+ KxR 30 Q—B7+ K—R1 31 R—R1+ Q—R4 32 RxQ+ and 33 N—B6.

    27 Q—R6   P—N4

A critical position for Black. The threat was 28 QxP+! KxQ 29 PxP+ K—N1 or N2 30 PxP+ KxP 31 R—R7 mate, a very pretty picture. Spassky himself claims that Black can defend successfully by 27 ... QxKP 28 PxP Q—N2 29 QxP+ QxQ 30 RxQ+ K—N1 when White would have to play 31 NxKP PxP (31 ... RxN? 32 P—N7) 32 R—R7 RxN (32 ... B—B4 33 N—Q6) 33 RxP+ and 34 R—R6+ with perpetual. However, as Bronstein pointed out White wins by 30 P—N7+ exploiting the pin on the queen!

27 ... B—B4 looks the natural defensive move but then comes 28 P—Q6 QxKP (28 ... Q—K3 29 N—Q5! QxN 30 PxP BxP 31 RxB wins) 29 PxP Q—N2 30 QxP+ QxQ 31 RxQ+ K—N1 32 N—Q5 PxP 33 QR—R1 and White wins the exchange by 34

N—K7+ and is left with a murderously strong passed pawn on K7. Hence the ugly text is forced.

28 RxP   P—B3

After the alternative 28 ... R—N1 29 KR—N1 B—B4 White gets a very favourable ending by exchanging both pairs of rooks and winning the KP by 32 Q—B4.

29 R—N6!   PxP
30 P—Q6   Q—KB2
31 N—Q5

As in other variations considered earlier, White gets the better of it once he is able to augment his pressure by bringing the knight into the attack. Spassky now gives the following variations to illustrate how difficult Black's position is.

I 31 ... B—B4 32 R—B6! Q—N2 33 QxQ+ KxQ 34 P—R6+ K—R1 35 R—B1 wins.

II 31 ... P—K6 32 R(1)—N1 and a. 32 ... B—B4 33 R—N7 R—KN1 34 P—Q7! wins, b. 32 ... R—N1 33 N—B6 P—K7 34 K—Q2 P—B6+ 35 PxP Q—R7+ 36 K—K3 wins, c. 32 ... P—K7 33 R—B6 P—K8(Q)+ (or 33 ... R—N1 34 RxQ RxR+ 35 K—B2 B—B4+ 36 RxB P—K8(Q) 37 R—B8+ RxR 38 QxR+ R—N1 39 Q—B6+ R—N2 40 N—K3!! threatening 41 P—R6 and 41 P—Q7) 34 KRxQ Q—N2 (34 ... Q—N1 35 R—N6!) 35 QxQ+ KxQ 36 P—R6+ K—R1 (36 ... K—N1 37 N—K7+ K—R1 38 RxR+, 39 NxB and 40 P—Q7 wins) 37 RxP with a won ending because of his strong passed pawn and the back row mate threats.

31 ....   R—K3
32 KR—N1

Threatening 33 N—K7 followed

by 34 RxR and 35 N—N6+.

32 ....   RxR
33 PxR   Q—KN2
34 Q—R2!   P—K6

With both players very short of time, Black finds an ingenious resource. 35 PxP seems to win out of hand because of 35 ... Q moves 36 QxP+ but in fact Black does not move his queen but replies 35 ... P—K7! and is out of all danger.

35 NxP   R—B5

But here he misses the logical follow-up to his last move. Having diverted the knight he should try 35 ... P—B6 hoping for 36 PxP P—K5. White can however, simply play 36 P—N4 and if 36 ... B—K3 to keep the knight out of Q5 then 37 PxP Q—B3 38 R—B1 QxR+ 39 NxQ RxN+ 40 K—B2 B—B4+ 41 KxP R—B8+ 42 K—N2! R—B7+ 43 QxR BxQ 44 P—Q7 wins.

36 N—Q5   R—N5

Or 36 ... R—Q5 37 N—B6! P—R3 38 N—K8 and 39 QxKP+.

37 RxR   BxR
38 QxP+

Forcing an easily won ending with his knight proving a strong piece in conjunction with his passed pawns.

38 ....   QxQ
39 PxQ   B—B4
40 N—B6   P—QR4

Now it was time to seal and Black resigned without waiting any further as he cannot force the exchange of all White's pawns which is his only hope of drawing, e.g. 41 P—Q7 BxQP 42 NxB P—K5 43 N—B6 P—K6 44 N—Q5 and now P—N5 is never a threat.

76 Havana Olympiad 1966
Black: Parma
Pirc Defence

1 P—K4	P—Q3
2 P—Q4	N—KB3
3 N—QB3	P—KN3
4 N—B3	B—N2
5 B—K2	

The most solid line. If White wishes to proceed more aggressively then he must play 4 P—B4 the previous move.

5	0—0
6 0—0	B—N5

This is generally considered Black's best, although the semi-waiting 6 ... P—B3 is also in line with the sophisticated concepts of this modern defence. The text aims at exerting pressure on White's Q4.

7 B—K3	N—B3
8 Q—Q2	P—K4
9 P—Q5	

Black has carried out his plan of attacking the black squares in the centre, and White must now come to a decision about his QP. 9 PxP is a good alternative as White keeps a slight advantage after 9 ... PxP 10 QR—Q1 QxQ 11 RxQ KR—Q1 12 KR—Q1 RxR 13 RxR N—K1 14 N—Q5 BxN 15 PxB! (guarding the KP safely; if 15 BxB then 15 ... N—Q5 16 B—Q1 P—B3 17 N—N4 N—Q3 18 P—QB3 NxP!) 15 ... N—Q5 16 B—Q1 N—K3 17 P—QB3 B—B1 18 B—R4! Larsen-Ivkov and Reshevsky-Ivkov, Santa-Monica 1966, while if Black plays to keep queens on by 10 ... Q—K2 then 11 B—KN5 BxN 12 BxB N—Q5 13 N—Q5! Andersson-Mecking, Beverwijk 1971.

9	N—K2
10 QR—Q1	N—Q2

Black's first inaccuracy. Naturally he is eager to take the initiative by advancing P—KB4, but White's next move forces him to exchange his good bishop for White's bad one. Hence he should remove White's knight at once by 10 ... BxN and only then 11 BxB N—Q2. As an alternative he could try Vasiukov's plan of 10 ... B—Q2 followed by N—R4 and then P—KB4 (Geller-Vasiukov, Kislovodsk 1968, though Geller had played 10 P—QR4 instead of 10 QR—Q1). ·

11 N—KN5!

Now the knight lives and will prove an embarrassing piece due to the threat of N—K6 if Black plays P—KB4.

11	BxB
12 NxB	P—KR3
13 N—R3	K—R2
14 P—QB4	P—KB4
15 P—B3	

The position looks very much like a King's Indian except that White's knights are on unusual squares. He should exploit this difference by playing 15 PxP and if 15 ... PxP then 16 P—B4 when Black's usual reply (in similar King's Indian formation) of 16 ... PxP would here be bad because of 17 KNxP threatening 18 N—K6, while 16 ... NxP would leave White some advantage by 16 P—B3 followed by N—B2—K4. White's knight at K2 would then serve the useful role of ruling out

N—Q5 by Black.

15 ....   N—KB3

A second inaccuracy. 15 ... P—B5 was stronger and if the bishop retreats then P—KN4 with the usual attacking chances on the K side. Spassky actually intended 15 ... P—B5 16 KNxP PxN 17 NxP but then discovered that the counter sacrifice 17 ... RxN! 18 BxR P—KN4 followed by a later N—N3 would give Black considerable play on the dark squares.

16 PxP   PxP

17 P—B4

Correcting his previous error at the cost of a tempo.

17 ....   N—K5

Parma in Informator prefers 17 ... N—N5 18 PxP NxB 19 QxN PxP but White then gets a bind on the White squares by 20 P—KN4 and if 20 ... PxP 21 Q—K4+ K—R1 22 QxNP R—N1 (22 ... P—K5 23 QxP BxP 24 KN—B4 threatening 25 N—K6 or 25 QxN!) 23 Q—R5!

18 Q—B2   Q—K1

19 N—B2

A natural-looking move but 19 PxP PxP 20 N—B2 is better as Black's centre pawns would then come under pressure — the White KR attacks KB5 and P—Q6 is a strong threat as after PxP RxP the rook is strongly placed with pressure, amongst other things, on the Black KRP.

19 ....   NxN

20 RxN   P—K5

Now his centre pawns are comparatively safe.

21 B—Q4   P—B4?

The losing error as the weakness of his QP and Q4 square are much more serious evils than the one he is seeking to vaoid — the

knight entry at K6. Simply 21 ... KR—N1 22 BxB RxB 23 N—Q4 Q—Q2 24 N—K6 R—N5 would leave him with a defensible position — pressure on the KN file and possibilities such as N—N3—R5 or N—N3—B1 or N—N1—B3—R4.

22 PxP e.p.   BxB

23 NxB   NxP

24 Q—B3!

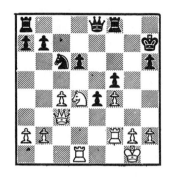

The obvious 24 N—N5 would permit Black a measure of consolidation by 24 ... N—N5 25 Q—B3 N—Q6 26 KR—B1 (26 R—K2 NxBP) 26 ... Q—K2.

24 ....   Q—K2

This loses quickly. He could prolong the fight by 24 ... NxN 25 QxN Q—K3.

25 N—B2!!

A superb Nimzovichian move as the knight is excellently placed on the blockading square at K3 attacking the second weak pawn at KB5 and defending QB4 and KN2 against possible pressure.

25 ....   QR—Q1

26 KR—Q2   Q—K3

27 N—K3   N—K2

Losing a pawn. He had to guard the QNP by 27 ... P—N3 though after 28 Q—R3 R—B3 29

R—Q5 he is tied down hand and foot.

28	Q—N4	N—N3
39	RxP	Q—K2
30	P—KN3	R—B3
31	P—B5	

Now it is clearly gone.

31	....	KRxR
32	RxR	Resigns

He loses at least another pawn (32 ... RxR 33 PxR Q—Q2 34 Q—B5).

77 Sochi 1967
Black: Langeweg
Queen's Gambit Declined

1	P—Q4	N—KB3
2	N—KB3	P—Q4
3	P—B4	P—K3
4	N—B3	P—B4

At one time the Semi-Tarrasch was thought to give Black an easier game than the Orthodox QGD lines with B—KN5, but decades of experience have shown that this is not really true. As this particular game shows White has many dynamic chances due to the presence of many pieces which cannot easily be exchanged.

5	BPxP	NxP
6	P—K3	N—QB3
7	B—B4	

Botvinnik's move threatening 8 BxN PxB 9 PxP, and so forcing Black to a decision in the centre.

7	....	PxP
8	PxP	NxN

Black normally retains his options here by 8 ... B—K2 since he may wish to play N—KB3 subsequently, so as to threaten the QP and safeguard his K side. After 8 ... B—K2 Black has no reason to fear 9 BxN PxB 10 Q—N3 because of 10 ... N—QN5! 11 0—0 (Otherwise N—Q6+ is

awkward to meet) 11 ... B—KB4 threatening 12 ... B—B7 or 12 ... N—B7.

9	PxN	B—K2
10	0—0	0—0
11	B—Q3	

As the bishop is unguarded it is difficult to achieve a breakthrough by P—Q5 (N—R4!), so White turns his attention to the K side where Black has only one minor piece available for the defence.

11	....	P—QN3
12	Q—K2	

A more usual attacking formation is 12 Q—B2 P—N3 (12 ... P—KR3 13 Q—K2 and 14 Q—K4) 13 B—R6. The text envisages a slower onslaught keeping a careful eye on the possibilities of expanding in the centre by P—QB4 and P—Q5.

12	....	B—N2
13	B—N2	Q—Q4

The queen ultimately gets into trouble as White's fine 15th move snuffs out all Black's intended counter play on the long white diagonal 13 ... B—B3 is the sound way to play it.

14 P—B4	Q—KR4
15 B—K4!	KR—K1
16 KR—Q1	

The threat of P—Q5 now becomes very serious as the pawn will be able to advance as far as the seventh in some variations due to the absence of suitable blockading forces.

16	N—R4
17 BxB	NxB
18 QR—B1	

Building up the tension and preparing to use this rook along the third rank to harrass the enemy queen. ˙18 P—Q5 is less good now that Black has two minor pieces controlling the blockading squares at Q3 and QB4.

18	B—B1
19 R—B3!	KR—B1

A strange move that leaves his QR out of it for the rest of the game. Black was presumably worried about the threat of 20 R—K3 followed by 21 P—Q5 but 19 ... QR—B1 20 R—K3 QR—Q1 looks sounder even though after 21 R—K5 Q—N3 22 R—KN5 Q—R3 23 B—B1 Black still has a very uncomfortable position.

20 P—Q5

A strong advance whose main point is not the creation of a passed pawn but the concentration of White's pieces on the K side where he will have a marked local superiority.

20	N—B4
21 R—K3	PxP

The threat of 22 R—K5 followed by B—B1 or N—R4 and R—R5 attacking the queen without any quarter forces Black into this further concession. Now

the queen will be able to escape along the third row to QB3 or Q3.

22 RxP	Q—R3
23 N—Q4!	

Now that the KP has vanished the threat of N—B5 followed by a concentrated attack on KN7 is decisive. Black finds an ingenious counter based on back row mate possibilities but it proves inadequate as White's piece co-ordination is superior.

23 .... N—R5

Not 23 ... P—N3 24 N—B5! still, nor 23 ... P—B3 24 R—N3 with the threats of 25 R—R5 or 25 N—B5.

24 N—B5	Q—QB3
25 BxP!	QxR

The position both players had envisaged, but Spassky had seen further. Note that 25 ... QxP loses to 26 R—KN3 QxQ (26 ... Q—B8+ 27 Q—B1) 27 N—R6 mate, and 25 ... BxB simply to 26 N—K7+.

26 N—R6+!	KxB
27 Q—N4+	Resigns

It is mate in all variations, the prettiest being 27 ... K—B3 38 N—N8.

78 Moscow 1967
Black: Bilek
Sicilian Defence

1 P—K4	P—QB4
2 N—KB3	P—Q3
3 P—Q4	PxP
4 NxP	N—KB3
5 N—QB3	N—B3
6 B—KN5	B—Q2

One of the modern dynamic reassessments in this most dynamic opening. For decades it was taken for granted that White's threatened 7 BxN was so strong that it had to be prevented by 6 ... P—K3. Now, however, it is thought that the two bishops and open KN file are adequate compensation for Black.

7 Q—Q2 P—QR3

This is no longer strictly necessary as KN—N5, normally so strong in the Rauzer attack, loses its point when Black has not weakened his QP by P—K3. Current preference is for 7 ... R—B1 intending 8 ... NxN followed by 9 ... Q—R4 or even the bold exchange sacrifice 9 ... RxN.

8 0—0—0 R—B1
9 P—B4   P—KR3

Forcing the bishop to declare its intentions. Black probably has no other reasonable move as 9 ... P—K3 would allow 10 N—B3 with the awkward threat of 11 P—K5 (see game No. 56, Spassky-Taimanov). Polugaevsky, however thinks 9 ... P—QN4 playable.

10 BxN NPxB
11 B—K2 P—KR4

In such positions Black cannot allow B—R5 when the pin is very strong (e.g. White may be able to follow up by P—B5 and then N—K6). Black's provocative opening play (seven pawn moves out of eleven) cries out to a player of a classical turn of mind for condign punishment and Spassky is just the sort of player to oblige!

12 K—N1 P—K3
13 KR—B1 P—N4

Two more pawn moves! Yet it is far from easy for White to create a breach in the solid. mass of pawns round the Black monarch.

14 NxN RxN

After 14 ... BxN comes 15 Q—K3 threatening 16 N—Q5.

15 B—B3

Preparing the manoeuvre N—K2—B4.

15 .... R—B4
16 P—B5

At last decisive action!

16 .... Q—R4?

This weakens the squares around his king (especially Q2). Black would do better to drive the knight away by 16 ... P—N5 before it can get to the fine central square at K4. After 16 ... P—N5 17 N—K2 Q—N3 18 N—Q4 Black remains under severe pressure, but after the text the pressure is transformed into a quick win for White.

17 PxP PxP

17 ... BxP 18 N—Q5! and despite the opposite bishops resulting from 18 ... QxQ 19 RxQ

BxN 20 PxB White has a much superior ending with his threat of doubling on the K file.

18 P—K5!

At a stroke White improves the mobility of his minor pieces and plays to penetrate on the Q file or KB file.

18 ....   RxP

Not 18 ... QPxP? 19 QxB mate, while after 18 ... BPxP comes 19 Q—N5 P—K5 (otherwise 20 BxP+) 20 BxP+! still RxB 21 RxB+ KxR 22 R—KB1+ K—K1 23 Q—N8+ K—K2 24 Q—B8 mate.

19 Q—B4   R—KB4

After 19 ... P—B4 20 Q—N5 or 19 ... B—K2 20 N—K4 followed by 21 NxQP+ or 21 NxBP+ as appropriate, White breaks through at once.

20 Q—N3   R—N4

20 ... K—B2 looks a better chance. White then continues 21 N—K4 P—Q4 22 Q—QN8! when 23 N—Q6+ is now a strong threat and 22 ... PxN allows 23 RxB+ K—N1 24 Q—K8 etc.

21 Q—R4

Black has driven the queen to a slightly less threatening square but still has to decide how to counter the threat of N—K4.

21 ....   P—Q4

Or 21 ... Q—Q1 22 N—K4 R—KB4 23 N—N3 etc.

22 BxQP!

Naturally White must play to open lines in the centre.

22 ....   PxB

This loses quickly. 22 ... B—K2 would hang on as 23 N—K4 is met by 23 ... RxB 24 RxR PxR 25 NxP+ K—Q1 and the pin saves Black. However, after the simple 22 ... B—K2 23 B—N3 White could follow up by 24 Q—Q4 or 24 N—K4 or even 24

KR—K1 with an easy win. If 22 ... RxB then 23 NxR PxN 24 QxBP with an immediate win.

23 RxBP   KR—N1

Not 23 ... R—N5 24 R—K1+ B—K2 (24 ... K—Q1 25 RxB+ K—B2 26 Q—Q8+) 25 RxB+! KxR (25 ... K—Q1 26 Q—K1) 26 NxP+ K—K1 27 R—B8+! KxR 28 Q—K7+ K—N1 29 N—B6 mate. If 23 ... R—K4 then simply 24 Q—Q4.

24 NxP

The last obstacle in the centre disappears. Note that the White queen guards K1 so that Black cannot play for a back row mate by 24 ... RxN. However, that was Black's best chance of prolonging the game as the knight is much too strong a piece.

24 ....   B—N5?

Apparently shutting out the queen with gain of time, but White now has a forced win.

25 RxB+   Resigns

25 ... KxR 26 R—KB1+ K—K1 (26 ... B—B4 27 RxB+ RxR 28 Q—K7 mate or 27 ... K—K1 28 RxR RxR 29 QxR Q—K8+ 30 Q—B1) 27 N—B6+ K moves 28 NxR with decisive material gain.

After Black's incorrect 16th move the Black queen has played a 'spectator's role in the game.

79 Moscow 1967
White: Uhlmann
Queen's Gambit Declined

1 P—Q4	N—KB3
2 P—QB4	P—K3
3 N—KB3	

Uhlmann favours this move, preferring to meet the Queen's Indian or Bogoljubov-Indian (or as here the Queen's Gambit) rather than a Nimzoindian.

3	P—Q4
4 N—B3	B—K2

Spassky prefers the Orthodox Defence to the Semi-Tarrasch 4 ... P—B4. Perhaps he already knew what he demonstrated in the fifth game of his return match with Petrosian — that this variation is not so easy to play for Black as was once thought. (See game No. 87).

5 B—N5	0—0
6 P—K3	P—KR3
7 B—R4	P—QN3

Tartakower's variation in which the Black knight remains at home to guard, for the moment, the white squares at QR3 and QB3 which have been weakened by the text move. In modern times this system has proved quite popular, at least amongst those players who adopt the QGD in preference to one of the Indian defensive systems.

8 Q—B2

The most aggressive counter intending to castle long and try for a pawn storm on the other side (compare this game with Spassky-Bobotsov No. 78).

8	B—N2
9 BxN	

Rubinstein preferred the immediate 9 0—0—0 which leads to a very complicated game.

9	BxB
10 PxP	PxP
11 0—0—0	

Now White obviously intends P—KN4, P—KR4 and then P—N5 to open lines for an attack. Black counters on the other side.

11	P—B4
12 P—KN4	

Consistent play. White can also try for pressure in the centre by 12 PxP when however, Black can equalise either by Reshevsky's 12 ... BxN 13 QxB N—Q2! 14 P—B6 BxP! or the pawn sacrifice 12 ... PxP 13 NxP BxN 14 B—B4 N—Q2! 15 BxB R—N1

12	PxP
13 PxP	

If 13 NxP then simply 13 ... N—B3 striving to open his bishop's central black diagonal. White really needs his knight on KB3 so as to support P—N5 and to have a subsequent N—KN5 in reserve.

13	N—B3
14 P—KR4	P—N3

If 14 ... Q—Q3 then White prevents Q—B5+ by 15 Q—Q2. The text slightly weakens the Black king position but improves the mobility of both KB and king, so giving Black a greater choice of defensive possibilities.

15 P—N5

Neyshtadt in his authoritative

book on the QGD suggests as a response to Black's last move that White could try for an attack on the white squares by 15 P—R5 and if 15 ... P—KN4 then 16 Q—B5 N—N5 17 N—K5.

15 ....   PxP
16 P—R5

Neyshtadt here claims that the text leads to a decisive line opening for White as if 16 ... P—N5 then 17 PxP PxN 18 P—N7! winning. However, Spassky finds a much better defence. Note that the alternative White plan of 16 PxP would give Black a sound defence either by 16 ... B—N2 or quite simply by 16 ... BxP+ and if 17 K—N1 then 17 ... N—N5 18 Q—K2 R—K1 and White's queen is embarrassed for a good square. Certainly it is not clear how White can then make use of the open KR file.

16 ....   K—N2!
17 PxP

This opens the KR file before White has managed to play a major piece to support his KR, and in a move or two the whole attack looks ludicrously unsound. Uhlmann was probably regretting that he had not completed his development by 15 B—N5 or 15 B—K2 so as to be able to play QR—N1 before breaking open the K side. Even now it was not too late for 17 B—N5 so as to play BxN and thus reduce the pressure on his QP.

17 ....   PxP
18 B—N5   P—N5!

19 Q—Q2

An unsound sacrifice, but he did not really have a good move. Thus if 19 QR—N1 then 19 ... B—N4+ 20 NxB QxN+ 21 K—N1 NxP with advantage, while if 19 BxN BxB 20 N—K5 (20 QR—N1 B—Q2 threatening 21 ... B—B4) 20 ... BxN 21 PxB Q—N4+ and Black's pieces are very well placed for attack or defence, while White still has no genuine threats.

19 ....   PxN
20 Q—R6+   K—B2
21 Q—R7+   B—KN2
22 R—R3

Presumably both players saw up to here and Uhlmann must have thought he had a good attack as if 22 ... Q—B3 then 23 NxP Q—B4 24 B—B4. Spassky finds convincing refutation.

22 ....   R—R1!
Resigns

After 23 RxP+ Q—B3! 24 RxQ+ KxQ 25 NxP+ K—B2 the queen is trapped and Black is a piece up in a simplified position.

A game of theoretical significance.

80 Spartakiad, Moscow 1967
Black: Petrosian
French Defence

1 P—K4	P—K3
2 P—Q4	P—Q4
3 N—QB3	N—KB3
4 B—N5	PxP

Petrosian is one · of the few modern players to favour this cramped defensive system, as the passive positions which result from it are hardly to the taste of the great majority of modern grandmasters who favour systems which offer greater counter chances for Black.

5 NxP	QN—Q2
6 NxN+	NxN
7 N—B3	P—B4
8 B—N5+	

A simplifying line instead of the more complicated 8 B—QB4 or 8 B—Q3. Thus a game from their 1966 match went 8 B—Q3 B—K2 9 PxP Q—R4+ 10 P—B3 QxP(4) 11 Q—K2 B—Q2 12 N—K5 B—B3 with approximate equality. Spassky was hardly likely to repeat Tal's unfortunate choice of 8 Q—Q3 when Tal-Petrosian, Curacao 1962 continued 8 ... B—K2 9 BxN BxB 10 Q—N5+ B—Q2 11 QxNP R—QN1 12 QxRP RxP and Black had a very promising game.

8	B—Q2
9 BxB+	QxB
10 BxN	

White can still try for complications by Simagin's suggestion 10 Q—K2 intending castling long. The text clearly shows that White wishes to work on the slight advantage of a Q side pawn majority, while Black's King side

pawns are slightly devalued by the doubled pawn.

10	PxB
11 P—B3	

The second important feature of the position is the comparative value of the remaining minor piece on each side. The text ensures White's knight a fine central outpost.

11	PxP

Hoping to simplify even further by the exchange either of minor pieces or of queens, but Spassky's 13th move avoids this. An interesting alternative was 11 ... R—KN1 followed by castling long, but this is hardly in Petrosian's style.

12 NxP	B—B4

Black offered a draw here.

13 Q—B3!	0—0—0

Knowing Petrosian's penchant for exchange sacrifices, one might expect here 13 ... BxN 14 0—0—0 R—QB1?! 15 K—N1 RxP 16 PxR Q—N4+ 17 K—R1 B—K4 but after 18 R—Q3 White threatens both 19 QxNP and 19 R—QN1 and should be able to force a win in the long run.

14 0—0—0	Q—K2

Exchanging minor pieces first by 14 ... BxN 15 RxB Q—K2 is less good as after 16 QR—Q1 RxR 17 RxR R—Q1 White's rook could be usefully employed along the fourth rank by 18 R—KB4 or 18 R—KR4 and if 18 ... Q—Q2 the counter attack is broken by 19 R—B4+ K—N1 20 R—Q4 Q—K2 21 RxR+, 22 Q—N3+ and 23

Q—N7 with good chances in the queen ending. After the text White plays to avoid the exchange of minor pieces as the knight may well prove the superior piece in an ending.

15 N—N3   B—N3
16 P—N4!

An excellent blockading move reducing the mobility of Black's King side pawns.

16 ....   RxR+

The paradoxical 16 ... P—B4 was also possible as after 17 PxP Q—N4+ 18 K—B2 QxP+ 19 QxQ PxQ the mobile bishop gives Black good drawing chances in the ending.

17 RxR   P—KR4
18 P—KR3

Maintaing the status-quo. After 18 PxP? P—B4 threatening Q—R5 or Q—N4+ the White KRP would come under pressure.

18 ....   PxP
19 PxP   R—R7

Black must have felt quite happy at this stage as if 20 R—Q2 P—K4 and White's knight is out of it and White has a rather passisve position. However, Spassky plays a stronger move which shows that Black should have carried on consistently with the plan of exchanging major pieces by 19 ... R—Q1.

20 N—Q4   P—QR3

If 20 ... BxN 21 RxB then White would again have a powerful rook on the 4th row and would threaten 22 R—KB4 R—R3 23 P—N5!

21 R—Q2   K—N1
22 P—N4

White can now finally set his Q side pawn advance in motion.

22 ....   R—R1
23 N—N3   R—QB1

24 K—N2   R—B5

An impressive looking move, but it is not linked with any concrete plan and leaves the rook on an unguarded square. 24 ... R—Q1 still looks a better drawing chance.

25 P—QR4   P—K4

25 .... P—R4 would prove ineffective as White replies 26 Q—Q3 and if 26 ... RxKNP then 27 PxP B—R2 28 Q—N5 with a strong attack.

26 P—R5!

Once the bishop is drawn away from the defence of Q1 White's control of the Q file will begin to tell.

26 ....   B—R2

If 26 ... B—B2 then 27 N—B5.

27. Q—Q3!   R—B5

Practically forced unless Black is prepared to go into completely passive defence by 27 ... R—B2 when the ending after 28 Q—Q8+ QxQ 29 RxQ+ R—B1 30 RxR+ KxR 31 P—B3! is very favourable to White. If Black snatches a pawn by 27 ... RxKNP then 28 P—N5! PxP 29 QxP threatening 30 R—Q7 and White has a winning attack.

28 P—B3   P—K5
29 PxP   RxKP
30 R—R2

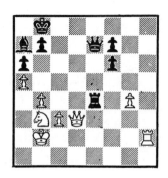

White's threats now become acute. Naturally Black makes room for his king and tries to activate his bishop.

30 ....   B—K6
31 R—R8+   K—R2
32 Q—Q5

A fine move emphasising his domination of the white squares. As the threat of 33 R—Q8 followed by R—Q7 is very strong, Black must drive the queen away straight away. 32 ... Q—K3? would lose at once to 33 Q—Q8.

32 ....   R—K4
33 Q—Q3   R—K5

Repetition?

34 R—KN8!

No!

34 ....   B—N4?

A time trouble blunder, but Black's defence was very difficult. 34 ... R—K3 was his best move.

35 N—Q4!

The knight now enters the game with decisive effect.

35 ....   B—K6

Realising his error, but too late.

36 P—QN5!

Threatening 37 P—N6 mate. If 36 ... PxP then 37 NxP+ K—R3 38 R—R8 mate! He cannot give his king more space by 36 ... P—N3 because of 37 N—B6+. So...

36 ....   BxN
37 QxB+   Resigns

37 ... RxQ 38 P—N6 is a pretty mate.

A remarkable victory from an apparently rather barren position.

81 Spartakiad, Moscow 1967
Black: Suetin
Sicilian Defence

1 P—K4   P—QB4
2 N—KB3   N—QB3
3 N—B3

A useful waiting move to see which system Black intends. 3 ... P—QR3 can be met by 4 P—Q3 and 5 P—KN3 and 3 ... P—K3 by 4 B—N5 transpsoing into a promising line of the Nimzovich-Rossolimo attack 3 B—N5.

3 ....   P—K3
4 P—Q4

Spassky however, prefers a more open fight.

4 ....   PxP
5 NxP   Q—B2
6 B—K3   P—QR3

7 N—N3

Apparently illogical after his last move guarding this knight, and in fact 7 B—Q3 is quite playable. However, the knight on N3 can be useful in taking the sting out of Black's traditional counter-play (... N—QR4). By controlling QB5 White prepares P—B4 without having to worry about a possible ... B—B4 in reply.

7 ....   N—B3
8 P—B4   B—N5

Dubious. The black squared bishop is normally needed on K2. White's doubled QBPs are no great weakness as Suetin found great weakness as Suetin found both in this game and in the following famous miniature: 1 P—K4 P—QB4 2 N—KB3 P—K3 3 P—Q4 PxP 4 NxP P—QR3 5 B—Q3 N—K2 6 N—QB3 QN—B3 7 N—N3 N—N3 8 0—0 P—N4 9 B—K3 P—Q3 10 P—B4 B—K2 11 Q—R5! B—B3 12 QR—Q1 BxN? 13 PxB Q—B2 14 R—Q2 QN—K2 15 N—Q4 B—Q2 16 P—B5! PxP 17 PxP N—K4 18 N—K6! BxN 19 PxB P—KN3 20 QxN! PxQ 21 PxP+ Resigns, as he loses much material after 21 ... K—Q2 22 B—B5+ K—B3 23 B—K4+ N—Q4 24 BxN+ K—Q3 35 BxR+ K—K2 26 B—N5+ etc. (Tal-Suetin, Tbilisi 1969-70).

9 B—Q3	0—0
10 0—0	BxN

There is a well known Russian proverb which Soviet players and annotators love to quote, "Kto skazal A..." i.e. "Once you've said 'A' you have to say 'B'." Having pinned the knight he must now remove it as 10 ... P—Q3 11 N—R4 P—QN4 12 N—N6 R—N1 involves giving up both bishops for knights after 13 NxB R(B1)xN 14 P—B3.

11 PxB	P—Q3

11 ... P—Q4 12 P—K5 N—K5 13 P—B4 leaves him struggling to maintain his precarious hold on the centre.

12 R—B3	P—K4
13 P—B5!	P—Q4
14 R—N3	

Now White clearly has a strong attack as if 14 ... PxP there comes 15 B—R6 P—KN3 16 PxP RPxP 17 BxR KxB 18 B—K2 and should win on material.

14	K—R1
15 PxP	N—K2

After 15 ... NxP White can either transpose into the game by 16 B—B5 QN—K2 (16 ... NxP 17 Q—K1 N—Q4 18 RxP! KxR 19 Q—N3+ K—R1 20 BxR wins) or play the direct 16 Q—R5 NxB 17 P—B6 P—KN3 18 Q—R6 R—KN1 19 QxN B—K3 20 N—Q2 intending to return to the attack by Q—R6 and N—K4—N5.

16 B—B5	KNxP
17 Q—N4	R—KN1

Or 17 ... P—KN3 18 R—R3 with the strong threat of 19 Q—KR4, so Black does best to remove his rook from the pin. However, the boxed-in position of his king means that from now on White can operate with the threat of RxRP+ followed by Q—R5 mate.

18 R—R3	N—KB3
19 Q—N5	

Threatening 20 BxN QxB 21 RxP+ NxR (forced) 22 QxQ.

19	QN—Q4
20 R—KB1	

To meet 20 ... N—B5 by 21 RxN PxR 22 R—R6! (but not 22 B—K7 Q—N3+!) with a winning attack. e.g. 22 ... R—K1 23 RxN! PxR 24 QxP+ K—N1 25 B—Q4 or 22 ... B—Q2 23 RxN! PxR 24 QxP+ R—N2 25 B—Q4 R(1)—KN1 26 QxBP etc. Naturally 22 ... PxR fails to 23 QxN+ R—N2 24 B—B8. Note in all this how Black is far too pre-occupied with the defence of his king to spare even a moment to threaten the doubled QBP.

20	P—QN3

20 ... NxP? 21 B—K7! Q—N3+ 22 K—R1 threatening 23 Q—R4 and 24 BxN.

21 B—K4	B—N2

His best defence was 21 ... PxB 22 BxN B—N2 (not 22 ... R—N1 23 N—Q2' B—N2 24 N—K4!)

playing for exchanges. After 23 BxB QxB 24 NxP White's extra pawn is of no real value.

22 BxN	BxB?

Now he must lose. 22 ... PxB transpsoing into the last note is essential. White's best reply would then be 23 BxB QxB 24 Q—K3 taking control of his K4 square and threatening two pawns. However, Black should be able to hold on for a long time as he has broken the force of the attack.

23 B—K7!

Surely Suetin should have seen that this old theme was 'on' again?

23	Q—B3
24 R—R6!	

This too has been in the air for several moves. The dual threat of 25 RxN and 25 BxN PxB 26 RxP+! forces Black into a lost ending.

24	N—K5
25 RxQ	NxQ
26 R—Q6!	

It is more important to simultaneously get rid of opposite coloured bishops and his doubled isolated pawn than to snatch the QNP which is doomed anyway.

26	BxN
27 RPxB	

So that the QRP is not en prise on move 28.

27	N—K5
28 RxP	NxP
29 P—B6	KR—K1

Or 29 ... N—Q4 30 R—N7 PxP (30 ... NxB 31 PxN P—B3 32 R—Q1, 33 R(7)—Q7 and 34 R—Q8) 31 BxP+ (31 RxP?! K—N2! is less clear) 31 ... NxB 32 RxN R—N2 33 P—B4 with more active rooks and a 'runner' which is far from the enemy king.

30 PxP+	KxP
31 R—N7	N—K7+

The only way to guard his KBP.

32 K—R1	N—B5
33 P—N3	N—N3
34 B—Q6	N—R1

"Some knights don't leap, they limp" (Tartakower).

35 P—B4	K—N3
36 P—KN4!	

White's pieces are so well placed that he can usefully play to weave a mating net round the enemy king.

36	R—K3
37 P—B5	K—N4
38 P—R3	P—K5

A last desperate chance. Among White's threats was 39 R—QB1 followed by 40 P—B6 to queen the pawn and so win the exchange at least.

39 K—N2	P—K6
40 B—B4+	K—N3
41 R—N6!	P—K7
42 R—K1	R—QB1
43 P—N4	P—QR4
44 RxP	PxP
45 R(2)xR+	PxR
46 B—K5!	

An ideal demonstration of the superiority of centralised bishop against offside knight. Now 46 ... RxP 47 BxN and 46 ... N—B2? 47 RxP+ K—N4 48 K—N3 and 49 P—R4 mate have to be rejected, so even resignation was perhaps called for. (46 ... K—B2? 47 R—N7+).

46	P—R4
47 RxP+	K—B2
48 R—QN6	PxP
49 PxP	K—K2

Not 49 ... N—N3? 50 R—B6+ winning a piece.

50 BxN	RxB
51 RxP	K—K3
52 R—QB4	K—Q4

53 R—B1	R—KN1		57 K—B5	R—B1+
54 K—N3	K—B3		58 K—K6	R—KN1
55 K—B4	R—B1+		59 R—KN1	Resings
56 K—N5	R—N1+			

82 6th match game, Candidates 1968
Black: Geller
Sicilian Defence

1 P—K4	P—QB4
2 N—QB3	P—Q3
3 P—KN3	N—QB3
4 B—N2	P—KN3
5 P—Q3	B—N2
6 P—B4	

A more aggressive plan than the usual KN—K2. White plays his knight to a more natural square and reserves K2 for the other knight in case it is driven away by P—QN4—N5.

6	N—B3

Geller persists in his plan of the 2nd and 4th games in both of which he had a good opening, even though he lost both games in the end. 6 ... P—K3 intending KN—K2 followed if necessary by P—B4 is a strong and flexible alternative.

7 N—B3	0—0
8 0—0	R—N1

After the match, Geller thought 8 ... B—N5 9 P—KR3 BxN 10 BxB N—Q5 better.

9 P—KR3

An improvement on 9 N—KR4 which Spassky had played in his 1966 match with Petrosian and in the 2nd game with Geller. Experience had shown him that a headlong attack on the K side by P—B5 gives Black too much counter play due to the latter's control of his K4. It is better then to complete development by B—K3 (without being worried by a N—KN5 from Black) and then play for a Dutch type attack with P—KN4, Q—K1, Q—R4 etc.

9	P—QN4
10 P—R3	

A remarkable concept, hoping to deter Black's 'programmed' move P—N5 by the threat of opening the QR file.

10	P—QR4
11 B—K3	P—N5
12 PxP	RPxP
13 N—K2	B—N2
14 P—N3	

Another defensive move on the Q side.

In the 4th game Spassky had played 14 Q—Q2 when his queen had become tied down to the defence of the QBP. Now that menial task is assigned to the QR.

14	R—R1

Black gets equality by changing his plan — 14 ... N—Q2 15 R—B1 P—K3 16 P—N4 P—Q4.

15 R—B1	R—R7
16 P—N4!	

At last an aggressive gesture by White. It takes great confidence to make so many concessions to Black before obtaining counter play oneself, but Spassky has confidence in the potential energy of his army on the K side.

16 ....   Q—R1?

The beginning of a plan that takes too much time and leaves his queen away from home when the White attack finally gathers momentum. It was now high time for Black to play a prophylactic move e.g. 16 ... P—K3! to meet 17 P—B5? by 17 .... KPxP 18 KPxP R—K1. Then 17 Q—K1 is met by 17 ... B—QR3 and 18 Q—R4? loses a pawn to 18 ... BxP. Geller also gives 16 ... P—Q4 17 P—K5 N—Q2 18 Q—R4 P—K3 as a sound defensive line.

17 Q—K1   Q—R3

The same defensive idea as in the last note — 18 Q—R4? NxP!

18 Q—B2   N—R2

Too slow. 18 ... N—Q2 is the right move.

19 P—B5!   N—N4
20 PxP

Rather a surprising decision as 20 N—B4 so as to follow-up with P—N5 looks a strong plan, but the opening of the KB file is a much quicker way of launching a strong attack as the exchange sacrifice RxN(B6) to remove the main defending piece soon comes into the reckoning.

20 ....   RPxP

After 20 ... BPxP weakening his K3, Black has to go back on the defensive e.g. 21 N—B4 B—B1 22 N—N5 N—B2, but this was a better chance as he retains the option of expelling the knights by P—K4 and P—R3, whereas now the N on KN5 becomes a real thorn in his flesh.

21 N—N5!   N—R6

Black has carried out his plan of intensifying Q side pressure to

breaking point, but as the subsequent course of the game shows, Spassky's judgement is much sounder — the attack on the king is a much more powerful factor.

22 Q—R4   R—B1
23 RxN!   PxR
24 Q—R7+   K—B1
25 NxP!

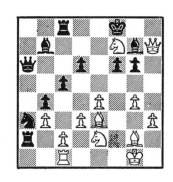

Possibly it was this move which Geller failed for foresee in his previous analysis. 25 ... KxN now loses to 26 B—R6 R—KN1 27 N—B4 RxP 28 R—B1 and Black must give up a great deal of material to avoid mate (28 ... K—B1 29 NxP+ K—B2 30 N—B4 — 30 N—R8+ is also good — 30 ... K—B1 31 N—R5 BxB 32 QxB+! K—K2 33 Q—R7+ K—Q1 34 NxP! etc.)

25 ....   RxP
26 B—R6!   RxR+

Or 26 ... RxN 27 QxB+ K—K1 (27 ... K—K2 28 N—N5+ mates) 28 N—N5! PxN 29 BxP and mates, or 26 ... QxP 27 QxB+ K—K1 28 RxR NxR 29 N—B4 with a winning attack.

27 NxR   KxN

Or 27 ... BxB 28 NxB K—K1 29 N—N8 K—B1 30 N—K7 and mates.

28 QxB+ K—K1

Or 28 ... K—K3 29 P—N5 PxP 30 BxP R—K1 31 P—R4 P—Q4 (otherwise 32 B—R3 is mate) 32 PxP+ K—Q3 (32 ... BxP loses the queen after 33 QxP+) 33 B—B4+ and 34 BxR mate.

29 P—N5

Here too this brings White's bishops into play with decisive effect. However in the time scramble, Spassky misses the quicker win 29 P—K5 BxB 30

P—K6!

29 .... P—B4

30 QxP+ K—Q2

Or 30 ... K—Q1 31 Q—B7 R—B2 (otherwise 32 P—N6 etc. getting a second queen) 32 Q—B8+ K—Q2 33 P—N6 R—B1 34 P—N7 Q—R1 35 P—N8(Q) etc.

31 Q—B7+ K—B3

32 PxP+ Resigns

After the exchange of queens on QN7 White marches his KBP home to queen.

83 7th match game, Candidates 1968
Black: Korchnoy
King's Indian Defence

1 P—Q4 N—KB3
2 P—QB4 P—KN3
3 N—QB3 B—N2

Korchnoy rarely plays the King's Indian, normally preferring the Grunfeld.

4 P—K4 P—Q3
5 P—B3 0—0
6 B—K3 N—B3
7 KN—K2 P—QR3
8 N—B1

Spassky's favourite move which he had already adopted against Gheorghiu (Students' Olympiad, 1962) and Jansa (Tel-Aviv Olympiad, 1964). I must take the opportunity here of correcting a double error in my book on the 1968 Candidates matches, where it is stated that the Gheorghiu game was played in the late fifties and that Spassky played 8 Q—Q2 in that game.

8 .... P—K4

9 P—Q5 N—Q5
10 N—N3 NxN

The Gheorghiu game went 10 ... P—B4 11 PxP e.p. PxP 12 NxN PxN 13 BxQP P—B4 14 B—K3 R—N1 15 Q—B2 B—K3 16 B—K2 N—Q2 17 0—0 N—K4 18 P—QN3 N—B3 19 Q—Q2 and Black had inadequate compensation for the pawn.

11 QxN

Recapturing with the pawn is more usual, but White gets Q side pressure in both cases. In fact Korchnoy had already written on his score sheet, 11 PxN P—B4 so the text is a shrewd psychological choice.

11 .... P—B4

As White has already vacated Q1 for his rook this leaves Black tied down permanently to his weak QP. He should try the more orthodox plan of 11 ... N—R4 and 12 ... P—KB4 or else 11 ... N—Q2 and then P—N3 and P—QR4 adopting a defensive attitude.

12 PxP e.p.   PxP
13 0—0—0!   B—K3?

Too eager to bring his R to QN1 and also based upon an error in analysis. 13 ... R—K1 or 13 ... Q—K2 intending 14 ... R—Q1 are better moves. Black actually thought that 13 ... Q—K2 14 Q—N6 was good for White over-looking that 14 ... B—N2 is quite all right for Black.

14 Q—R3   N—K1

After this Black remains completely passive, but 14 ... P—Q4 is bad because of 15 BPxP PxP 16 PxP and if 16 ... BxP 17 B—KN5 or 16 ... NxP 17 B—QB4 R—B1 (not 17 ... NxB 18 RxQ NxB because of 19 QxR+!) 18 BxN BxB 19 K—N1 and Black must give up the exchange for inadequate compensation.

15 P—R4!   P—B3?

All these pawn moves weaken crucial squares, in this case his K3. 15 ... B—B3 is his best chance of making a fight hoping to play B—K2. Then if 16 B—R6 he must offer a draw by repetition by 16 ... B—N2.

16 P—B5!

Whereas Spassky's pawn moves are very strong.

16 ....   R—B2

Once again 16 ... P—Q4 loses material after 17 PxP PxP 18 B—QB4 as there is then a pin on the diagonal QR2/KN8 as well as on the Q file. (18 ... N—B2 19 NxP BxN 20 BxN+ NxB 21 Q—N3.)

17 Q—R4

The attack on the QBP gains time to exchange white square

bishops thus punishing Black for his 15th move.

17 ....   Q—B2
18 B—QB4   BxB
19 QxB   B—B1
20 P—R5!

Now to keep the KR file closed by 20 ... P—N4 would weaken his KB4 giving White a chance to try a subsequent N—K2—N3—B5.

20 ....   PxBP

This looks awful, but his pieces were all so badly placed that he does not have a good move at his disposal.

21 PxP   PxP
22 Q—K6

Much stronger than 22 BxP letting Black get rid of his crippled bishop.

22 ....   R—Q1

Or 22 ... N—Q3 23 BxP N—N4 24 BxB R(1)xB (24 ... NxN 25 B—Q6 Q—R4 26 PxN QxP+ 27 K—N1 and Black has no compensation for the piece). 25 R—R6 K—N2 26 QR—R1 threatening mate in two by 27 RxP+ KxR 28 Q—N4.

23 RxR   QxR
24 R—Q1

It was better to leave the rook on the KR file. The most precise was 24 QxQBP Q—Q6 25 BxP which leaves Black with a resignable game e.g. 25 ... Q—B5 26 QxN QxB 27 K—N1 followed by 28 N—Q5.

24 ....   Q—K2
25 QxQBP   N—B2

(See diagram next column.)

26 Q—N6!

A move that Kotov in his book ((Secrets of Chess Thinking" (English title "Think Like a Grandmaster") praises as the sort of 'creeping move' that changes

the position significantly despite its insignificant appearance. The point is that Black threatens 26 ... Q—K3 exploiting the unguarded White queen to force exchanges. Kotov believes that such moves are very hard to find.

26 ....   K—N2

Now 26 ... Q—K3 is met by 27 BxP with the win of a sound pawn. Black's best chance was 26 ... P—B5 which keeps material level for the moment, though after 27 Q—N8 with the threat 28 R—Q8 White has much the better of it, but not 27 N—Q5 NxN 28 RxN P—B6! 29 PxP Q—R6+.

27 N—Q5!   Q—K3

Or 27 ... NxN 28 RxN P—B5 29 QxRP.

28 BxP   BxB
29 QxB   N—N4

Exchanging knights leaves a hopeless ending after 30 RxN.

30 Q—K3   Q—B3+
31 K—N1   N—Q5
32 R—QB1

Snuffing out Black's temporary initiative.

32 ....   Q—N4

Or 32 ... Q—Q3 33 R—R1 returning to the attack.

33 N—B7   Q—K7

Now White wins quickly, but Black had only a choice of evils. (33 ... Q—Q2 34 NxP; 33 ... Q—N2 34 N—K8+ and 35 N—Q6; 33 ... Q—N3 34 N—K8+ K—B1 35 R—B8 K—K2 36 N—B7 and 37 N—Q5+).

34 N—K6+   K—R2

Or 34 ... K—N1 35 R—B8+ K—R2 36 QxQ NxQ 37 R—QR8 winning a second pawn, but not 35 Q—R6? Q—Q6+.

35 Q—R6+!   Resigns

The sort of mating finale that grandmasters permit only when in grave time trouble.

84 Lugano Olympiad 1968
Black: Porath
French Defence

1 P—K4   P—K3
2 P—Q4   P—Q4
3 N—QB3   N—KB3
4 B—N5   PxP

A passive system, but one imagines that the Israeli veteran was thinking in terms of playing a strategically clear system in which he might draw by accurate defence.

5 NxP   QN—Q2
6 KN—B3

An essential feature of modern master play is to hold the whip hand by avoiding variations in which you suspect your opponent has prepared thoroughly. 6 NxN+ had been played in the game against Petrosian a year before (game No.   ), so White varies.

6 ....   B—K2
7 NxN+   BxN

Black decides to play for further exchanges.

8 BxB

An unusual move. 8 Q—Q2 is normally tried so that after 8 ... BxB 9 NxB N—B3 10 0—0—0 the knight is a slight threat to the enemy K side.

8 ....   QxB
9 B—B4   P—B4

Obviously not 9 ... P—K4? 10 PxP NxP? 11 Q—K2 0—0 12 NxN when 12 ... R—K1 fails to 13 ... BxP+.

10 Q—K2

An attacking idea that Tal is very fond of. The QP is sacrificed temporarily so that after 10 ... PxP 11 0—0—0 White can quickly concentrate his rooks in the centre (11 ... P—K4? 12 RxP).

10 ....   0—0
11 0—0—0   P—QR3

Since 11 ... P—QN3 to develop his bishop fails to 12 Q—K4 R—N1 13 Q—B6 with development difficulties for Black he has to get his bishop out in this long winded way.

12 Q—K3!   PxP

12 ... P—QN4 does not seem much better as after 13 B—Q3 PxP White's rook had admittedly been prevented from recaptruing, but White has 14 Q—K4 Q—R3+ 15 N—N5! and if 15 ... QxN+ 16

P—KB4 winning the exchange.

13 RxP   P—QN4
14 B—Q3   P—N3

The threat was 15 Q—K4 or 15 BxP+. If 14 ... R—R2? then 15 R—KR4 with a double attack and if 14 ... R—N1 then 15 R—KR4 P—N3 (15 ... P—R3 16 Q—K4) 16 N—N5 P—KR4 17 P—KN4 with a swift attack on the weakened K side. These variations show what attacking strength lies in the formation R on Q4, B on Q3.

15 R—Q1

White has no need to concentrate on the K side as Black's inability to develop his bishop due to the hanging knight at Q2 is very serious.

15 ....   N—B4

After this Black has no way of saving the game. The knight had to remain where it was, ready to go to KB1 or KB3 for the defence of his king. Black should try 15 ... Q—K2 and then N—B3 when he can finally move his bishop.

16 N—K5   Q—K2

After 16 ... NxB+ 17 KRxN Black has to watch out for N—Q7 as well as Q—K4 followed by N—B6 or R—KR3. 16 ... B—N2 is met by 17 R—KB4 Q—K2 18 N—N4 with strong threats on the black squares. Hence Black decides he must play another prophylactic move before moving his bishop.

17 B—K2   P—B3

A counsel of despair, but 17 ... B—N2 loses to 18 N—Q7 KR—QB1 (18 ... KR—Q1 19 NxN winning a piece, or 18 ... KR—K1 19 Q—K5!) 19 N—N6.

18 N—B6   Q—QB2

18 ... Q—QN2 19 B—B3 or 18

... Q—KB2 19 R—Q8 are clearly no better.

19 R—Q8   N—N2

Trying to expel the invader. 19 ... QxN 20 Q—R6 R—K1 21 B—B3 or 19 ... B—N2 20 QxN QRxR (otherwise 21 QxR mate) 21 N—K7+ lose at once.

20 RxR+   KxR
21 B—B3

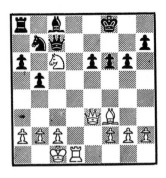

Now Black's pieces are all tangled up in the corner and Black has no reasonable move.

21 ....   K—N2
22 Q—R3

22 N—Q8 would win material (22 ... R—N1 23 BxN and 24 NxP+ but White has this even more devastating move, leaving the Black rook no safe square.

22 ....   K—B2

Not 22 ... B—Q2? 23 Q—K7+ and meanwhile White threatened 23 Q—K7+ winning the exchange.

23 P—KN3!

Zugzwang.

23 ....   P—K4
24 N—Q8+   K—N1

Not 24 ... K—K1 25 B—B6+. nor 24 ... K—N2 25 BxN BxB 26 N—K6+.

25 B—Q5+   Resigns

Black is forced into the variation of the last note as 25 ... K—R1 allows mate in one.

85 Lugano Olympiad, 1968
White: Larsen
Queen's Gambit Declined

1 N—KB3	N—KB3
2 P—B4	P—K3
3 N—B3	P—Q4
4 P—Q4	B—K2
5 B—B4	0—0
6 P—K3	QN—Q2

With the White bishop at KB4 and not KN5 Black could immediately play 6 ... P—B4 but the quiet text is quite in order.

7 R—B1   P—B3
8 P—KR3

An unnecessary precaution. 8 P—QR3 would be a better move allowing him to play P—B5 safely later on. Then if 8 ... N—R4 9 B—K5! is strong.

8 ....   P—QR3
9 P—QR3

If his pawn were on QR3 he could now safely play 9 P—B5 whereas now that move is met by 9 ... P—QN3 10 P—QN4 P—QR4 11 P—QR3 RPxP 12 RPxP PxP 13 NPxP B—R3! and Black is quite well placed having eliminated his bad bishop.

9	PxP
10 BxP	P—QN4
11 B—QR2	B—N2
12 0—0	

12 P—K4 may be playable but after 12 ... P—B4 White would have to play the sharp 13 P—Q5 is he wished to achieve anything, so the safer text is perhaps more sensible for the moment.

12	P—B4
13 P—Q5	

Now this leads to simplifying exchanges, so 13 N—K5 looks a better prospect for complex play.

13	NxP
14 NxN	BxN
15 BxB	PxB
16 QxP	N—B3

The psychological background of games played at the Olympiad has to be borne in mind here. Spassky's task with Black on top board is not to lose, while his colleagues on the lower boards try to deal severely with the less experienced Danes. Larsen feels honour bound to play for a win especially to counterbalance the impression caused by his severe loss to Spassky in the Candidates' match a few months earlier. Hence Spassky offers the exchange of queens and Larsen chooses the most aggressive move in reply.

17 Q—N7	R—K1
18 KR—Q1	Q—B1
19 QxQ	

Or 19 Q—N6 P—B5.

19	QRxQ
20 B—Q6?	

Hoping to get at Black's Q side pawns but White is beginning to play with fire and 20 K—B1 was a much sounder plan.

20	K—B1

21 K—B1	N—K5!
22 BxB+	KxB
23 R—Q5	QR—Q1
24 R—R5?	

White runs great risks of having his rook cut off from the main activity in the centre. 24 R—K5+ and exchanging rooks with a likely draw was correct.

24	P—R3
25 P—QN4	P—B5!
26 P—QR4	

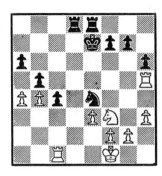

Clearly it was because of this move that White left his rook on the fifth rank. Spassky's next two moves show that the plan was misconceived.

26	K—B3
27 PxP	P—N3!
28 RxRP?	

A better chance was 28 R—R4 so as to try and get the rook back into play.

28	PxP
29 N—Q4?	

Not realising the danger. He should still try 29 R—R4.

29	N—Q7+
30 K—N1	

A bitter necessity.

30	N—N6!
31 NxN	PxN
32 R—N1?	

This loses 32 R—R4 was still best.

| 32 .... | R—K5! |
| 33 P—N3 | |

Otherwise 33 ... K—N2 wins the rook that has strayed so far away from home.

| 33 .... | RxNP |
| 34 R—R4 | RxR |

| 35 PxR | R—Q6 |
| 36 K—N2 | |

Or 36 K—B1 K—K4 37 K—K2 R—B6 38 K—Q2 P—N5 39 P—B3 K—Q4 and wins quickly.

| 36 .... | K—K4 |

Resigns

Larsen's well known optimism was severly punished in this game.

86 4th game, World Championship, 1969
White: Petrosian
Queen's Gambit Declined

1 P—QB4	P—K3
2 P—Q4	P—Q4
3 N—QB3	P—QB4

Considered suspect for decades the Tarrasch Defence was rehabilitated by Spassky in this match and played a large part in his success.

4 BPxP	KPxP
5 N—B3	N—QB3
6 P—KN3	N—B3
7 B—N2	B—K2
8 0—0	0—0
9 B—N5	

Petrosian persisted in this move throughout the match thus showing clearly that he considers it superior to the classical plan thought up by Reti. (9 PxP BxP 10 N—QR4 B—K2 11 B—K3) in which Black has the gambit move 9 ... P—Q5.

| 9 .... | PxP |

A playable alternative seeking exchanges is 9 ´ ... N—K5 as adopted by Capablanca in his 1909 match with Marshall.

| 10 KNxP | P—KR3 |

| 11 B—K3 | B—KN5 |
| 12 N—N3 | |

Or 12 P—KR3 B—K3 13 R—B1 Q—Q2 14 K—R2 N—K4 15 Q—R4 QxQ 16 NxQ N—B5 with equality (Korchnoy-Spassky XXIV USSR 1957.) In the 12th ˙game Petrosian obtained some pressure by 12 Q—R4 N—QR4 13 QR—Q1 N—B5 14 B—B1 Q—B1 15 Q—B2.

12	B—K3
13 R—B1	R—K1
14 R—K1	

In the 2nd game 14 N—QN5 Q—Q2 15 N(5)—Q4 B—KR6 left Black with no difficulties. It is a useful precaution to guard the KP and prepare B—R1 as an answer to B—KR6.

14	Q—Q2
15 B—B5	QR—B1
16 BxB	QxB
17 P—K3	KR—Q1
18 Q—K2	B—N5!

Better than the tempting 18 .... P—Q5 when 19 NxP NxN 20 PxN RxP 21 N—N5 RxR 22

NxR!

19 P—B3

A weakening of the KP. 19 Q—B1 is more in the Petrosain style.

19 ....   B—B4

20 QR—Q1   N—K4

Black has weaknesses on the dark squares but his pieces are developed harmoniously and he has targets on the light squares.

21 N—Q4

Or 21 NxP RxN 22 RxR NxR 23 P—K4 N—Q6! 24 QxN N—N5 and Black has a fine position.

21 ....   B—N3

22 B—R3   R—B5?!

A bold move that leads to complex play as the rook is rather exposed on this square. However, the safe 22 ... R—N1 left it pretty level, whereas now both sides have chances.

23 P—KN4

This awkward looking move threatens 24 P—B4 and then 25 NxP, but further weakens the K side.

23 ....   N—B3

24 P—N3   R—N5

25 Q—Q2   R—N3

26 QN—K2?

Petrosian failed to see here that the logical move 26 N—R4 continuing his threats to the wandering rook could not be met by 26 ... NxN 27 PxN R—K3 because 28 P—N5 wins the exchange. Black would have to reply 26 N—R4 R—R3 and after 27 B—B1 NxN 28 PxN (28 QxN R—B3 29 QxRP P—R4! with good K side play) 28 ... R—K3 29 N—B5 RxR+ 30 RxR Q—B2 31 R—K5 the game is probably level, but White retains some initiative on the dark squares. Having failed to discover this

logical continuation Petrosian clearly became unsettled and his next few moves reveal that in the expressive phrase "he has lost the thread."

26 ....   B—R2

27 B—N2

The first uncertain move. 27 B—B1 or 27 N—B4 P—KN4 28 N(B4)—K2 were better.

27 ....   R—K1

28 N—N3

The second uncertain move. 28 N—B4 was still correct.

28 ....   NxN

29 PxN

Playing for exchanges. Capturing with the queen was better.

29 ....   R—K3

30 RxR   QxR

31 R—QB1

To play for further exchanges by 31 K—B2 was more consistent.

31 ....   B—N3

Preparing to put his knight on R2 and then his queen on KB3 with a strong attacking formation.

32 B—B1?

32 K—B2 was still much better.

32 ....   N—R2

33 Q—B4   N—B1

A more promising line was 33 ... Q—N3 34 R—B5 N—N4 35 RxP Q—QB3 36 Q—Q6 Q—B6 with various awkward threats. However, the text is unpleasant enough to meet (Petrosian had quarter of an hour left on the clock and Spassky 25 minutes at this point.)

34 R—B5

34 Q—K5! was a better drawing chance hoping for 34 ... QxQ 35 PxQ RxP 36 P—B4 and 37 P—B5 shutting in the enemy bishop. Black would do better to play in this 35 ... N—K3 36 K—B2

P—Q5 but then 37 N—B5 and White should draw.

34 ....   B—N8

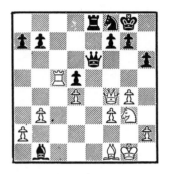

Now the game becomes tense.
35 P—QR4   N—N3
36 Q—Q2   Q—KB3
37 K—B2?

Up to now Petrosian has defended correctly, but once he allows the knight to come to KB5

his position becomes much too difficult. 37 R—B1 was his last chance, forcing 37 ... N—R5 and after 38 B—N2 B—N3 39 K—B2 Black has only a slight initiative.

37 ....   N—B5!
38 P—R5

Or 38 R—B3 N—K3 39 N—K2 Q—R5+ 40 K—N1 P—KR4!

38 ....   B—Q6!
39 N—B5

Not 39 BxB QxP+, nor 39 Q—B3 Q—R5 40 K—N1 BxB and Black wins.

39 ....   Q—N4!
40 N—K3

Otherwise 40 ... N—R6+.

40 ....   Q—R5+
41 K—N1   BxB

Spassky sealed this after five minutes and Petrosain resigned without resuming, as 42 NxB R—K7 or 42 KxB Q—R6+ are clear wins for Black (43 K—K1 RxN+, or 43 K—N1 RxN).

87 5th game, World Championship, 1969
Black: Petrosian
Queen's Gambit Declined

1 P—QB4	N—KB3
2 N—QB3	P—K3
3 N—B3	P—Q4
4 P—Q4	P—B4
5 BPxP	NxP
6 P—K4	NxN
7 PxN	PxP
8 PxP	B—N5+

These exchanges were long thought to give Black easy equality so that the more restrained 6 P—K3 was the norm in

master chess of the last two decades.

9 B—Q2	BxB+
10 QxB	0—0
11 B—B4	N—B3
12 0—0—0	P—QN3
13 QR—Q1	

This move had been tried in the thirties but preference was normally given to the formation with rooks on Q1 and QB1. Spassky's formation with rooks on Q1 and K1 is basically more aggressive.

13 ....   B—N2

After this game in which Black soon got into difficulties, whereas theory gives it as equal, there were a number of improvements suggested. The main consensus of opinion was that 13 ... N—R4 to drive the bishop away from the support of P—Q5 was called for. However, it is nothing like so simple as the game Polugaevsky-Tal, XXXVII USSR later in 1969 showed. (13 ... N—R4 14 B—Q3 B—N2 15 KR—K1 R—B1 16 P—Q5! PxP 17 P—K5! N—B5 18 Q—B4 and White has a threatening position in return for his pawn. In fact after Tal's 18 ... N—N7 there followed the Greek gift 19 BxP+ KxB 20 N—N5+ and White's attack is sufficient to win in the long run).

14 KR—K1

On making this move Spassky's clock showed only seven minutes taken and Petrosian's seventeen.

14 ....   R—B1

Now Black sinks into difficulties. He should try 14 ... N—R4 15 B—Q3 Q—Q3 to rob the White queen of KB4 and to meet 16 P—Q5 by 16 ... P—K4 blocking the position.

15 P—Q5!   PxP

After this White gets the better of it due to his well posted bishop. Petrosian rejected 15 ... N—R4 fearing 16 PxP but this sacrifice is nothing to worry about (16 ... QxQ 17 PxP+ K—R1 18 NxQ NxB 19 NxN RxN 20 P—K5 B—B1 21 P—K6 BxP 22 RxB P—N3 and 23 ... K—N2.) As Spassky confirmed after the Polugaevsky-Tal game, his prepared answer would have been 16

B—Q3 and if 16 ... PxP 17 P—K5 while 16 ... Q—Q3 can be met by 17 PxP QxKP 18 N—Q4 and in this fluid position White has very active pieces.

16 BxP

White would also get a promising position from 16 PxP N—R4 17 B—B1 Q—Q3 18 N—N5 QR—Q1 19 Q—Q3 and Black has to take away the blockader by 16 ... Q—R3.

16 ....   N—R4

After this the knight plays a very minor role in the struggle. However, Black's game was already far from easy and the improvement suggested by the critics 16 ... Q—K2 is met by 17 Q—B4 R—B2 (17 ... P—KR3 18 N—R4 and 19 N—B5) 18 P—KR4 N—Q1 19 Q—N3 N—K3 20 N—K5 with the threat of advancing the KBP.

17 Q—B4   Q—B2
18 Q—B5   BxB

Petrosian clearly realised that he was now in great trouble as he thought twenty minutes over the exchange, his longest period of thinking in the whole game. 18 ... P—KR3 to prevent 19 N—N5 is met by 19 BxB QxB 20 R—Q7 R—B2 21 KR—Q1.

19 PxB   Q—B7

Black's position is very poor so he plays to exchange queens. 19 ... N—B5 is met by 20 N—N5 P—N3 21 Q—R3 P—KR4 22 N—K4 N—Q3 23 N—B6+ K—N2 24 Q—KN3 with a powerful attack, (25 NxP+ or 25 Q—K5 in the offing). 19 ... Q—Q3 is no good either because of 20 N—N5 Q—N3 (20 ... P—N3 21 Q—R3 P—R4 22 Q—KB3 with the threat of N—K4—B6+) 21 QxQ RPxQ 22 P—Q6 N—N2 23 P—Q7

QR—Q1 24 R—K7 N—B4 25 R—Q6 and Black is completely tied up.

20 Q—B4

20 QxQ RxQ 21 R—K7 was also very strong but Black's bare K side and inability to block the passed pawn suggests to White that he should keep the pressure on.

20 ....   QxRP

The commentators criticised this, but in fact Black has no constructive move.

21 P—Q6   QR—Q1
22 P—Q7   Q—B5
23 Q—B5   P—KR3

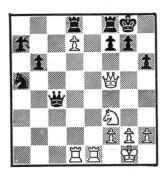

Or 23 ... Q—B3 24 N—K5 Q—K3 25 Q—B2 followed by 26 Q—B7 with decisive effect.

24 R—QB1   Q—R3
25 R—B7   P—QN4
26 N—Q4   Q—QN3

With all his men pressed to the edge of the board Black is lost, but a better resistance is put up by 26 ... Q—Q3 27 NxP Q—Q7 28 R—KB1 N—N6 29 RxP N—Q5 30 NxN QxN 31 R—N7 P—N3 32 Q—QN5 K—N2 but White will ultimately win if necessary by advancing his K side pawns to open lines against the king.

27 R—B8!   N—N2

Not 27 ... QxN 28 RxR RxR 29 R—K8+, nor 27 ... P—N5 28 R—K8! QxN 29 RxKR+ RxR 30 RxR+ KxR 31 Q—B5+! QxQ 32 P—Q8(Q) mate, nor again 27 ... P—N3 28 RxR RxR 29 QxQNP.

28 N—B6   N—Q3

Black's last gasp, but White now has an elegant finish.

29 NxR   NxQ
30 N—B6   Resigns

88 19th game, World Championship, 1969
Black: Petrosian
Sicilian Defence

1 P—K4   P—QB4

Spassky led at this stage by 9½ points to 8½ but, as defending champion, Petrosian had merely to draw the match to remain world title holder. One would therefore expect him to play a solid line as Black, such as the Petroff or the Closed Lopez, hoping to score the single win needed when he was White and to draw all the other games. Hence the choice of opening is rather risky.

2 N—KB3   P—Q3
3 P—Q4   PxP

4 NxP   N—KB3
5 N—QB3   P—QR3
6 B—KN5   QN—Q2

6 ... P—K3 is more usual when after 7 P—B4 B—K2 8 Q—B3 Q—B2, White is at a loss as to how to post his KB actively, whereas after the text he puts it on a strong square at once.

7 B—QB4   Q—R4

Not 7 ... P—K3 when BxKP gives a promising attack. In Tal-Juchtman, 1956 and Tal-Bilek, 1964 Black tried 7 ... P—R3 but after 8 BxN! NxB 9 Q—K2! White had rather the better of it as 0—0—0 and then P—K5 becomes very threatening for the second player.

8 Q—Q2   P—KR3

Varying from Spassky's well known game with Polugaevsky (see game No. 25).

9 BxN   NxB
10 0—0—0

The same plan as in Tal-Bilek. Now Black is badly behind in development and his position does not look very promising.

10 ....   P—K3

10 ... P—K4 has been suggested so as to rule out a subsequent breakthrough by White with P—K5. However, after 11 N—B5 BxN 12 PxB R—B1 13 B—N3 White has a firm grip on the white squares and the better game.

11 KR—K1

White could also play the prophylactic 11 B—N3 when a game Kuijpers-Damjanovic, Beverwijk 1966 continued 11 ... B—Q2 12 P—B4 B—K2 13 K—N1 Q—B2 14 KR—K1 R—Q1 15 P—N4 P—KN4 16 N—B5! and White won.

11 ....   B—K2?

Intending to castle short, but as the subsequent course of the game shows, White finds no great difficulty in assaulting the enemy king there. A better chance was 11 ... B—Q2 12 P—B4 0—0—0 e.g. 13 P—K5 P—Q4! or 13 P—B5 P—Q4! 14 KPxP PxBP or 14 BPxP PxB 15 PxB+ RxP and Black is not too badly placed.

12 P—B4

12 K—N1 was possibly more accurate as before castling Black would have to retreat his queen to a more passive position (12 K—N1 0—0? 13 N—Q5!)

12 ....   0—0
13 B—-N3   R—K1

Preparing to defend his K3 against White's threat of an ultimate P—K5 when the moves PxP or P—K4 would both cede White control of the • important Q5 square and "lengthen" his bishop's diagonal.

14 K—N1   B—B1
15 P—N4!

White has fully consolidated his position and must undertake something definite. He boldly sacrifices a pawn which if not captured will advance with great effect e.g. 15 ... P—QN4 16 P—N5 PxP 17 PxP N—R4 18 P—N6! PxP 19 Q—N5. Black's best defence is probably 15 ... P—K4 though after 16 PxP PxP (16 ... QxP 17 N—B3 and 18 P—N5) 17 N—B5 BxN 18 NPxB QR—Q1 19 Q—N2 White gets an attack along the KN file and has the more aggressive bishop.

15 ....   NxNP
16 Q—N2   N—B3

Or 16 ... P—K4 17 N—B5 with strong threats.

17 R—N1

Now the main threat is P—B5

to bring his bishop into the attack on the king, but Black has also to take account of a possible P—K5. Thus if now 17 ... Q—QB4 as suggested by Averbakh, then 18 N—B3 B—Q2 19 P—K5! with great effect.

17 ....   B—Q2

At last the bishop comes out and if now 18 N—B3 preparing P—K5 then 18 ... B—B3.

18 P—B5!   K—R1

Far from best as White now makes very effective use of the open KB file. Black had to try 18 ... P—K4 or even 18 ˙ ... PxP though White's ultimate Q—N6 would prove hard to meet.

19 QR—KB1 Q—Q1

Geller recommended 19 ... P—K4 but then White plays 20 N—K6 and if 20 ... PxN 21 PxP BxP then 22 RxN! with decisive effect. Still, two better chances of putting up a real resistance were either 19 ... PxP 20 NxP BxN 21 RxB Q—Q1 22 BxP R—K4 and 19 ... Q—K4 when White continues 20 N—B3 Q—B5 21 Q—R3 threatening 22 N—KN5 or if 20 ... Q—B4 then 21 P—KR4 intending N—KN5 or N—K1—Q3.

20 PxP   PxP

Yet another inferior move. 20 ... BxP would let him exchange one attacking piece. White would continue 21 NxB PxN 22 N—K2 and if 22 ... P—K4 to prevent 23 N—B4 then 23 B—B7 winning the exchange, (23 ... R—K2 24 RxN!) White could also try the more complicated 22 P—K5 PxP 23 N—K4 N—R4 24 Q—N6! Q—R5 (not 24 ... N—B5 25 RxN PxR 26 P—B3 with the winning threat of 26 B—B2) 25 R—N4 Q—R6 26 B—B4 with a variety of threats.

21 P—K5!

White could ˙also win by 21 N—B3 threatening 22 N—KR4 and 22 P—K5 but the text is much more decisive, as it gives White use of his K4 for his QN which is the only piece as yet not participating in the attack.

21 ....   PxP
22 N—K4   N—R4

The only move for if 22 ... PxN (22 ... NxN? 23 RxB+! mates) 23 NxN P—KN4 (otherwise 24 Q—N6) 24 Q—R3 R—K2. 25 RxP B—N2 26 RxB! KxR 27 R—N1+ with a mating attack.

23 Q—N6!

Penetrating further on the White squares. Black replies with an outright blunder but after the objectively correct move 23 ... N—B5 White wins by 24 RxN PxR 25 N—KB3 (25 P—B3 to play B—B2 should also win but Black can put up a fight by 25 ... B—B3) 25 ... Q—N3 (25 ... Q—R4 26 N—B6 Q—KB4 27 QxRP+ mating). Now the main threat of either knight to N5 has been stopped (26 ... QxR mate!) but after Geller's 27 R—N5!! (not 27 R—N2 or 27 Q—N4!) it is all over — 27 ... Q—Q1 27 N—K5!

23 ....   PxN?

Played after sixteen minutes thought.

24 N—N5!   Resigns

Black has to give up his queen by 24 ... QxN to prevent mate. If 24 ... PxN then 25 QxN+ K—N1 26 Q—B7+ K—R1 27 R—B3 and mates.

One of the shortest decisive games in world championship matches and full of the sort of tactics that the chess public loves.

1969-70 WORTHY CHAMPION

The heading of this section seems justified when one bears in mind the widespread feeling in the chess world that Petrosian's manner of play and his results were not really worthy of a world champion even in a period when the title holder tends to be, in Botvinnik's words, first amongst equals.

I well remember how in 1968 and 1969 (before Spassky's victory) it was seriously suggested in some circles that the world championship system should be changed to that which applies in hundred square draughts. This would mean that the title would be competed for annually by means of a match in one year and by means of a tournament in the next. This proposal is now rarely mentioned in view of Spassky's convincing results in the period since he won the title, and especially after his Siegen victory over Fischer (No. 98).

The best games in this section are the fine attack against Petrosian (No. 88) the vigorous finish against Ciric (No.93), and the quiet victory over Larsen in which superior positional judgement turns a drawish looking game into a win in a short space of time (No. 85).

89 San Juan 1969
Black: Kavalek
King's Indian Defence

1 P—Q4	N—KB3	6 B—K3	P—QR3
2 P—QB4	P—KN3	7 B—Q3	P—QN4?
3 N—QB3	B—N2		
4 P—K4	P—Q3		
5 P—B3	P—B3		

A move that must have brought happy memories to Spassky's mind (see Spassky-Evans game No. 51).

Black plays this too early. He should castle or else play 7 ... QN—Q2 as in Spassky-Penrose, Palma 1969. True the champion won that game too but only after a long fight and Black was not then reduced to such shambles in the opening as now occurs.

8 P—K5!

This disrupts Black's game. He should try and keep the position closed by 8 ... KN—Q2 9 P—B4 N—N3 instead of which he commits a further inaccuracy which leaves him struggling for the rest of the game to get his pieces on to reasonable squares.

8 ....   QPxP
9 QPxP   N—N1

Naturally not 9 ... N—R4 10 P—KN4, while if 10 ... KN—Q2 11 P—B4 N—N3 12 PxP RPxP 13 B—K4! and the open Q file leaves Black worse off than in the variation given in the last note (13 ... N—B5 14 QxQ+ KxQ 15 0—0—0+ and 16 B—QB5! threatening 17 NxP)

10 P—B4'   N—R3
11 N—B3   B—B4

Trying to exchange White's better bishop, but Spassky does not oblige! If 11 ... N—B4 then 12 B—KB2 and the knight has few prospects other than retreating to KR3.

12 B—K2!

Now the open Q file again works against Black, as, after an exchange of queens, White has little trouble in exploiting his much superior placed men to harrass Black all over the board. Perhaps Black should now take the heroic decision of keeping queens on by 12 ... Q—B2 or Q—B1 but he decides wrongly that he can get reasonable play by attacking White's KP.

12 ....   QxQ+
13 RxQ   P—B3

Tarrasch would certainly describe Black's pawn formation here as "ugly" and he would be right.

14 N—Q4!

To exchange Black's well placed bishop and generally open up the game so as to make use of his superior development. Black must have been very annoyed to find that White can blithely ignore the pressure on his KP.

14 ....   BPxP
15 PxKP   0—0

Since the knight is hanging (15 ... BxP?? 16 BxN) one would expect here 15 ... N—B2 or 15 ... N—N5 to make a virtue of necessity. However, after 15 ... N—B2 there comes 16 NxB PxN 17 P—K6! N—Q3 (17 ... N—K4 18 0—0 as in the game) 18 B—R5+ K—B1 19 P—B5! N—N2 20 0—0 wins out of hand. If 15 ... N—N5 then 16 NxB PxN 17 BxN PxB 18 P—K6! 0—0 19 R—KB1 and after the exchange of rooks Black is paralysed by his inability to develop his Q side.

16 0—0   N—B2

If 16 ... P—K3 then the QB is in grave danger after 17 P—KR3 threatening 18 P—KN4.

17 NxB   PxN
18 P—K6   N—K4

If 18 ... N—Q1 then not 19 B—Q3 P—B5! but 19 B—N4! NxP (19 ... PxB 20 RxR+ and 21 RxN again with complete paralysis) 20 BxP N—B2 21 B—QN6! N—K1 22 B—K6+ K—R1 23 RxR+ and 24 R—Q8 wins at once. Or if 18 ... N—Q3 19 B—B5 B—K4 20 B—R5 threatening the murderous 21 KR—K1.

19 P—KN4!

Once the KB file is opened Black's back row becomes too weak e.g. 19 ... BPxP 20 RxR+ BxR 21 R—Q8 or 19 ... NxNP 20 BxN BxN 21 PxB PxB 22 B—R6! R—K1 23 R—B7 or 23 R—Q4 with a mating attack.

19	P—B5
20 RxP	R—K1
21 KR—Q4	

Forcing the decisive penetration on Q8.

21	P—B4
22 R—Q8	QN—B3

(See diagram next column.)

At last, but too late!

23 RxR+	RxR
24 PxP	N—Q5

A desperate attempt at counter play. After 24 ... PxP 25 BxBP P—N5 26 N—Q5 etc., White wins easily.

25 PxP	R—R1
26 BxN	PxB

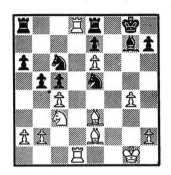

27 N—Q5	Resigns

If 27 ... P—Q6 28 BxP NxB 29 RxN RxP 30 NxP+ K—B1 31 N—B5 with the threat of 32 R—Q8+ finishes it.

90 Palma de Majorca 1969
Black: Penrose
King's Indian Defence

1 P—Q4	N—KB3
2 P—QB4	P—KN3
3 N—QB3	B—N2
4 P—K4	P—Q3
5 P—B3	P—B3
6 B—K3	P—QR3

The British Champion was perhaps unwise to choose an opening variation against which the World Champion always plays so well (see games 49 and 89).

7 B—Q3
After 7 P—QR4 P—QR4 followed by N—R3 Black has a fair game.

7 ....   QN—Q2
Not repeating Kavalek's mis-

take of 7 ... P—QN4? 8 P—K5.

8 KN—K2	P—QN4
9 Q—Q2	B—N2
10 0—0	

The point of Black's deferment of castling is seen in the variation 10 B—R6 BxB 11 QxB Q—R4 and as 12 Q—N7 R—KN1 13 Q—R6 P—K4 gains control of QB4 or K4 for the Black QN, White has achieved little by his queen foray.

10	0—0
11 P—QN3	P—K4
12 P—Q5	P—N5!
13 N—Q1	

Rather passive. 13 N—R4 looks more natural but after 13 ...

P—B4 followed by P—QR4 and N—N3, Black is well on his way to creating counter play on the QR file.

13 ....   P—B4?

But here the move is out of place and Black gradually finds that he cannot free his cramped position. The crucial line was 13 ... PxP 14 BPxP NxQP! 15 PxN P—K5 16 PxP BxR 17 QxP Q—B2 18 QN—B3 B—N7 19 R—N1 P—QR4 20 Q—Q4 (20 Q—R4 N—B4!) 20 ... B—R6! (21 B—KR6? B—B4) and as Black has retained his KB and diverted the White rook from the open files, he can look forward to the future with confidence. The correct judgement of such lines is of course a most exacting task, and for a long time it does in fact appear that Black's solid position cannot be broken down.

14 P—N4	K—R1
15 N—B2	N—KN1
16 N—N3	Q—R5
17 K—N2	

The trap is a little too obvious. 17 B—N5 does not win the queen but merely lets Black exchange his more active bishop by 17 ... B—R3, whereas now 17 ... B—R3 18 P—N5 B—N2 19 N—N4 does leave the queen in grave danger, (19 ... P—B4 20 PxP e.p. QNxP 21 B—N5 or 20 ... BxP 21 NxB QxN 22 P—B4 PxP 23 BxKBP N—K4? 24 B—R6 N—B6 25 Q—K3 NxB 26 QxN(R6) and the pinned knight is a source of concern).

17	P—R3
18 P—QR3!	
17	P—R3
18 P—QR3!	

A correct change of front since after Black's last move there is no longer any favourable way of opening lines on the K side.

18	P—QR4
19 R—R2	N(Q2)—B3
20 KR—QR1	N—R2

It was better to defend the Q-side by 20 ... QR—N1 21 PxP RPxP 22 R—R7 when the invading rook can be expelled by N—R2 followed by B—KB3—Q1—N3.

21 PxP	RPxP
22 RxR	RxR
23 RxR	BxR
24 Q—R2	B—N2
25 Q—R7	Q—K2

The position Penrose was playing for. Indeed it is difficult to see how White can find a winning plan as Black has few real weaknesses. A common saying in such positions is "It is as difficult for White to win as it is for Black to draw". White can tack about, prepare the best possible piece formation before opening lines, and threaten various sacrifices to open the way for the advance of two united passed pawns.

26 B—K2!

Freeing Q3 for his knight.

26 ....   N(R2)—B3

An alternative defence was 26 ... Q—B2 restricting the mobility of the enemy queen (see move 29) and after 27 P—B4 P—B3 28 N—Q3 B—KB1 the sacrifice played in the actual game would not work.

27 P—B4	PxP
28 BxKBP	N—K1
29 Q—N8!	B—Q5
30 N—Q3	P—B3

Once again Black seems to be out of danger now that he has activated his KB and ruled out P—K5. However, White still has one line remaining chance of opening lines — the advance of the KRP.

31 B—B3   Q—Q2
32 P—R4!   K—R2
33 P—R5   P—N4

Doubtless played with a sigh of relief. The weakening of KB4 does not seem too significant and the bishop is driven away so that the pressure on the QP is diminished.

34 B—Q2   B—K4

It may be better to play 34 ... N—N2 but then 35 P—K5! BPxP 35 B—K4+ K—R1 36 B—N6 threatening N—K4—B6 is hard to meet.

35 B—K3   N—K2

Black is about to play 35 ... Q—B1 with a safe draw, but now comes a winning sacrifice.

36 NxB   BPxN
37 BxBP!   PxB
38 QxP   N—N1

Or 38 ... Q—Q3 39 Q—R1 followed by 40 P—K5.

39 Q—N8   N(K)—B3
40 N—B5   N—K2

Even at this late stage Black still seems safe since if 41 P—K5 NxN 42 PxN P—N5! or 41 NxN QxN 42 P—K5 N—K1. Now however, we get the brilliant coup-de-grace.

41 NxP!   N(K)xP

Or 41 ... KxN 42 Q—B8+ K—R1 44 QxN+ and 45 QxP with four pawns for the knight.

42 BPxN   KxN
43 Q—B8+   Q—N2
44 QxP   N—Q2

Still hoping to blockade the KP.

45 Q—Q6+   K—R2
46 P—K5!   K—R1

Or 46 ... NxP 47 B—K4+ K—R1 48 Q—N8+ winning knight then bishop.

47 P—R6   Q—R2
48 P—K6   Q—B7+

Or 48 ... N—B3 49 Q—N8+ N—N1 50 Q—K5+ and mates.

49 K—N3   Resigns

91 Rest of World - USSR, Belgrade 1970
White: Larsen
Larsen's Opening

One of the most interesting innovations suggested in recent years, is that players or officials should take a note, not only of the moves but also of the time taken over them. Bronstein is one of the keenest supporters of this idea and applied it in watching this famous game. Readers may be interested in his record of the times, so after each move there is given in brackets the time taken over it.

1 P—QN3 (0)

Larsen often plays this move thereby confirming his position as the truest follower of Nimzovich amongst contemporary grandmasters.

1 ....   P—K4 (0)
2 B—N2 (0)   N—QB3 (0)
3 P—QB4 (0)

This makes the game into a sort of English or reversed Sicilian. A more independent line results from the immediate 3 N—KB3 or 3 P—K3. In the latter event the game could continue 3 P—K3 P—Q4 3 B—N5 B—Q3 5 P—KB4 a line quoted in books dating from the middle of the last century!

3 ....   N—B3 (0)
4 N—KB3 (0)

Here again 4 P—K3 comes into serious consideration so as to meet 4 ... P—Q4 by 5 PxP NxP 6 B—N5 or as Larsen played against Spassky at Leiden, a few weeks after this game 6 P—QR3 B—Q3 7 Q—B2 0—0 8 N—KB3 Q—K2 9 N—B3 NxN 10 QxN P—B4 11 B—N5! with equality.

4 ....   P—K5 (1)

4 ... P—Q3 is quite feasible, but Spassky decides to take up the challenge.

5 N—Q4 (1)   B—B4 (4)
6 NxN (0)   QPxN (1)
7 P—K3 (1)   B—B4 (4)

Naturally Black plays to render the QP backward.

8 Q—B2 (3)   Q—K2 (1)
9 B—K2 (5)   0—0—0 (4)

This position bears comparison with the one arising from the Nimzovich variation of the Sicilian Defence, namely 1 P—K4 P—QB4 2 N—KB3 N—KB3 3 P—K5 N—Q4 4 N—B3 NxN 5 QPxN P—K3 6 B—KB4 N—B3 7 Q—Q2 B—K2 8 0—0—0 Q—B2 9 B—B4 P—QN3 10 KR—K1 B—N2 in which Black has a difficult but playable game. If Larsen had borne this in mind he would not have committed the error that he now perpetrates — but then, as Bronstein's figures show, Larsen did not attach any great significance to the move.

10 P—B4? (2)

White should develop his knight by 10 N—B3, while 10 BxN QxB 11 N—B3 putting pressure on the KP was also a reasonable idea.

10 ....   N—N5! (4)

White's last move weakened his K side and so Black who has a free development for his pieces begins to use them with nasty threats of 11 ... Q—R5+ 12 P—N3 Q—R6 or 11 ... RxP?! or piece sacrifices at K6.

11 P—N3 (15)

At last Larsen realises the seriousness of his position. 11 BxN Q—R5+ 12 P—N3 (moving the king is the lesser evil) 12 ... QxB would leave him chronically weak on the white squares.

11 ....   P—KR4 (18)

Black could already consider 11 ... RxP 12 NxR NxKP 13 Q—B3 R—Q1 with dangerous threats but the vigorous text is much more difficult to meet.

12 P—KR3 (6)

After 12 N—B3 the sacrifice · 12 ... RxP is sufficient to win, e.g. 13 QxR BxP 14 Q—Q1 (14

Q—B2 B—B7+ 15 K—Q2 — to prevent 15 ... N—K6 with check — 15 ... P—K6+) 14 ... B—B7+ 15 K—B1 P—R5! and 16 ... PxP, while if 13 KxR then 13 ... BxP+ 14 K—Q1 R—Q1+ 15 K—K1 B—B7+ etc.

12 ....   P—R5 (6)

After this fine move, the hall with over two thousand spectators, bubbled over with enthusiasm. B.H.Wood and I who were sitting in the front rows feverishly analysed the acceptance of the offer, on a portable set, especially the variation beginning 13 BxN. After some initial scepticism our conclusion was that Black should win, but I must admit in all honesty that we did not find Spassky's coup de grace at move 14.

13 PxN (53)

If 13 BxN then 13 ... BxB 14 PxB PxP 15 R—N1 R—R8!! as in the game 16 RxR P—N7 17 R—N1 Q—R5+ 18 K—K2 QxP+ 19 K—K1 Q—N6+ 20 K—K2 (or 20 K—Q1 Q—B7 21 QxP QxR+ wins) 20 ... Q—B6+ 21 K—K1 B—K2! with decisive mating threats, e.g. 22 P—Q4 PxP e.p. 23 QxNP P—Q7+ 24 NxP B—R5+ 25 Q—N3 QxKP+ etc.

13 ....   PxP (1)

14 R—N1 (0)   R—R8!! (17)

Here apparently the excitement in the hall transmitted itself to Spassky and he spent some time checking whether White had any defence. The answer is no!

15 RxR (4)

If 15 K—B1 then 15 ... RxR+ 16 KxR Q—R5 and mates.

15 ....   P—N7 (3)

16 R—B1 (4)

If 16 R—N1 Q—R5+ 17 K—Q1 Q—R8 18 Q—B3 QxR+ 19 K—B2 Q—B7 20 PxB and now Black can win either by 20 ... P—N8(Q) or 20 ... QxB 21 N—R3 B—N5! winning the queen as 21 ... Q—Q6+ 22 K—B1 P—N8(Q)+ cannot be permitted.

16 ....   Q—R5+ (1)

17 K—Q1 (1)   PxR(Q)+ (0)

Resigns

Mate is forced after 18 BxQ BxP+.

One of the most startling games of modern times, and one that along with number 99 (Fischer) provides convincing proof that Spassky is a more than worthy world champion.

92 Leiden 1970
Black: Donner
French Defence

1 P—K4	P—K3
2 P—Q4	P—Q4
3 N—QB3	N—KB3
4 B—N5	PxP
5 NxP	B—K2
6 BxN	BxB
7 N—KB3	B—Q2

Tried without success by Petrosian in the 1965 match

8 Q—Q2	B—B3
9 NxB+	QxN
10 N—K5	0—0
11 0—0—0	R—Q1

An improvement on Petrosian's, weakening 11 ... N—Q2, but White still has a good game with his strong knight on K5 and his greater space control. Was Donner really wise to choose a variation which the great men and their seconds must have looked at very carefully and in which Spassky must have felt very much at home?

12 Q—K3

Away from the line of the rook. Development of the bishop can wait a move or two.

12 ....   B—K1

Why play the bishop to B3 unless one is prepared to leave it there or exchange it? 12 ... N—Q2 looks best as White cannot so easily play the attacking line of the previous game, though after 13 NxB PxN 14 P—KB4 or 14 P—KN3 he still has an advantage.

13 P—KN3	N—Q2
14 B—N2	P—B3

A regrettable necessity as 14 ... QR—N1 would not make it any easier for him to achieve the freeing P—QB4.

15 P—KB4	Q—K2
16 P—KR4	

Ready for the attack, Black in his parlous situation decides he must exchange his bad bishop, but weakens his KP.

16 ....   P—B3

The patient plan was preferable e.g. 16 ... N—B1 followed by QR—B1, P—QN3 and P—QB4.

17 N—B3	B—R4
18 B—R3!	

Immediately fastening upon the weak point.

18	BxN
19 QxB	N—B1

19 ... P—K4? is even worse as after 20 QPxP PxP there is the highly unpleasant check 21 Q—N3+ K—B1 (to guard the queen — 21 ... Q—B2?? 22 B—K6 or 21 ... K—R1 22 QxP and wins a piece due to the pin as 22 ... QR—N1 is met by 23 RxN!) 22 PxP and then the killing 23 KR—B1+

20 KR—K1	Q—B2
21 B—B1!	

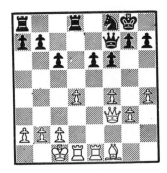

Not the sort of move everybody would think of at once but the last note indicates that the diagonal QN3/KN8 is a key to the position.

| 21 .... | R—Q3 |
| 22 B—B4 | QR—Q1? |

The wild 22 ... P—QN4 is met by 23 BxNP, so Black moves his unguarded rook. However, the main threat was P—B5 so Black had to try 22 ... P—KB4 and White would have to manoeuvre round and safeguard his QP before breaking through by P—KN4 and possibly P—R5.

| 23 P—B5! | RxQP |
| 24 PxP | RxR+ |

This loses without a fight. 24 ... Q—K2 was imperative though after 25 Q—R3! to remove the blockader, White should win, e.g. 25 ... QxQ 26 P—K7+ RxB 27 PxQ or 25 ... N—N3 26 P—R5! RxB 27 PxN RxR+ 28 RxR QxP 29 R—Q8+ and mates, or 25 ... P—QB4 26 QxRP RxR+ (26 ... RxB 27 RxR and 28 P—K7) 27 RxR RxR+ 28 KxR N—N3 29 QxNP! etc.

| 25 RxR | RxR+ |
| 26 QxR | Resigns |

After 26 ... Q—K2 the blockader is forcibly removed by 27 Q—Q8! pinning the knight and so preventing N—N3.

93 IBM Amsterdam 1970
Black: Ciric
Queen's Gambit Declined

1 P—Q4	P—Q4
2 P—QB4	P—K3
3 N—KB3	N—KB3
4 P—KN3	B—K2
5 B—N2	O—O
6 O—O	P—QB3

A sound defence preparing P—QN3 which if played at once gives White some initiative with 7 PxP or 7 N—K5. The text also allows him to recapture in the centre with the BP.

7 P—N3	QN—Q2
8 B—N2	P—QN3
9 QN—Q2	B—N2
10 R—B1	R—B1
11 P—K3	

White has the very slight advantage that he can post his queen at the safe square K2 whereas Black has no such haven for his consort.

| 11 .... | P—B4 |

11 ... R—B2 intending to put the queen at R1 at once may be sounder, e.g. 12 N—K5 P—B4 13 Q—K2 Q—R1 14 BPxP KPxP 15 NxN NxN 16 PxP PxP 17 P—K4 R—K1 (Keres-Ragozin, XIV USSR 1945).

| 12 Q—K2 | R—B2 |

Returning to the Ragozin method.

| 13 BPxP | BxP |

.A bold decision allowing White a strong central push. Simply 13 ... KPxP should hold the balance.

| 14 P—K4 | B—N2 |
| 15 P—K5 | N—Q4 |

16 N—B4   Q—R1

He should try 16 ... B—R3 preventing White's next move, but it was hard to see how strong the pawn sacrifice really is.

17 N—Q6!   BxN

Or 17 ... B—QB3 18 PxP NxBP 19 N—Q4 threatening 20 NxB or 20 Q—N4.

18 PxB   R—B3
19 PxP   PxP

Or 19 ... NxP 20 N—N5 with threats of 21 Q—K5 21 Q—R5 or even 21 BxP.

20 N—N5!

An excellent attacking move threatening amongst other things 21 NxKP (21 ... R—K1 22 Q—N4!) so Black now has little choice.

20 ....   RxP
21 KR—Q1!

Quite the strongest move pinning the knight and bringing his last inactive piece into play. The tempting 21 NxRP KxN 22 Q—R5+ K—N1 23 BxP KxB 24 Q—N4+ K—R1 25 R—B4 has the vital flaw 21 ... N—B6! 22 BxN BxB with counter threats on the long white diagonal.

21 ....   R—R3

To break the pin and remove the rook from a square where it is a tactical weakness. Thus 21 ... QN—B3 loses to 22 QBxN PxB 23 Q—R5! PxN 24 QxNP+ K—R1 25 Q—K5+ and 26 QxR. The best defensive chance however, is 21 ... P—KR3 22 N—K4 R—R3 23 Q—N4 P—B3 though after 24 NxQBP NxN 25 RxN(B5) White's bishops give him the better of it (25 ... N—K6? 26 PxN BxB 27 R—Q7 R—B2 28 RxR KxR 29 R—B7+).

22 Q—K4

The start of a devastating attack.

22 ....   P—B4

Or 22 ... QN—B3 23 QBxN winning a piece, or 22 ... P—N3 23 NxRP!

23 Q—QB4   Q—K1

The threat was 24 NxKP but the weakness of the KP cannot be so easily covered.

24 R—K1   RxP

Black can find no defence, so he throws himself on the sword. Thus 24 ... K—R1 to escape from the dangerous diagonal is met by 25 BxN PxB (25 ... BxB 26 QxR) 26 RxQ PxQ 27 R—K7, while 24 ... R—N3 is met by 25 RxP! RxR 26 BxN BxB 27 QxB etc.

25 RxP   Q—R1

He has to guard the knight.

26 BxN

A surprising decision, as 26 R—K7 or 26 R—Q6 look very strong. Clearly Spassky did not wish to pass up the chance to finish the game with a queen sacrifice.

26 ....   BxB
27 Q—KR4   P—KR3
28 QxP

He could also win by· 28 RxRP but the lovely text is more decisive and prettier (28 ... PxQ 29 R—KN6 mate).

| 28 .... | N—B3 |
| 29 RxN! | Resigns |

The finish could be 29 ... RxR
30 Q—R7+ K—B1 31 Q—R8+

K—K2 (31 ... B—N1 32 BxR) 32
QxP+ R—B2 33 NxR B—R8 (33
... BxN 34 R—K1+) 34 N—K5+
and mate next move.

94 IBM Amsterdam 1970
Black: Langeweg
King's Indian Defence

1	P—Q4	N—KB3
2	P—QB4	P—KN3
3	N—QB3	B—N2
4	P—K4	P—Q3
5	P—B3	0—0
6	B—K3	N—B3
7	KN—K2	R—N1

A strange looking move but not pointless as Black intends to challenge in the centre by P—QR3 and P—QN4 when the rook will find useful employment.

8 N—B1 P—K4
9 N—N3

A crucial line here is 9 P—Q5 N—Q5 offering a pawn for strong black squares play. If White then plays 10 N—N3 questioning the knight outpost, Black can continue 10 ... P—B4 11 PxP e.p. PxP activating his rook. The game shows that Langeweg has the same idea in mind.

9 .... R—K1

A bold attempt to unsettle the champion, but it doesn't come off and 9 ... PxP 10 NxP N—KR4 was to be preferred.

10 P—Q5 N—Q5

The thematic move, and anyway 10 ... N—K2 would leave his QRP en prise.

11 NxN PxN

12 BxP P—B4
13 B—K3!

Spassky produces an important innovation as Boleslavsky's authoritative book on the King's Indian considers the pawn sacrifice very promising on the basis of the game Bagirov-Bobolovich, Semi-final XXXIV USSR Championship, which continued 13 B—B2? P—QN4! 14 PxP NxKP 15 PxN (15 NxN P—B4) BxN+! 16 PxB RxP+ with a strong attack. Spassky points out that Black has a good alternative in the immediate 13 ... NxKP 14 PxN BxN+ 15 PxB RxP+ and if 16 K—Q2 then 16 ... Q—N4+ 17 K—B2 Q—B4! with an advantageous position due to the threats of discovered check or simply 18 ... QxB+. The text keeps the K side closed.

13 .... P—QN4?

Black decides to proceed along the lines of the Bobolovich game, but he should instead try 13 ... N—R4 intending to exploit the half open K file by P—B4. White can consolidate by 14 B—Q3 and 15 0—0 but Black has a good grip on the black squares and attacking chances with a timely

Q--R5 or B—K4 and Q—B3.
14 PxP   NxKP?
Too much of a slavish imitation. 14 ... N—R4 was still best.
15 PxN   BxN+
16 PxB   RxKP
17 Q—Q2!
Black was relying on the more obvious 17 Q—B3 when after 17 ... Q—K2 18 K—Q2 Black develops his bishop with gain of time by 18 ... B—N5. Then 19 Q—N3 R—K1 20 R—K1 R—R5 gives him considerable chances of justifying his heavy sacrifices.
17 ....   Q—R5+
Now 17 ... Q—K2 18 K—B2 leaves Black with hardly any prospects so he plays to weaken White's KB3 square.
18 P—N3   Q—K2
19 K—B2   Q—B3+
20 K—N1
The attack has been liquidated and there is no weak point for Black to strike at.

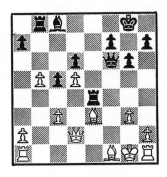

20 ....   B—N5
Or 20 ... Q—B6 21 B—KB4!
21 B—N5   Q—K4
22 B—KB4   Resigns
After 22 ... Q—K2 23 P—KR3 B—B6 24 R—R2! followed by 25 R—B2 White has firmly guarded his K2 square (25 B—N2? R—K7!) and brought his king into perfect safety.

95 IBM Amsterdam, 1970
White: Jongsma
Sicilian Defence

1 P—K4	P—QB4
2 N—KB3	P—Q3
3 P—Q4	PxP
4 NxP	N—KB3
5 N—QB3	P—K3
6 P—KN3	B—K2
7 B—N2	0—0
8 0—0	P—QR3

Clearly Black cannot yet develop his knight by 8 ... N—B3

because of 9 NxN PxN 10 P—K5!
9 B—K3
Too slow. The normal plan is to fianchetto this piece so 9 P—N3 or 9 QN—K2 are the correct moves here (see game 4).

9	Q—B2
10 Q—K2	N—B3
11 QR—Q1	B—Q2
12 P—KR3	

Continuing his slow build-up, but, as the course of the game shows, development without a concrete plan is insufficient against Black's Q side pressure. This had already been shown in a game Dubinin-Estrin, 1962 which went 12 N—N3 P—QN4 13 P—QR3 QR—N1! 14 P—B4 P—N5 15 PxP NxNP when White was already forced to take up a defensive attitude by 16 R—B1 because of the threat 16 ... NxP 17 QxN B—R5!

12 ....   P—QN4
13 P—R3   KR—B1

This move which also came in the Estrin game is the prelude to strong pressure on the White Q side.

14 P—B4

At last a sign of White's desire to engage Black on the other side of the board, but the gesture comes much too late.

14 ....   QR—N1
15 NxN

Further inconsistency. 15 P—KN4 is the only justification for his last two moves.

15 ....   BxN
16 B—B1

An honest confession of his inaccuracy at move 9.

16 ....   P—QR4
17 KR—K1

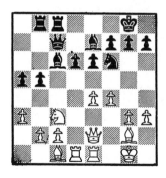

Preparing an instructive blunder. Strange though it may look his best move was the further retreat 17 N—N1, though naturally Black had much the better of it after 17 ... P—N5 when White has to take account of the threat 18 ... B—N4.

17 ....   P—N5
18 PxP   PxP
19 N—Q5?

He had to try 19 N—N1.

19 ....   PxN
20 PxP

White had seen so far and saw that he wins back the piece. The champion however, has seen just a little further.

20 ....   B—Q2!
Resigns

21 QxB R—K1 and the queen is lost!

96 Siegen Olympiad 1970
White: Vizantiadis
Queen's Gambit Accepted

1 P—Q4   P—Q4
2 P—QB4   PxP

3 N—QB3
3 N—KB3 is usual so as to pre—

vent the following freeing move.

 3 ....   P—K4
 4 P—Q5

Not 4 PxP QxQ+ 5 NxQ N—QB3 6 N—KB3 B—K3 with an easy development for Black who can later proceed to attack the KP.

 4 ....   P—QR3
 5 P—QR4

Not 5 Q—R4+? P—QN4 6 NxP? B—Q2! nor 5 P—K4 P—QN4 6 P—QR4 P—N5 7 N—R2 and now not 7 ... P—KB4 (Golombek-Alekhine, Margate 1935) but 7 ... N—KB3 with advantage.

 5 ....   N—KB3
 6 B—N5   QN—Q2
 7 P—K4   P—R3
 8 BxN

Abandoning his better bishop. 8 B—R4 was stronger.

 8 ....   NxB
 9 BxP   B—QN5

9 ... B—Q3 at once seems best.

 10 Q—B2   0—0
 11 N—B3   B—Q3

Losing a tempo 11 ... Q—K2 looks more consistent. Still Black retains the advantage as White's centre pawns make his White square bishop a poor piece.

 12 0—0   N—R4

Preparing to exploit the black squares, while White's only possible plan of pressure on the QB file is foiled by the fine defensive formation P—QR3, B—Q3.

 13 N—K2   B—KN5
 14 N—Q2

He must avoid the doubled pawn, but Black's pieces now occupy even more threatening squares.

 14 ....   Q—N4!
 15 N—KN3?

15 P—B3 was essential.

 15 ....   N—B5

Of course!

 16 N—N3   P—KR4
 17 P—B3   B—Q2
 18 K—R1   P—KN3
 19 R—KN1

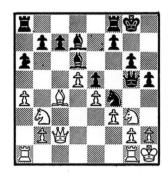

White's poor opening and his subsequent errors have left him with a thankless task. He would like to exchange the powerful Black knight, but the threat of 19 ... P—R5 has to be attended to first. However, 19 Q—B2 looks slightly better than the horrible text move which leaves his king with no flight square and invites a smothered mate.

 19 ....   P—KB4
 20 N—K2

Yet another concession. 20 N—QB1 intending 21 N—Q3 was at least a logical plan.

 20 ....   PxP
 21 NxN

Not 21 QxP? B—KB4 22 Q—K3 N—R6! 23 QxQ N—B7 mate.

 21 ....   RxN
 22 PxP   QR—KB1
 23 Q—B1   K—N2

Inviting his opponent to "exploit the pin" by 24 P—N3 when there comes 24 ... B—KN5!, and 25 ... B—B6+ is a grave threat.

24 B—K2   Q—K2
25 N—Q2

Hurrying back to guard the king.

25 ....   P—B3!
26 B—B4

He had to make the further concession of 26 PxP BxP as the bishop was needed to guard his KB3.

26 ....   R—B7
27 N—B3

Otherwise 27 ... B—QN5 will force this anyway.

27 ....   R(1)xN!
Resigns

The attractive finish would be 28 PxR RxP+! 29 KxR Q—R5+ 30 K—N2 and now either 30 ... B—R6+ or 30 ... B—QB4 force mate.

97 Siegen Olympiad 1970
Black: Kostro
Queen's Gambit Declined

1 P—Q4   P—Q4
2 P—QB4   P—QB3
3 N—KB3   N—KB3
4 N—B3   P—K3
5 B—N5   P—KR3

A move which has a bad reputation. Older theory was that after 6 BxN QxB 7 Q—N3! preventing 7 ... B—N5 White could use his control of K4 to advance 8 P—K4 with advantage. However, then Black might have some compensation in his two bishops, so Spassky prefers a pawn sacrifice with which he had already been successful against Pachman in the 1967 Moscow Grandmasters' event.

6 B—R4   PxP
7 P—K4   P—KN4

"In for a penny in for a pound" or as the Russian proverb has it "having said A you have to say B". 7 ... P—QN4 8 P—K5 would merely be a transposition.

8 B—N3   P—N4

After 8 ... B—N5 White has the gambit 9 BxP NxP 10 0—0 with plenty of open lines for his pieces.

9 B—K2

Against Pachman, Spassky went 9 Q—B2 P—KN5 10 N—K5 QxP 11 R—Q1 Q—N3 12 B—K2 QN—Q2 `13 0—0 B—K2 14 NxKNP with a complicated game which he eventually won. The text with its emphasis on quicker development seems a more reliable continuation.

9 ....   B—QN2

9 ... P—QN5 would win the KP in return for the QBP but is a very loosening move.

10 0—0   QN—Q2

If 10 ... B—K2 then 11 N—K5 to follow up by 12 P—B4 opening the KB file, while 10 ... B—N2 would weaken his Q3 allowing 11 P—K5 N—Q4 12 N—K4.

11 P—Q5!

With development complete, White opens the centre to get at

the uncastled king.

11 ....   BPxP

Not 11 ... KPxP 12 PxP NxP 13 NxN PxN 14 BxP! and if 14 ... QPxB then 15 R—K1+ B—K2 16 B—Q6. Meanwhile the threat was 12 N—Q4 or 12 PxP (either) and then 13 N—Q4.

12 PxP!

Spassky is not to be appeased by the exchange (12 NxQNP NxP!). It is more important to open the K file.

12 ....   Q—N3

12 ... P—QN3 13 PxP PxN 14 PxN+ QxP would achieve the exchange of queens but after 15 PxP the loose QBP (N—K5) and the open files in the centre leave White with much the better game. 12 ... NxP looks a better prospect but after 13 NxQN the threat is 14 N—Q6+ and the QBP is again loose.

13 PxP   PxP

14 N—Q4   B—B4

Or 14 ... P—R3 15 B—R5+ and 16 R—K1 with decisive effect.

15 KNxNP   O—O

16 B—B3

Not 16 BxP? Q—B3! Now it is just a mopping-up operation.

16 ....   BxB

17 QxB   QR—B1

17 ... P—R3? loses the queen to 18 B—B7

18 QR—Q1   Q—B3

19 Q—K2   N—Q4

He cannot guard all his weak points as 19 ... KR—K1 20 N—Q6 is decisive.

20 N—Q6!   BxN

21 QxP+   K—N2

Or 21 ... R—KB2 22 NxN BxB 23 N—K7+.

22 BxB   Resigns

98 Siegen Olympiad 1970
Black: Fischer
Grunfeld Defence

1 P—Q4	N—KB3
2 P—QB4	P—KN3
3 N—QB3	P—Q4
4 PxP	

Accepting the challenge to repeat the opening of their previous encounter at Santa-Monica, 1966 (game No. 76).

4	NxP
5 P—K4	NxN
6 PxN	B—N2
7 B—QB4	P—QB4
8 N—K2	N—B3
9 B—K3	O—O

10 0—0   Q—B2
11 R—B1   R—Q1
12 P—KR3

In 1966 Spassky played 12 Q—K1 but afterwards came to the conclusion that on 12 ... Q—R4 Black had equality. Hence he returns to a little played move first employed, we think, in Gligoric-Smyslov, Yugoslavia-USSR match 1959.

12 ....   P—N3
13 P—KB4   P—K3
14 Q—K1   N—R4

Capturing the QP allows an ultimate B—Q5 discovering an attack on the queen and rook when Black loses the exchange. The Gligoric-Smyslov game went, 14 ... B—N2 15 Q—B2 (the aggressive 15 P—B5 is a better choice) 15 ... N—R4 16 B—Q3 P—B4 and Black had a good game.

15 B—Q3   P—B4

The programmed move to block White's expansion by P—B5, and to induce the positional error 16 P—K5? when 16 ... P—B5 17 B—N1 B—N2 gives Black a fine position.

16 P—N4

White boldly strikes out. 16 R—Q1 would transpose in essence into the Santa-Monica game with White having lost a tempo.

16 ....   PxKP
17 BxP   B—N2
18 N—N3   N—B5
19 BxB

Not 19 B—B2 when Black has 19 ... BxB 20 QxB N—Q7! 21 QxP+ K—R1 22 KR—Q1 N—B6+ 23 K—R1 R—K1 24 Q—Q5 N—R5 with powerful threats of 24 ... QR—Q1 and 24 ... QxP. This variation confirms the impression that the opening variation is not very promising for White.

19 ....   QxB
20 B—B2   Q—B3
21 Q—K2

21 PxP? N—Q7 threatening 22 ... N—B6+.

21 ....   PxP
22 PxP   P—QN4

Black clearly has the better of it with his pressure on the QP, but the weakness of his KP and the pin on his knight are tactical factors that must not be underestimated.

23 N—K4!

The passive 23 KR—Q1 would be much worse — Black replies 23 ... R—KB1 followed by QR—Q1 and White is permanently tied down.

23 ....   BxP

To exchange his good bishop for White's defensive one is a decision not to be taken lightly especially as White's knight is poised to exploit the weak square which now arises at KB3. Still the capture arises logically from his previous play and does give Black some counter play on the Q file, especially with the threat of R—Q7. Vasiukov gives a line showing that Black cannot hope to win by quieter play:- 23 ... R—KB1 24 N—B5 QR—K1 25 P—QR4 P—QR3 26 NxRP QxN 27 PxP QxP 28 QxN, or in this 27 ... Q—R6 28 RxN QxKRP 29 B—K1 R—Q1 30 B—N4! RxBP (30 ... R—B2 31 Q—B3) 31 QxP+ K—R1 32 RxR Q—N6+ 33 K—R1 QxR 34 R—B8.

24 N—N5

24 BxB RxB 25 N—B6+ ^{v}—N2 26 P—N5 QR—Q1 is quite satisfactory for Black as he threatens

27 ... R—-Q7.
24 ....   BxB+
Playing to win. Returning the
pawn by 24 ... B—B3 would leave
it level.

25 RxB   R—Q3
The first error. 25 ... R—K1
looks more passive and gives up
temporarily the control of the Q
file. However, the rook on Q3
gives White an invaluable tempo
later for redeploying his knight.

26 R—K1   Q—N3
The move Fischer had relied
on, pinning the rook so as to
meet 27 NxKP by 27 ... R—K1 28
P—B5 R—Q7 29 Q—B3 RxP.
However, White is not finished
even then, as he can continue 30
R(1)—KB1 (not 30 PxP? RxR 31
QxR   RxN)   with   attacking
chances.

27 N—K4!   R—Q5
Black could keep material
equality by 27 ... R—B3 when
White would probably continue
28 R—Q1.

28 N—B6+   K—R1
29 QxP

The majority of commentators
consider that this move took
Fischer by surprise since now 29
... R—Q8 seems to win a piece

for Black. (30 QxQ? RxR+ or 30
K—N2 RxR 31 QxR? QxN or 30
K—B1? QxQ). However, Spassky
had prepared the fine answer 30
Q—B7! winning, e.g. 30 ... RxR+
31   K—N2   N—K6+   (or   31   ...
Q—B3+ 32 K—N3 R—KN8+ 33
K—R4 RxP+ 34 KxR N—K6+ 35
K—N5 Q—-B4+ 36 P—B5) 32
K—B3 (not 32 K—N3 N—B4+! 33
PxN Q—K6+ and 34 ... Q—K2)
32 ... Q—B3+ 33 K—N3 R—N8+
34 K—R4 RxP+ 35 PxR Q—R8+
36 K—N5 R—QB1 (or 36 ... NxP
37   KxN   Q—N8+   38   K—R3
Q—R8+ 39 K—N3 Q—N8+ 40
R—KN2 Q—K8+   41   K—N4
Q—KR3 42 R—N3 and Black has
run out of checks.) 37 Q—Q7!
R—QN1 38 Q—Q4 (analysis by
Vasiukov). If in fact this is what
Fischer had overlooked, it is a
terrible psychological shock, and
from now on his play deteriorates.

29 ....   R—Q3
Exchanging queens gives White
the fresh threat of 31 R—K7 e.g.
29 ... QxQ 30 RxQ K—N2 31
P—N5 R—KB1 32 R(2)—K2!
threatening 33 R—K7+ R—B2 34
R—K8 R—B1 35 R(2)—K7+.

30 Q—K4   R—KB1?
Black could still keep it level
by 30 ... QR—Q1, e.g. 31 P—N5
R—Q7 32 R(1)—KB1 RxR 33
RxR Q—K6 34 QxQ (34 Q—N7
Q—N6+) 34 ... R—Q8+ etc.

31 P—N5   R—Q7
32 R(1)—KB1!
White   could   also   play   32
R(1)—K2   N—Q3   33   Q—K7
R—B2! 34 QxR when after 34 ...
QxR+ 35 KxQ RxR+ 36 KxR
NxQ 37 K—Q3 White's active
king   gives   him   a   considerable
advantage.

32 ....   Q—B2?
Defending   against   33   Q—K7

but allowing White a winning sequence of moves. Black could still get into an ending in which he would stand only slightly worse by 32 ... RxR 33 RxR Q—K6 34 QxQ (34 Q—N7 Q—N6+ and draws) 34 ... NxQ 35 R—Q2.

33 RxR!   NxR
34 Q—Q4!   R—Q1

Obviously not 34 ... NxR 35 N—K8+. Objectively Black should try 34 ... Q—N3 though after 35 QxQ PxQ 36 R—B1 N—B5 37 P—QR4 N—Q3 38 R—B6! N—K1 39 NxN RxN 40 PxP the ending is very much in White's favour.

35 N—Q5+   K—N1

35 ... Q—N2 loses the knight whereas now 36 QxN? Q—B4+ saves Black.

36 R—B2!   N—B5
37 R—K2

Now White wins by force as 38 R—K7 is threatened and 37 ... Q—N3 loses to 38 R—K8+! K—B2 39 QxQ.

37 ....   R—Q3
38 R—K8+   K—B2
39 R—KB8+   Resigns

Black loses his queen after 39 ... KxR 40 Q—R8+ while 39 ... K—K3 40 NxQ with check is also decisive.

Not a great game of chess, but one in which the result was far more important than the game.

RECENT EVENTS

1971 was a fairly quiet year for Spassky. Indeed it might almost be claimed that he had caught 'Petrosian's Disease', so rare were his appearances and so middling his results.

Between the Siegen Olympiad (September 1970) and the Gothenburg tournament of July 1971 he did not play a single serious game, spending most of his time resting. He did, however, undertake a crowded tour of the Soviet Far East, and naturally enough he was in great demand as a commentator when the epic series of Candidates' Matches were being assessed. In his comments on these he showed, and not for the first time, a feeling of empathy for Bobby Fischer which some psychologists might consider a positive handicap when it comes to a World Championship Match with the phenomenal American.

However Spassky showed himself a good prophet since in various interviews after the Fischer-Taimanov match he was already talking in terms of a 1972 match with Fischer. This was a prospect, he felt, which would give him a 'creative boost'.

Spassky's play at Gothenburg rather lacked bite, and he had to be satisfied with third place. He could console himself that he was up against opponents who were determined to give of their best against the world title holder.

It is not certain that the same could be said of his next appearance in the Soviet Team Championship in August where he played just four games for one of the weaker sides 'Lokomotiv'. An eye-witness of that event writes that the Soviet public now looks upon Spassky "as a god, and the only defence against Fischer" (and this even before the Petrosian-Fischer match in Buenos Aires!).

Spassky's showing in the Canadian Open in September was also disappointing, though allowance must be made for the novelty of the experience. No World Champion has ever been exposed before to the hurly-burly of a swiss open event with a varied entry. Was the Russian bear merely dozing as some commentators thought, or was he in genuinely bad form? The answer to this question is probably 'neither'. To win a swiss system tournament requires a different kind of technique from the "win with white, draw with black" approach that prevails at the highest levels. Playing in another swiss open tournament, this time at Toronto, Spassky failed to take top honours and finished in a tie for 3rd-4th places.

The last event of 1971 was a great one — the Alekhine Memorial Tournament in Moscow. Spassky started badly and at one time had a minus score thanks to losses to Petrosian and Korchnoy. Eventually he pulled up at the expense of some of the lower placed players, and his final placing of 6th-7th was a moderate success.

Perhaps these recent lapses are no more indicative of Spassky's future than were those from the period before the 1968 candidates' cycle. Certainly, there are good grounds for believing that perhaps we are now already in the era of Fischer, but no matter what the result of the 1972 title match, no-one can deny Spassky his place amongst the greatest players of all time.

99 Gothenburg 1971
Black: Kinnmark
Nimzoindian

1 P—Q4	N—KB3	7 PxB	P—K4
2 P—QB4	P—K3	8 N—K2	P—KR3
3 N—QB3	B—N5		
4 B—N5	0—0		

8 ... QN—Q2 first, is wiser pre-· paring to recapture with knight.

9 BxN

A dubious move based on the tactical trick 5 P—K4?! P—B4! and Black gets adequate counterplay by his dual threat of 6 ... Q—R4 and 6 ... PxP. (7 P—K5 PxP 8 QxP N—B3 9 Q—K3 N—KN5! or 9 Q—B4 Q—R4!)

White could try 9 B—R4 but after 9 ... P—KN4 10 B—N3 P—K5 and 11 ... P—QN3 Black would have some counterplay on the Q-side to make up for his weakened K-side. After the text White has harmonious development and soon builds up strong threats.

5 P—K3

After this restraining developing move White's centre is firm and the pin on the Black knight cannot now be relieved by P—KR3 and P—KN4 without serious weakening of the castled position.

9	QxB
10 N—N3	

He must prevent 10 ... B—B4 exchanging his powerful bishop.

5	P—Q3
6 B—Q3	BxN+

10 ....   P—B3

Doubling the pawn before White can˙ prevent this by 7 KN—K2.

Deciding that he must shut out the bishop even at the cost· of undoubling the pawn. 10 ... N—B3 11 0—0 P—QN3 (or 11 ... N—K2) is too slow as after 12 P—B4!

White has the very strong threat of opening the KB file or of P—KB5 followed by N—R5 and then Q—N4 or P—B6 with a violent attack.

11	0—0	P—Q4
12	P—B4	PxQP?

Inconsistent. He must play 12 P—K5 though after 13 B—K2 the threats of P—KB5 and N—R5 are still awkward to meet and the central pawn chain could be vulnerable to the old Queen's Gambit idea of PxP followed by P—B4 'playing the gambit a second time'.

13	P(3)xP	Q—K2
14	Q—B3	N—Q2?

A decisive mistake after which his bishop is temporarily shut out of the game. 14 ... R—K1 15 QR—K1 is quite pointless so his only chance of making a fight lay in 14 ... PxP 15 BxP B—K3 though after 16 B—Q3 White still has much the better of it. 14 ... B—N5? 15 QxB QxP+ 16 K—R1 QxB 17 N—B5 would be suicide of course as his K-side is left defenceless. (17 ... P—KN3 18 NxP+ K—N2 19 QR—Q1 QxBP — 19 ... Q—K5 20 QR—K1! — 20 P—B5! etc.)

15	PxP	PxP
16	N—B5	Q—R6

Or 18 ... Q—K3 19 QxP! with decisive advantage.

17 Q—N4!

White has now accumulated enough pressure to leave the bishop to its fate, but he must strike quickly before Black consolidates by N—B3.

White could get a more decisive attack by 17 Q—N3! P—KN3 18 NxP+ K—N2 19 N—B5+ K—B3 (19 ... K—R1 20 QR—Q1 PxN? 21 Q—R4+ K—N2 22 Q—N5+ K—R1

23 Q—R6+ K—N1 24 BxP wins) 20 Q—N5+ K—K3 21 N—N7+ K—Q3 22 KR—Q1 and then P—K4, or 18 ... K—R2 19 N—N4! QxB 20 Q—R4+ K—N1 21 R—B3 R—K1 22 R—R3 K—B1 23 Q—N5! keeping the king confined. The slight drawback to the text is that it places the queen on a more vulnerable square.

17	....	P—KN3
18	NxP+	K—R2

Or 18 ... K—N2 (the best defence since 19 NxP now fails to 19 ... QxB) 19 N—B5+ K—N1 (19 ... K—R1 20 Q—R4+ K—N1 21 Q—R6 PxN 22 R—B3 N—B3 23 R—N3+ N—N5 24 RxN+! mates or 19 ... K—B3 20 Q—N5+ K—K3 21 N—N7+ K—Q3 22 QR—Q1 followed by 23 P—B5) 20 QR—Q1 N—B3! 21 N—R6+ K—N2 22 Q—N5 N—K5 (22 ... R—R1 23 NxP! and otherwise White continues 23 P—B5) 23 QxQP N—B6 (23 ... KxN 24 BxN! QxKP+ 25 K—R1 and wins) 24 Q—KN5 NxR 25 RxN and White will get a decisive attack by 26 P—B5 since 25 R—R1 still fails to 26 NxP, e.g. 26 ... KxN 27 QxP+ K—B1 28 Q—B6+ K—N1 29 B—B4+ K—R2 30 Q—R4+ K—N2 31 Q—N5+ mating or winning a great deal of material.

| 19 | NxP! | QxB |

Not 19 ... RxN 20 QxP+ K—R1
21 QxR QxB 22 R—B3 N—N3 23
R—N3 and mates.

20 P—B5!

This is the move that Black
can be forgiven for not seeing, yet
as the analysis in the previous
notes shows it is a key move in
nearly all variations. Now 20 ...
RxN? 21 PxP+ K moves 22 PxR
and 20 QxP+ 21 K—R1 or even
20 ... PxP 21 RxP QxP+ 22
K—R1 N—B3 23 Q—R4+ K—N1
24 Q—R8+ KxN 25 RxN+ all
lose, so Black must fall back to
defend his KN3.

20 ....   Q—R3

Not 20 ... P—KN4 21 NxP+
and wins quickly.

21 N—N5+   K—N1

Or 21 ... K—N2 22 N—K6+ etc.

22 Q—R4.   N—B3

Or 22 ... R—B3 23 Q—R7+
K—B1 24 N—K6+ (24 PxP is also
good) 24 ... K—K1 25 N—B7+
winning the queen, or 22 ...
R—B2 23 NxR KxN 24 Q—R7+
and 25 PxP.

23 PxP

Dr. Tarrasch would almost certainly say of this pawn that it
"wirkt wie eine Figur" (i.e. plays
the part of a piece.) the threats
now are 24 RxN RxR 25 Q—R7+
K—B1 26 P—N7+ and also 24
Q—R7+ NxQ 25 PxN+ K—N2 26
RxR Q—R3 27 R—N8+ K—B3 28
R—B1+ and then 29 P—R8(Q)+
or 29 RxR according to Black's
reply. These variations show that
not only does the former KBP
'work like a piece, but even has
ambitions to become the strongest
of the pieces!

23 ....   K—N2
24 N—R7   Resigns

The finish could be 24 ...
B—Q2 (24 ... KxP 25 NxR+) 25
NxR RxN 26 RxN! RxR (26 ...
QxR 27 Q—R7 mate) 27 Q—R7+
K—B1 28 P—N7+ and 29
P—N8(Q)+.

This game won first brilliancy
prize at the Gothenburg
tournament.

100 Alekhine Memorial Tournament, Moscow 1971
Black: Gheorghiu
King's Indian Defence

1	P—Q4	N—KB3	
2	P—QB4	P—KN3	
3	N—QB3	B—N2	
4	P—K4	P—Q3	
5	P—B3	P—B4?!	

A strange choice for Gheorghiu
because he had reached a
minutely advantageous position
(as White) in this line against

Fischer in the 1970 Olympiad.

6	PxP	PxP	
7	QxQ+	KxQ	
8	B—K3	KN—Q2	
9	0—0—0	P—N3	
10	P—B4!		

Gheorghiu-Fischer went 10
KN—K2 N—B3 11 P—B4 B—N2
12 P—KN3 N—R4 13 B—R3

P—K3.
10 ....   BxN
11 PxB   B—N2

Black's position is a little cramped but while the position remains relatively closed White's two bishops are not very active and his advantage only slight.

12 N—B3   K—K1

Not 12 ... BxP? 13 N—N5 winning.

13 P—K5

After 13 B—Q3 N—KB3 14 P—K5 N—N5 15 B—N1 N—KR3 Black has a tenable position.

13 ....   BxN!?

If 13 ... N—QB3 14 B—K2 and Black has no play. Now the issue revolves around White's ability to open up the position and thereby increase the scope of his bishops.

14 PxB   P—B4!

Necessary, in order to retain control over White's K4 square. If 14 ... N—QB3 15 B—Q3 P—K3 16 B—K4 R—QB1 17 R—Q6 N—K2 18 KR—Q1 N—B1, White can continue with 19 B—N7 R—QN1 20 B—R6 followed by 21 B—N5+ winning at once.

15 PxP e.p.!

15 R—Q5 allows Black to consolidate by 15 ... N—B1 followed by ... N—K3.

15 ....   NxP
16 P—B5!

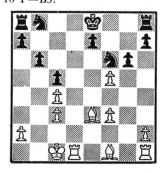

Black cannot accept this sacrifice because after 16 ... PxP 17 B—R3 P—K3 18 R—Q6 K—B2 19 KR—Q1 Black is tied down. 18 ... K—K2 (instead of 18 ... K—B2) is no better because after 19 KR—Q1 QN—Q2 20 B—N5 N—K4 21 BxP! Black is lost.

16 ....   N—B3
17 PxNP   PxP
18 B—N5

Now that White has cleared the air on the K side his two bishops are very active.

18 ....   K—B2

If 18 ... N—K4 19 R—K1!

19 P—KR4   QR—Q1
20 R—K1   R—Q3
21 R—R2   N—R2?!

Better was 21 ... R—K3

22 B—Q2   N—B3
23 K—B2   R—K3
24 RxR   KxR
25 B—Q3   K—B2
26 B—B4   N—KR4?

The start of a time-wasting manoeuvre. Better was 26 ... P—K3 followed by N—K2 and N—B4.

27 B—N5!   N—N6
28 R—R3   N—KR4

28 ... N—B4 is met by 29 P—R5.

29 P—B4   N—B3.
30 R—N3   R—KN1
31 P—B5!   N—K4

After 31 ... PxP 32 BxP Black is no better off than in the game.

32 PxP+   NxP
33 R—K3   N—B1
34 B—B5

Now neither of Black's knights can move.

34 ....   P—K3
35 R—R3   R—N3
36 P—R4   N(B3)—R2
37 B—B4!   Resigns

Black's forces are so congested on the K side that he cannot prevent White winning his Q side pawns. White will simply play P—QR5 and if PxP then B—Q6 followed by BxBP and Black's QRPs will fall. After P—R5, if Black allows White to exchange pawns at QN6, he has no defence to the threat of B—B7.·

A textbook example of the power of two bishops over two knights.

FIND THE WINNING CONTINUATION!

In each of the positions which follow (all of which are taken from Spassky's games) there is a clear-cut continuation which forces a winning position in a few moves. The number of moves required to establish the win is given in brackets.

More and more players in English speaking countries are coming to recognise the advantages of the algebraic notation, so it will not be amiss to give the solutions in that notation which, after all, Spassky learned at his mother's knee and has used ever since!

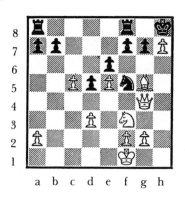

1 Spassky v Melik-Pashayan
White to move (4)

2 Spassky v Taimanov
White to move (7)

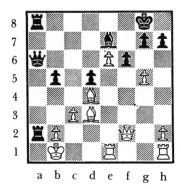

3 Spassky v Kozma
White to move (5)

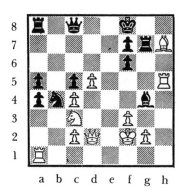

4 Spassky v Ufimtsev
White to move (5)

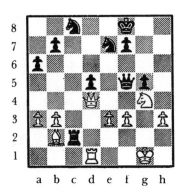

5 Spassky v Aronin
White to move (6)

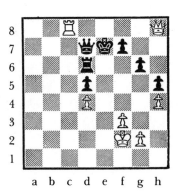

6 Spassky v Tal
White to move (7)

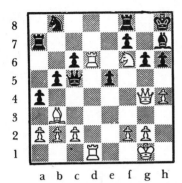

7 Spassky v Foguelman
White to Move (10)

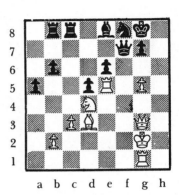

8 Spassky v Matanovic
White to move (4)

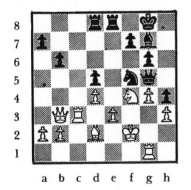

9 Kagan v Spassky
Black to move (3)

10 Spassky v Ivkov
White to move (6)

11 Hartoch v Spassky
Black to move (7)

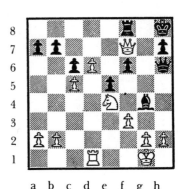

12 Spassky v Czerniak
White to move (6)

13 Spassky v Holmov
White to move (6)

14 Spassky v Unzicker
White to move (10)

SOLUTIONS

1 Spassky v Melik-Pashayan, USSR Semi-final 1954.
1 Bf6 Rac8 (1 ... gxf6 2 exf6 followed by 3 Nd4, as if 2 ... Kxh7, then 3 Qh5+ Kg8 4 Ng5) 2Nd4 gxf6 4 exf6 Resigns. ·

2 Spassky v Taimanov, XXII USSR 1955.
1 Nxb5 axb5 (1 ... Rc8 2 Qh5+ Qf7 3 Rd8+! Rxd8 4 Nxc7+) ,2 Qh5+ Qf7 (2 ... Ng6 3 Rxa8+ Bxa8 4 Nxg6 Qf7 5 Qg4) 3 Rxa8+ Bxa8 4 Rd8+! Kxd8 5 Qxf7 gxh4 6 Qxf6 Rg8 and White wins without too much trouble with his mobile queen opposed to Black's scattered. forces. Taimanov dragged the game on another 19 moves before finally resigning.

3 Spassky v Kozma, Students Olympiad 1955.
Black has given up a piece for an attack, but ... 1 gxf6 gxf6 2 Rhg1+ Kf8 (2 ... Kh8 3 Qxf6+) 3 Qxf6+! Resigns. The finish would be 3 ... Bxf6 4 Bc5+ Be7 5 Ref1+ mating.

4 Spassky v Ufimtsev, USSR Semi-final 1957.
1 Bf5! (not 1 fxg4 Qxg4 2 Qh6 Qxg2+ 3 Ke3 Re8+ and Black has at least perpetual check) 1 ... Bxf5 2 Rh8+ Rg8 3 Qh6+ Ke7 4 Re1+ Kd7 (4 ... Be6 5 Rxe6+ Qxe6!? 6 Rxg8! wins) 5 Qxf6 Resigns.

5 Spassky v Aronin, USSR Semi-final 1957.
1 Qh8+ Ng8 2 Bg7+ Ke7 3 Qxg8 Nd6 (3 ... Qxf3 4 Bf6✣ Ke6 5 Qe8+ Kd6 6 Be5+ Kc5 7 Qxc8+ etc.) 4 Bf6+ Ke6 5 Qd8 Nc8 6 e4! and Black lost on time.

6 Spassky v Tal, XXV USSR 1958.
Spassky's famous loss! He played 1 Qf8+ Kf6 2 Re8 but after 2 ... Re6 3 Qh8+ Kf5 4 Qh6 Kf6 White has no more than a draw. Chekhover subsequently pointed out what had been missed by both players — 1 g4! to use his pawns to take vital squares off the enemy king. Now 1 ... hxg4 2 Qf8+ Kf6 3 fxg4 Re6 (or 3 ... Rc6 4 Re8 Rc2+ 5 Kf3 Rc3+ 6 Kf4 Qc7+ 7 Re5!) 4 Rc3 Re4 5 Rf3+ Ke6 6 g5 etc. Or 1 ... Re6 2 g5 Rc6 3 Qf8+ Ke6 4 Re8+ Kf5 5 Re7 Rc2+ 6 Kg3 Qd6+ 7 Re5+ and wins.

7 Spassky v Foguelman, Mar del Plata 1960.
1 Nxh7 axb3 (1 ... Kxh7 2 Bxf7! decisively weakening the g6 square.)
2 Nxf8 bxc2 3 Nxg6+ fxg6 4 Rd8+ Kg7 (4 ... Kh7 5 Rcl with a simple
win.) 5 Rg8+! Kxg8 6 Qxg6+ Rg7 (6 ... Kf8 7 Qf6+ and 8 Rd8+) 7 Rd8+
Qf8 8 Rxf8+ Kxf8 9 Qxc2 Kg8 10 Qc5 Resigns.

8 Spassky v Matanovic Havana 1962.
1 Rfl Qe7 (1 ... Qh5 2 g6 Qh6 3 Rg5 and 4 Rhl) 2 g6 Rc4 3 Rh5
Rxd4 4 Rxf8+ Resigns as mate is forced in five.

9 Kagan v Spassky, Winnipeg, 1967.
1 ... Nxe3 2 Bxe3 Rxe3 3 Rxe3 (3 Kxe3 ·Bxd4+ 4 Kxd4 Qxf4+ 5 Kd3
Qf3+ and 6 ... Qf2+ winning the loose rook) 3 ... Qxf4+ Resigns.

10 Spassky v Ivkov, Palma de Mallorca 1968.
1 Bc3 e5 (1 ... Bxc3 2 Qxc3 Rxdl+ 3 Rxdl Rg8 4 Rd8!) 2 Qg3 Bxf2+
(2 ... g6 3 Bxd4 and 4 Qe5+ or 2 ... Rg8 3 Bxg8 Rxg8 4 Bxd4 exd4 5
Rxc7) 3 Qxf2 Qxf2+ 4 Kxf2 Ned5 5 Bxe5! Rxe5 6 Rxc7 Resigns.

11 Hartoch v Spassky, Amsterdam 1970.
1 ... Be8! (1 ... Rxg2? 2 Qf8+ Kf6 3 Qh8+ Kg5 4 Rxf5+! gxf5 5 Qxd4)
2 Rgl Qxgl+! 3 Kxgl Rxg2+ Resigns. (4 Khl Rh2+ 5 Kgl Reg2+ 6 Kfl
Bb5+ mating.

12 Spassky v Czerniak, Gothenburg 1971.
1 Qxf8+ Qxf8 2 fxg4 Qd8 3 d7 Kg8 (3 ...˙Kg7 4 Rd6) 4 Nxf6+! Kf7 5
Ne4 Ke7 6 Nd6! Resigns (6 ... Kxd7 7 Nxb7+ or 6 ... Qxd7 7 Nf5+).

13 Spassky v Holmov, USSR Teams Championship, Rostov 1971.
1 Qxh6! gxh6 2 Nf6+ Kh8 3 Nxd7+ Kg8 (3 ... Kh7 4 Nxf8+ and 5
Nd7) 4 Re8! Nc6 5 dxc6 Qa7 6 c7 Resigns.

14 Spassky v Unzicker, Santa Monica 1966.
1 Nf5! Bxd2 (1 ... Bf8 2 Nh6+ Kg7 — 2 ... Bxh6 3 Bxh6 with the
decisive threat of 4 Bg5 — 3 gxh5 Nxh5 4 Rxh5 gxh5 5 f4! Kxh6 6 f5+
Kg7 7 Qxh5 and 8 Rhl) 2 Qxd2 gxf5 (2 ... Nh7 3 Qh6) 3 Qh6 fxg4 4
fxg4 Bxg4 (4 ... Nxg4 5 Qxh5 and soon mates) 5 Rxf6 Qe7 6 Bdl! and
with the loss of the h pawn it is all over — 6 ... Bxdl 7 Rxdl Rec8 8
Rlfl Rxc3 9 Qxh5 Rc2+ 10 Khl Resigns.

SPASSKY'S PLAYING RECORD

		−	=	+	Position
1952	Leningrad Championship	6	7	0	2
1953	Bucharest	8	8	3	4/5
1954	Young Masters Tournament	10	5	0	1
	Semi-final USSR Champ.	6	12	2	4
1955	XXII USSR Champ.	7	9	3	3/4
	Junior World Champ. Antwerp	13	2	1	1
	Interzonal Gothenburg	7	8	5	8/9
	Student Team Champ.	7	1	0	
1956	XXIII USSR Champ.	7	9	1	1/3
	Champ. play-off	0	1	3	3
	Candidates Tournament Amsterdam	3	13	2	3/8
	Semi-final USSR Champ.	7	9	3	1/5
1957	XXIV USSR Champ.	7	12	2	4/5
	Student Team Champ.	5	4	0	
	European Team Champ.	2	3	0	
	Semi-final USSR Champ.	7	11	1	1/2
1958	XXV USSR Champ.	7	7	4	5/6
	Students Team Champ.	4	5	0	
	Semi-final USSR Champ.	7	6	2	1/2
1959	XXVI USSR Champ.	8	9	2	2/3
	Moscow Central Chess Club	4	6	1	1/3
	Leningrad Champ.	11	6	0	1
	Semi-final USSR Champ.	9	5	1	1/2
	Spartakiad	4	4	0	
	Riga	10	3	0	1
1960	XXVII USSR Champ.	5	10	4	9/10
	Mar del Plata	12	3	0	1/2
	Student Team Champ.	0	2	1	

		W	D	L	
	USSR Team Champ.	3	5	0	
	'Trud' Champ.	8	7	0	1
	Semi-final USSR Champ.	8	8	1	1
1961	XXVIII USSR Champ.	7	8	4	5/6
	Leningrad Champ.	8	10	0	1/2
	XXIX USSR Champ.	10	9	1	1
1962	Students Team Champ.	6	3	0	2/3
	Havana Tournament	11	10	0	
	XV Olympiad Varna	8	6	0	
	USSR Team Champ.	4	4	0	5
	XXX USSR Champ.	9	7	3	
					2
1963	Semi-final USSR Champ.	6	9	0	1/3
	XXXI USSR Champ.	5	14	0	
					2
1964	Champ play-off.	1	2	1	1
	Zonal Tournament of Seven	4	6	2	1/4
	Interzonal Amsterdam	13	8	2	4
	Sochi	5	9	1	1
	Belgrade	9	8	0	
	XVI Olympiad Tel-Aviv	8	6	0	
1965	Candidates match with Keres	4	4	2	
	Candidates match with Geller	3	5	0	
	Trades Union Spartakiad	3	4	0	1/2
	Sochi	6	9	0	
	Candidates match with Tal	4	5	1	
	Hastings	6	3	0	1/2
1966	World Champ. match with Petrosian	3	17	4	1
	Santa Monica	5	13	0	
	USSR Team Champ.	0	9	1	
	Sochi	6	7	1	5/6
	XVII Olympiad Havana.	5	10	0	
1967	Beverwijk	7	8	0	1
	RSFSR Championship	6	5	0	1/2
	Moscow Grandmasters	4	11	2	6/8
	Spartakiad	3	5	0	
	Sochi	5	10	0	1/5
	Winnipeg	2	7	0	3/4
1968	Candidates match with Geller	3	5	0	
	Candidates match with Larsen	4	3	1	
	Candidates match with Korchnoy	4	5	1	
	XVIII Olympiad Lugano.	6	8	0	
	Palma	10	6	1	2/3

1969	World Champ. match with Petrosian	6	13	4	
	San Juan	8	7	0	1
	Palma	3	14	0	5
1970	USSR v Rest of World match	1	1	1	
	Leiden Match/tournament of four	2	10	0	1
	Amsterdam (IBM)	8	7	0	1/2
	XIV Olympiad Siegen	7	5	0	
1971	Gothenburg	5	6	0	3
	USSR Team Champ.	3	1	0	
	Vancouver, Canadian Open	7	4	0	1/2
	Toronto, Canadian National Exhibition	5	1	0	3/4
	Moscow, Alekhine Memorial	4	11	2	6/7

Index of Opponents

The numbers refer to games

Index of Openings

The numbers refer to games.